THE OFFICIAL ILLUSTRATED HISTORY OF EVERTON F.C.

FOREVER EVERTON

THE OFFICIAL ILLUSTRATED HISTORY OF EVERTON F.C.

FOR EVER EVERTON

NIL SATIS NISI OPTIMUM

STEPHEN F. KELLY

Macdonald
Queen Anne Press

A *Queen Anne Press* BOOK

© Stephen Kelly 1987

First published in Great Britain in 1987 by
Queen Anne Press, a division of
Macdonald & Co (Publishers) Ltd
3rd Floor
Greater London House
Hampstead Road
London NW1 7QX

A BPCC plc Company

British Library Cataloguing in Publication Data
Kelly, Stephen
    Forever Everton: the official Illustration of Everton FC.
    1. Everton Football Club – History
    I. Title
    796.334'63'0942753   GV943.6.E93
    ISBN 0–356–15055–0

Printed and bound in Great Britain by
Butler & Tanner Ltd, Frome and London

CONTENTS

FOR EVERTONIANS EVERYWHERE

To those outside Merseyside it might seem a heresy that having written a history of Liverpool Football Club, one should then embark on a similar project about their greatest rivals. Those on Merseyside however will understand that a close relationship has always existed between the two clubs and while they are rivals on the pitch they remain firm friends off it. The division between the clubs is not along religious or geographical grounds as in other cities but instead divides families, with husbands and wives, fathers and sons often split in their allegiance. And the evidence was there for all to see when the two rivals recently clashed at Wembley as supporters travelled south together and mingled freely on the terraces while at the end of the game the chant was not just for Everton and Liverpool but for 'Merseyside'. When I had completed *You'll Never Walk Alone*, many Evertonians asked if I would be writing a history of their club. With that encouragement I embarked on this volume and what follows is dedicated to them and to the support they have given the club during the bleak as well as the glory years.

This book could not however have been written without the co-operation of Everton Football Club, its officials, directors and players. My thanks must also go to those writers who have pioneered this path before me, producing valuable research and statistics. But in the end all responsibility for any errors or misrepresentations must of course lie with me.

I would especially like to thank football statistician, George Higham, who checked the manuscript and offered much advice. I should also like to thank the Association of Football Statisticians who unearthed some interesting records on the club's early history as well as the staff of the Liverpool Central Library for all their help.

Also my thanks to the many others who assisted me during the writing of this book, particularly my wife, Judith Rowe Jones, who despite being a Liverpool supporter offered much valuable advice. Thanks also to Stephen Boulton, Ray Spiller and Joe Mercer.

And last but not least my appreciation to my publishers and especially Alan Samson, Celia Kent and Clare Forte who worked so hard and professionally to make this a worthwhile publication.

No doubt there will be many whom I have omitted to mention. To those I have forgotten or neglected, my apologies. I hope it will be sufficient to add that they too have played their part in the history of a great club.

Stephen Kelly
Liverpool

INTRODUCTION

Back in 1928 Steve Bloomer, the legendary Derby County and England goalscorer, said of Everton that 'they always manage to serve up football of the highest scientific order,' and 'worship at the shrine of craft and science'. From that moment on Goodison Park became known as the 'School of Science'. And it is a description which has remained with them throughout the succeeding years with every outstanding Everton team dedicated to playing football of the highest quality.

Few clubs can boast the honours Everton have achieved. Nine League championships, runners up on seven occasions, four FA Cup victories, a further six appearances in the Final, a European trophy, plus two appearances in a League Cup Final. Only one team in the land can compare with them and that is their distinguished Merseyside neighbours, Liverpool.

Everton have never been a club simply content to win trophies. When they are won, it has to be done in style. Not for them the defensive wall or the long ball hit upfield for forwards to chase. Instead, they have prided themselves in attacking football, initiating their surges from defence through midfield and into attack. Skill and ability have always been to the fore and even in their darkest days they have remained true to their cause.

That heritage began with outstanding Corinthians like the former Blackburn Rovers inside-forward Edgar Chadwick, the English international Johnny Holt and the Scottish star Bob Kelso, who before the turn of the century mesmerised defences throughout the Football League with their sharp skills and fleeting footwork. The tradition continued into the Edwardian era with players such as Jack Sharp, Jimmy Settle and Jack Taylor, while the 1930s were dominated by names like Cliff Britton, Sam Chedgzoy, Warney Cresswell and Joe Mercer: all players who placed skill above endeavour. And in the modern age of football Goodison has continued to produce the same high calibre in Howard Kendall, Alan Ball

and Colin Harvey, while today Trevor Steven and Peter Reid have again created the impulse that has made Everton a force to be reckoned with.

Yet all this is to ignore Everton's greatest contribution to the game – the goalscorer. Throughout the club's history, it has been endowed with some of the most outstanding centre forwards soccer has ever known. Fred Geary who during the 1890s scored at the rate of a goal a game and Bertie Freeman who some years later created a First Division goalscoring record, set the standard for others to follow. And then there was the greatest of them all, Dixie Dean, whose feats alone have filled many a footballing book. But Dean was hardly the last. In later years Tommy Lawton, Fred Pickering, Alex Young, Bob Latchford and Gary Lineker have all provided the final strike that has helped make Everton such a power in the land.

During their 99 years in the Football League Everton have accumulated more points in the First Division race than any other team and can rightfully claim to be the all-time champions of English football. And it will be many years, if ever, before another team catches them. With such a record it is hardly surprising that Everton are envied throughout the footballing world. Wherever soccer is the talking point, you can be sure that those assembled will know of Everton but few will know of the detailed history and fascinating personalities that have created such a famous club.

This then is that history. It is a story rich in incident, abundant in skilled players, and concerned with the continual challenge for trophies and honours. It is about the players who have served the club; some gifted, some less so. And it is about the games; some outstanding, others not so exciting. Yet all have contributed in their own way to making Everton Football Club one of the best known in the world. Never has a club's motto *Nil Satis Nisi Optimum* been more appropriate. Loosely translated it means, 'Nothing but the best is good enough'.

Wayne Clarke, scorer of Everton's winning goal against Coventry in the 1987 Charity Shield, parades the latest Everton trophy around Wembley.

ST DOMINGO'S

Liverpool in the 1870s was a city at the height of its industrial might. Sailing vessels from all around the world cruised past the Mersey Bar and sailed down the river and into the port. Queen Victoria, then approaching her sixties and in the fourth decade of her reign, ruled supreme over the nation and its expanding Empire. The docks were all named after the great figures of the age, Huskisson, Albert, Victoria, Canning, Stanley and Coburg. The days of the slave trade may have been long past, but the port prospered even more now as four-masted schooners, Baltimore clippers, Cape Horners and barks brought sweet-smelling timbers from India, grain and wool from Australia, cotton from the Americas and sugar from the Caribbean. And in exchange Liverpool exported industrial equipment and machinery to the flourishing Empire overseas. Just across the River Mersey, in Birkenhead, the Cammell Laird shipyard was constructing not only sailing ships but iron vessels to transport this wealth of goods around the world. Passengers flocked into the city bound for the ships and a 15 guinea passage that would carry them to America, Australia or India, while the Cunard and White Star liners vied with each other in the race to capture the coveted Blue Riband for the fastest crossing of the Atlantic.

In the city there was work for thousands, with the population increasing each week to meet the demand for labourers. New homes were springing up to house the city's growing numbers, roads were built, glamorous shops were opened, while well laid out parks were cultivated. Victorian England was at its peak. Men and women worked long, arduous hours for only meagre rewards. But there was time for pleasure. Theatres and music halls were becoming the centres of mass entertainment. Any evening you could wander down Lime Street and see the likes of Sarah Bernhardt, Ellen Terry, Sir Henry Irving or Grimaldi in any one of a dozen theatres. And on Sunday the churches would be bursting to the aisles as the hard-working nation gave thanks for its pitiful returns.

For the first time in British history this new-found prosperity among the masses had made the nation leisure-conscious. Not all could afford the luxury of a one-penny seat at the Prince of Wales or the New Star Music Hall but had to take comfort in devising their own fun. And so it was that out of Victorian England sport sprang up as a popular pastime for the young and not so wealthy. Games, of course, were nothing new. Real tennis, bowls and boxing had been devised by the Elizabethans, but the Victorian era brought a flow of new sports into the public arena. Rugby, golf, cricket, hockey and association football suddenly emerged to satisfy a hungry nation.

In Liverpool rugby was the most important and socially acceptable team game, with clubs such as Waterloo, Wavertree, Liverpool and New Brighton. Baseball, too, was popular, though in time it would be overtaken by cricket, while baseball was being taken up with unparalleled success across the Atlantic. At the centre of all these sporting activities you could usually find the church, organising and motivating the young. Clerics believed earnestly that clean, healthy bodies automatically led to clean, healthy minds, and so encouraged as many sporting activities as they could fit into the calendar. On Sunday afternoons groups of young people could be found in most of the city's new parks, playing baseball or cricket, or simply wobbling unsteadily on old iron-framed bicycles.

Some churches had organised football teams as early as the 1870s, with St Peter's, St Benedict's and St John's of Bootle quick off the mark to field sides, but it was not until late in the decade that St Domingo's organised a team and took the first steps to creating what was to become Everton Football Club.

It was Methodism, the booming religion of the time, that was at the centre of so much of this activity. With its less rigid, more relaxed approach, the Methodist church appealed to working people, encouraging them to enjoy themselves. Three Methodist churches had been built in Liverpool during the latter half of the eighteenth century, at Bevington Hill, Chatham Place and Hotham Street. But, with the growth of Methodism, it was decided in 1869 to close them all down and build a new and larger church on a chosen site in Breckfield Road North, Everton. That year, the foundation stone of St Domingo's (and of two of Europe's greatest soccer clubs) was laid, with the church formally consecrated in May the following year. Six years later the Reverend Chambers was installed as the new vicar, in a move that was to bring fresh ideas and enthusiasm to

One of the earliest known photographs of Everton FC. Taken during the 1883/84 season when they had just won their first trophy, the Liverpool Cup, and were still playing at Priory Road in the Lancashire Association.

the church. Chambers was one of a new breed of clergymen – young, keen, outgoing and athletic. Not surprisingly, like other Methodist ministers, he wanted to introduce his parishioners to sport and within a year had set up a cricket club. But cricket was essentially a summer game, and when some of the younger members of his congregation asked in 1878 if they could organise a football club, Chambers readily agreed. And so St Domingo's Football Club kicked off in a small corner of nearby Stanley Park that winter, playing against a variety of local church teams. They carried their own goalposts to the ground, marked out their pitch and changed in nearby huts. It was typical Sunday League soccer.

A year later, as 1879 wound to its wintry conclusion, the club – flushed with their early success and keen to recruit the many non-churchgoers who wanted to play for them – took a step into the wider world by discarding their old title and adopting the name of the district where their church was situated, Everton. And so just a few days before Christmas, on

23 December 1879, Everton Football Club played its first match against St Peter's. Auspiciously, Everton won by six goals to nil and so began a sequence of events that was to lead to glory and fame which would spread well beyond the confines of Stanley Park and Liverpool. There were no reports of that game in the local press. Instead, the papers concentrated on a dangerous mutiny that was sweeping across India, and just a few days after that first match the Tay Bridge tragically collapsed, killing 75 people.

The names of the players in Everton's first-ever team will probably always remain unknown, but those who took part in the second match, another victory over St Peter's four weeks later, were W. Jones, T. Evans, J. Douglas, C. Hiles, S. Chalk (captain), R. W. Morris, A. White, F. Brettle, A. Wade, Smith and W. Williams. Fifty years on, Arthur Wade still had a link with the club as a director, while Will Cuff, another youngster playing in some of those early games, later served the club as secretary, director and chairman.

During 1880 Everton joined the thriving Lancashire Association and began playing against much tougher competition, with matches as far away as Bolton and Birkenhead. Drawn against Great Lever in the Association's cup, they returned home with a creditable 1–1 draw, only to be thrashed 8–1 in the replay at Stanley Park. But there were victories, principally around Liverpool, where they were fast becoming the most feared side in the city. Only 'Brutal Bootle' (so nicknamed because of their style of play) could offer Everton any serious challenge, and the clashes between the two could guarantee as many as 2,000 turning up in Stanley Park on a Saturday afternoon. It was the problem of such large crowds and the need for an enclosed ground which finally forced Everton to abandon Stanley Park and look for more suitable accommodation for their matches. A meeting was held in March 1882, in the Sandon Hotel, owned by John Houlding, to discuss the matter, where it was decided to rent a field owned by a Mr Cruitt off Priory Road for the following season.

John Houlding had started taking an interest in Everton when they began to use his public house for changing before their matches in Stanley Park and it had quickly become the club's unofficial headquarters. Houlding was a wealthy brewer and a self-made man who had started life working in a brewery before venturing out on his own by purchasing a small public house. Out of the success of that business he financed the purchase of a small brewery and profited comfortably for the remainder of his life. He was also a prominent member of the Working Men's Conservative Association and an Orangeman, and even represented the Everton ward as a Conservative Councillor for many years, finally becoming Lord Mayor of the city in 1897. But, although Houlding was to play a minor role in the early years of Everton Football Club, it was as chairman of Liverpool Football Club years later that he was to achieve greater notoriety.

Life at Priory Road began in earnest. A dressing-room and small stand were constructed and the first match, in which a Liverpool representative team drew with Walsall, brought gate receipts amounting to the grand sum of 14 shillings. The club continued to play matches against local teams like the Liverpool Ramblers and Haydock, as well as those from further afield, such as Hartford St John's from Cheshire and Burslem from the Potteries. And in that season, 1883/84, Everton won their first trophy.

They had been playing in the Liverpool Cup for a number of seasons without much success. In the previous year Bootle had beaten them in the semi-final, but this time Everton took their revenge with a 5–2 win and went on to defeat Earlestown 1–0 in the final. It was to be the first of many trophies. Success or no success, by the end of the season Mr Cruitt had grown weary of the noise and crowds that were flocking to Priory Road and Everton were told in no uncertain terms that they had to find another ground for their matches. Their next move would help create one of the greatest football teams of all time and one of the most famous grounds, but it would not be Everton's.

Everton did not have to search very long for a new ground. John Orrell, a friend of Houlding and a fellow brewer, had a patch of land in the Anfield Road and readily responded to their overtures. They could rent the ground, he replied, provided they kept it in a good state of repair and paid a donation each year to the Stanley Hospital in his name. And so, after just one year at Priory Road, Everton shifted their home to Anfield and played their first match there on 27 September 1884, beating Earlestown 5–0. Later that season they took on Bootle in the Liverpool Cup, winning 2–1, and marched on to face Earlestown in the final. But they were not to repeat their cup-winning exploits of the previous season and lost by a single goal, hotly disputed by the Everton players, who claimed the ball had not gone between the posts. In those days before goalnets referees often judged that shots had flashed between the posts when in fact they had gone well outside, but the introduction of nets would soon prevent such errors.

Everton continued in the Liverpool Association but were now widening their fixture list, with regular friendlies against Lancashire teams such as Blackburn Rovers, Bolton Wanderers, Blackburn Olympic and Accrington Stanley. Professionalism was also beginning to creep into the game. Until 1885 the Football Association had opposed the idea of professional footballers, but the game's growing popularity, along with the rich rewards that were resulting from high attendances, brought a more enlightened approach. As soon as professionalism was sanctioned, Everton were one of the first clubs to plunge into the new era of soccer and engaged their first professional players, George Dobson from Bolton, Alec Dick from Kilmarnock and George Farmer from Oswestry. During the early 1880s the club also signed its first Scot, Jack McGill, who came from Glasgow Rangers and later became club captain.

In the autumn of 1886 Everton entered the FA Cup for the first time, drawing Glasgow Rangers in the opening round, but were horrified to learn when Rangers arrived that some of their own players were ineligible; the club immediately withdrew, instead playing a friendly against the Scottish side, which they lost 1–0. The following season their Cup exploits suffered a similar fate when, after a series of disputed games with Bolton Wanderers, Everton were sus-pended for a month after again fielding ineligible players. To make matters worse, the Liverpool Association reacted by repossessing the Liverpool Cup from them in a move that resulted in Everton angrily withdrawing from the Association for a short spell.

By 1888 the proliferation of footballing associations in and around Lancashire and the Midlands was not only causing confusion but hampering the growth of the game. So in the spring of 1888 the Northern and Midland associations joined forces and formed the Football League. Everton, now boasting a couple of grandstands and all the amenities of a top football club, as well as a proud record, immediately applied for membership and were accepted, though only on the final vote, as founder members of the Football League, along with Accrington Stanley, Aston Villa, Blackburn Rovers, Bolton Wanderers, Burnley, Derby County, Notts County, Preston North End, Stoke, West Bromwich Albion and Wolverhampton Wanderers. It was the beginning of modern football.

The club began its history in the Football League on 8 September 1888 with a home game against Accrington, with Fleming scoring both goals in their 2–1 victory. Everton's team that day was Smalley, Ross, Dick, Dobson, Holt, R. Jones, Farmer, Chadwick, Lewis, Waugh and Fleming. A crowd of almost 10,000 turned up on that bright autumn Saturday and were entertained with a fast and skilful, though goalless, first half. Early in the second half the *Liverpool Daily Post* recorded that 'Fleming headed the first goal amidst tremendous cheering and waving of hats'. And before much longer there were more problems for the Lancashire side, when the Accrington goalkeeper, Horne, was in collision with the Everton forward Chadwick and fractured a rib. Horne was led off the field and McLennan had to take his place. By now Accrington were in disarray and Fleming soon capitalised with a second goal, driven in from Farmer's centre. The goal revitalised Accrington, who soon began to reorganise themselves and pressed Everton hard, hitting the bar and having a shot kicked off the line. Eventually they scrambled the ball into the goal, but although they attacked relentlessly they could not snatch an equaliser.

Everton's captain that day, and for the remainder

Everton's first captain, Nick Ross, arrived from Preston in 1888 but left after only one season following a bitter row with the club.

of the season, was a Scotsman, Nick Ross, who had arrived during the summer via Hearts and Preston. A defender, Ross was reckoned to be one of the foremost authorities on the game, and his transfer to Everton caught the imagination of the public. But his fame was also to figure as the principal element in a row between the club and its supporters. After a useful start to the season Everton ran into problems at Blackburn after fielding an under-strength side. In a dressing-room row McKinnon refused to play, and the ill-feeling which had been simmering beneath the surface since the opening of the season was suddenly made public. Within days it was splashed across the footballing papers. The argument was about who should choose the team – supporters and players demanded that Nick Ross should have a say and that it should not be left exclusively to the committee. There was no immediate solution, and as a result Everton's form suffered, while the letter pages of the local press argued the pros and cons of the debate and the terraces witnessed some unseemly crowd behaviour.

When the season ended, in February, Everton had played 22 games but finished an unimpressive eighth in the League, well behind the top team, Preston, who romped away with not only the title but also the

FA Cup. Although they had been quite successful at Anfield, having lost only three games, their away form was appalling, with one victory in 11 fixtures, most of these having been played in the New Year, when the row was in full flow.

As for Ross, he had had enough, and although Everton had been generously paying him £10 a month, twice the sum paid to other players, he returned to Preston, where he quickly won a championship medal and represented the Football League against the Football Alliance. Sadly he died from consumption just a few years later, at the early age of 31. The one-time slater had played only 19 games for Everton but holds the honour of being the club's first outstanding professional.

Everton had begun their footballing days playing in blue shirts with white stripes, but with new players arriving and donning their old club colours it had been decided in 1881 to bring some uniformity to the strip. And, as the club was short of money, the easiest solution was to dye all the kits black. The results looked rather drab, so someone had the bright idea of adding a two-inch-wide scarlet sash to the shirt, and Everton soon became known as 'The Black Watch'. The new colours did not last long, however, and the club switched to salmon pink shirts and blue shorts. This, too, did not please everyone and they were soon wearing ruby shirts with blue trimmings and navy-coloured shorts. It was not until a number of years later that they made their final switch to royal-blue shirts, white shorts and blue stockings.

The importance of Liverpool as a footballing city was recognised in March 1889, when Anfield staged its first international, a fixture between England and Ireland, which England won convincingly by six goals to one. In 1883 an international between the same two sides had been played at the Aigburth cricket ground, with England winning 7–0.

During the season 1889/90 there were changes on the committee and the team settled to some impressive performances. For much of the early season they tussled with Wolverhampton at the top of the table, winning one notable game against Stoke by eight goals to nil. A few fixtures later, however, the great Preston team led by the indefatigable Nick Ross arrived at Anfield and before 20,000 spectators trounced Everton by five goals to one. Although Everton went on to defeat Preston at Deepdale a month later, as well as knock seven past Aston Villa, 'Proud Preston' were in a class of their own. Yet Everton might have caught them but for unexpected defeats at Accrington and West Brom in the final matches of the season, which left them in second place, just two points adrift of the champions, Preston. Nevertheless it had been a stirring campaign and showed a promise that would soon be fulfilled.

Everton's 1890/91 season kicked off in early September with a 4–1 win at West Bromwich Albion, followed by a 5–0 defeat of Wolves at Anfield. Fred Geary scored a couple in each and then repeated his triumphs with two more the following week in the 5–0 defeat of Bolton. Everton were now looking like genuine championship contenders and in Geary had found a natural goalscorer. In their first seven games Everton had hit 27 goals with only four against.

Hopes were high, yet quite inexplicably the club lost their next three games as well as their top spot in the League. A week later 15,000 turned up at Anfield to watch Everton beat Sunderland and return to the top of the table, but a 2–0 defeat at Preston saw them tumble again. Geary had lost his touch and it began to look as if Everton would miss out once more. But then he suddenly hit form again as Everton swept to seven victories in the next eight games. Burnley were hit for seven and Aston Villa for five before Everton faced 'Proud Preston' at Anfield, and in the 'match of the season' went down disappointingly by a single goal.

The next week, with 700 supporters in tow, they travelled by special train to Turf Moor to tackle Burnley, and in driving sleet and snow gave two goals away in the final four minutes to lose by three goals to two. Everton looked to be in trouble and when they lost their final fixture by a single goal, at Sunderland, they left the field looking dejected. Luck, however, was on their side as news came through that 'Proud Preston' had also lost that afternoon. Everton were champions, pipping their rivals by just two points. They had lost seven games, two of them at home, and had scored 63 goals, with Geary the leading marksman on 20 goals, followed by Alfred Milward with a dozen and Edgar Chadwick with 10.

Geary was the star of the team with his sensational goalscoring exploits. Born in Nottingham, he had joined Everton in 1889 from Grimsby hitting 21 goals in his first season and then 20 in the championship season a year later. But he never quite matched those feats again, although he did score 19 goals a few seasons later. In 98 appearances he struck 86 goals, giving him a strike record rivalled only by Dixie Dean and Gary Lineker. In 1894 he left Everton and joined Liverpool but made only 45 appearances for the Reds before injury brought his career to a premature end. He was one of the club's earliest England internationals, winning two caps, the first against Ireland in 1890, when he scored a hat-trick in England's 9–1 victory. On the same day another England team with Everton's Johnny Holt at centre-half beat Wales 3–1 at Wrexham, so that both men tied for the honour of being the first Evertonian to wear an England shirt.

Holt had joined Everton from Bootle in 1888, where he had clearly learned a few tricks, not least of all how to tackle. Although only 5ft 4½ins, he was said to be one of the toughest centre-halves in the League, and played 225 games for Everton before joining Reading in 1898. In all he won 10 England caps, winning his final honour against Scotland in 1900.

Alongside Geary was the majestic Edgar Chadwick, who had joined Everton from Blackburn Rovers in the summer of 1888. A left-footed player, he formed an effective partnership with winger Alfred Milward and played regularly until the end of the century, making 300 appearances and scoring 110 goals. A confectioner in Blackburn during the week, he was said to have a dialect as broad as his smile. He won seven England caps and would have a major influence on Everton's fortunes over the next few years. In May 1899 he joined Burnley and later Southampton and became one of the first Englishmen to coach abroad, working in Holland and Germany.

His partner, the fine-moustached Alfred Milward, had signed from Great Marlow in 1888, the same year that Ross and Chadwick had joined the club. He was fast and skilful and liked nothing better than to

England international and outside left, Alfred Milward, joined Everton in 1888 and played over 200 games for the club during the next nine seasons, helping them to their first league championship.

John Houlding, a self-made businessman, Conservative councillor, Orangeman and city mayor, was a prominent supporter of Everton until the split when he remained at Anfield to form Liverpool Football Club.

sprint down the touchline before chipping delicate crosses into the goalmouth. Milward was another English international, winning four caps, and was one of five Everton players to be chosen for the England team against Scotland in 1891. After just over 200 League appearances and 85 goals he left Everton in 1897 and joined New Brighton Tower, the up-and-coming Wirral side.

Football was fast becoming one of the most popular spectator sports in the country, with crowds flocking to the matches. On Merseyside the game was given a boost in April 1890, when dock-workers were successful in the struggle for a $5\frac{1}{2}$-day week. That meant Saturday afternoon was free, and gates at Anfield began regularly to top the 20,000 mark. With so many fine players, Everton began the 1891/92 season hopeful that they could repeat the previous season's success. But just as a few seasons before, when events off the field had influenced results on it, so again backroom squabbles had their effect. This time the off-the-field row would be catastrophic and almost lead to the demise of the club.

It was with some justification that John Houlding had become known as 'King John'. He was not only a political power in the district but was now throwing his weight around elsewhere. His attitude to the club was proprietorial and his increasing influence over matters at Anfield was clearly to the distaste of many.

John Orrell, the owner of Anfield, had demanded an increase in rent for the ground and threatened to withdraw the tenancy unless certain alterations were

carried out. Houlding came up with a plan to counter Orrell. The club would form a limited liability company and approach Orrell with an offer to purchase the ground. This seemed a good idea, but what many had not realised until it became public was that Houlding himself had bought land adjoining Anfield and that the purchase of the ground also included the purchase of his land. Houlding stood to make a considerable gain from this transaction, and there was a furious row when the club's 279 members met on 25 January 1892 in the College, Shaw Street. Houlding's proposal was thrown out and Orrell reacted by giving the club notice to quit. So leave they did and immediately purchased a plot of land known as Mere Green Field on the other side of Stanley Park, in Goodison Road, for £8,090 12s 6d from Colonel Naylor-Leyland. A limited liability company was formed under the name of Everton Football Club and 500 £1 shares were issued.

Houlding was furious and immediately registered the name 'Everton Football Club' with himself, and for a short period there were officially two Evertons. But Houlding soon tired of that particular dispute and, with an empty ground, he instead re-registered his club in May 1892 as the Liverpool Association Football Club. He soon recruited 11 players and joined the Lancashire League for a season before winning election to the Football League. The rest is history.

Houlding's row with the majority of the Everton Football Club members was soon forgotten and in later years he reckoned the dispute had been provoked by the temperance members at the club, who had long opposed his association with brewing and public houses. Whatever the real cause of the argument, when Houlding died in 1902 the pall-bearers at his funeral were players from both clubs, while the flags at the two grounds fluttered at half-mast in tribute. Everton may have had their initial differences with 'King John', but there could be no denying his importance to soccer on Merseyside.

It had not been a good season for Everton. Even before the New Year they had lost half their fixtures and their crown was slipping. They improved marginally in the latter part of the season, but it was too late and they finished in fifth place, 14 points behind the eventual winners, Sunderland.

3

A PERMANENT HOME

Goodison Park was formally opened on 24 August 1892 by Lord Kinnaird, president of the Football Association. After a dinner at the Adelphi Hotel, Kinnaird and a host of city dignitaries travelled by carriage to the ground, where, after a short ceremony, an evening of athletic events was held, culminating with a magnificent firework display.

Kinnaird toasted the success of Everton and warned, as the *Liverpool Mercury* put it, that 'it was his endeavour to save the game from the taint of rowdyism and betting and he looked to the club to support him'. He added that 'any committee putting its foot down at any piece of rowdyism would, he was sure, receive the support both of players and spectators'.

Goodison was probably the finest ground in the country, with large double-baths, hot-water boilers, spacious dressing-rooms and even a changing-room for the referee. More than £3,000 had been spent on constructing the stadium. On three sides of the field there were tall covered stands, with a cinder banking on the remaining side and even a press stand. All in all it was reckoned there was adequate accommodation for more than 50,000 spectators. The directors of Everton, led by the chairman, George Mahon, who had inspired the move, had served the club and its supporters proud. The move to Goodison also led to the nickname 'The Toffees' because of Mother Noblett's toffee shop which stood close to the ground. Even today the toffeewoman still parades around the ground before games, dressed in her Victorian clothes and throwing Everton toffees to the crowd.

Goodison witnessed its first game on the evening of Thursday, 1 September 1892 with a friendly against Bolton Wanderers. Meanwhile, half a mile away, at Anfield, Liverpool Football Club kicked off with another friendly against Rotherham Town of the Midland League.

Everton's team that evening was Jardine, Howarth, Dewer, Boyle, Holt, Robertson, Latta, Maxwell, Geary, Chadwick and Milward, with Kelso as reserve. But while the Everton players were still admiring their new surroundings the Bolton team shot into a two-goal lead, and it looked as if the inauguration of Goodison might become an historical embarrassment. But Everton soon pulled their game together and came back to win by four goals to two.

In their first League fixture for the 1892/93 season, played at Goodison, Everton could only muster a 2–2 draw against Nottingham Forest, and then lost 4–1 away to Villa. It was not until the fourth game of the 1892/93 season that Goodison saw its first League victory, and it was worth waiting for: a 6–0 hammering of new club Newton Heath, who were later to become Manchester United. Such was the growing popularity of soccer that a second division had been added that season, also, of course, introducing the prospect of relegation. But there was never any danger that Everton would be struggling to remain in the division. On the contrary, they ended the season in third place behind champions Sunderland and Preston. In the five years since the League had been formed these three teams had dominated, with Preston yet to be out of the top two. But in February, at Goodison, 'Proud Preston' met their match, when Everton trounced them 6–0 before a crowd of over 35,000. 'The Prestonians were roasted,' wrote the football correspondent of the newly created *Liverpool Football Echo*, somewhat chauvinistically, and, indeed, it had been the heaviest defeat the Deepdale men had yet encountered.

Fred Geary was again the leading marksman, with 19, while Alex Latta hit 18. An outside-right, Latta had arrived at Everton in 1889 from Dumbarton Athletic and immediately forced his way into the team. Tall, slim and fast, the Scot had a keen eye for goal and netted 70 goals in 148 appearances for the club before signing for Liverpool in 1896. He had played twice for Scotland while with Dumbarton but was never capped again while at Goodison.

FA Cup Final 1893 Everton v Wolverhampton

Everton had entered the FA Cup on every occasion since joining the League but had shown little prospect of winning, failing each time to progress beyond the second round. Their best endeavour so far had been a thrilling 11–2 victory over Derby County in January 1890, which still remains their highest victory margin. But in 1893 they put together a stirring run that took them all the way to the final.

They opened their account at home in January with a match against Cup-holders West Brom and came out comfortable winners by four goals to one, with Geary netting a couple. Two weeks later they

faced Nottingham Forest, at Goodison, and again hit four goals, with Milward scoring twice.

The luck of the draw favoured Everton in the quarter-final as they once more came out of the hat with a home draw, although the opposition, Sheffield Wednesday, enjoying their first season in the League, were known gritty Yorkshire competitors. In the event, Chadwick set them on the road to the semi-finals with further goals from Geary and Maxwell in a 3–0 win.

The semi-finals pitted them against their greatest rivals, Preston, already winners of the Cup in 1889 and by far the most consistent and dangerous side in the League. The game played on 4 March at Bramhall Lane, Sheffield, attracted a crowd of 30,000. It was the first time Everton had played such an important game away from home and thousands of their supporters grabbed the opportunity to follow them. Everton led 2–0 at half-time but Preston, even though they were under strength through injuries, fought back magnificently to level the score.

The replay a fortnight later at Ewood Park, Blackburn, was another tough affair, with both defences on top this time. An even bigger crowd turned up to see the two sides battle out a second draw, this time 0–0. A third meeting was necessary, and on 20 March Everton eventually defeated their fellow Lancastrians 2–1 at Trent Bridge, Nottingham, with Chadwick's

The 1893 Cup final between Everton and Wolves was played at Fallowfield in Manchester where the huge crowd delayed the kick off. Everton eventually lost 1–0.

corner five minutes from time headed in by Gordon for the winner. Their prize was a final at Fallowfield, Manchester, against Wolverhampton Wanderers.

The Fallowfield stadium in Manchester was staging its first Cup Final. Indeed, it was the first time the final had been played outside London save for the replayed match at Derby in 1886. The old stadium still stands today after a long and colourful history as a major athletics track, a 'velodrome' for cycle races and now as the sports ground of Manchester University. But in 1893 the bumpy field in the suburbs of Manchester that was the home of the Manchester Athletic Club was the venue for England's premier soccer occasion.

The game was played on Saturday 25 March 1893 in brilliant spring sunshine that brought the crowds flocking to the Lancashire city. The kick-off had been scheduled for 3.30 p.m., but by 11.30 in the morning the queues had already started forming and an hour later more than 5,000 had found their way into the small ground. Manchester was just a couple of hours' train journey from Liverpool, so not surprisingly the game attracted thousands of Merseysiders, anticipating a triumphal day out.

Scottish international and former Preston player, Bob Kelso, won fame with Everton and starred in their first Cup final appearance.

'The sight', said the *Sporting Chronicle,* 'was one such as had never previously been seen at a football match in any part of the world.' A schoolboy game entertained the growing crowd before the final, and by the time it had ended the vast crowd had swelled on to the touchlines and there was grave danger either of a serious accident or of not being able to start the match. It was reckoned to be the biggest crowd that had seen a football match to that date, and the 192 Manchester police on patrol were clearly ill-equipped to deal with the mob. Fighting broke out between groups of supporters and policemen and to help quell the disturbances the band struck up, playing 'The Man Who Broke the Bank at Monte Carlo'. The 10,000-strong crowd in the far stand basking in the warm afternoon sunshine joined heartily in the chorus, just as the Wanderers emerged. Everton showed up a few minutes later, pushing and squeezing their way through the 45,000 spectators on to the pitch.

Everton were optimistic, having beaten Wolves the previous week in a League match at Molineux with a weakened side. Now, with most of their players fit again, surely they could improve on the four goals they had knocked past Wolves that day. But it was not to be.

Everton, as favourites, began the game at a cracking pace and clearly had the best of the first half. Their play was skilful and it was generally agreed that they were unlucky to be going in goalless at half-time. Whatever happened to the Wolverhampton players in the dressing-room, however, had a dramatic effect, as the Midlanders came out a transformed side. Everton were pinned back on the defensive, and with less than half an hour remaining the Wolves defender Allen took a chance shot at goal and the ball unluckily skated past Ben Williams in the Everton goal for the only score of the match. For the rest of the half Wolves continued to outplay the Merseysiders and, as the *Sporting Chronicle* put it, 'It was a very hard match, but not a particularly scientific one, and there is no denying the fact that the Wolves played in a most plucky fashion.'

Everton returned home disappointed, no doubt feeling that they had failed to produce the football they knew they were well capable of playing. And even the *Liverpool Football Echo,* in its special Cup Final edition, had to acknowledge that Everton had been outplayed. A few days later funeral cards, printed in Wolverhampton, began to circulate in Liverpool carrying a somewhat sour poem:

They came in all their glory
From that noted toffy Town,
To fight the famous Wolves
A team of English renown.

The Toffys came on boldly,
Their victory for to seek;
But now they go home gravely
O'er their troubles for to weep.

Farewell, farewell, dear old Everton,
No more for the Pot you will dribble;
You have lost it today through difficult play
And we'll shout farewell for ever and ever.

Everton Williams, Howarth, Kelso, Stewart, Holt, Boyle, Latta, Gordon, Maxwell, Chadwick, Milward.
Wolves Rose, Baugh, Swift, Malpass, Allen, Kinsey, Topham, Wykes, Butcher, Wood, Griffin.

For the remainder of the nineteenth century Everton continued to play an impressive brand of football that kept them in the highest echelons of the game. Most Saturdays they could field a team of half a dozen internationals and few sides came to Goodison and escaped with the points. By 1896 the *Sporting Chronicle* was able to report that Everton had as many as 30

T.D from sketch
A.A.F.

Everton beat Sheffield Wednesday 3–1 at Goodison in September 1894 with goals from Bell, Chadwick and McInnes.

registered professionals, an unusually large number even by today's standards. All the players were paid a good wage, usually between 15 and 20 shillings a week, with a bonus of £1 for every League win. During the 1893/94 season the club boasted no fewer than 12 internationals among their ranks.

Although Geary had gone by 1894, Edgar Chadwick was still displaying his fine touches and Alex Latta would tear at defences until 1896. Behind the 'Little Devil' Johnny Holt was the Scot Bob Kelso, who had joined Everton from Preston after spells with Renton and Newcastle West End. While at Renton he had won a Scottish Cup medal and had helped them defeat West Bromwich Albion in 1887 to claim the title 'champions of the world'. Everton converted him from a right-half into a fullback, but his being with an English club meant that he was ignored by the Scottish selectors and it was not until he returned north in 1896 to join Dundee that he added a further cap to the six he had won with Renton.

Scottish football was at its height in the closing years of the nineteenth century, and Everton were always quick to take advantage of a trip north to play friendlies. Glasgow Rangers, King's Park and Queen's Park all provided stiff opposition for the Blues, while many of Everton's finest players had Scottish origins.

John Bell signed for Everton in 1892, having just won a League championship medal with Dumbarton. Another Dumbarton import was Richard Boyle, who within four years of his arrival in 1890 had been appointed team captain. A centre-half, in the 10 years to the turn of the century he made 243 appearances for the club but was never capped by his country. Yet he was said to be the backbone of the Everton team and one of the most creative centre-halves ever to wear a blue shirt. He was not only strong in the tackle, and a fine passer of the ball, but was also capable of long daring runs upfield.

With this rich vein of Scottish skill Everton soon overcame the previous season's misfortune in the Cup Final. The 1893/94 season saw them in sixth position, with the highlight of the season the consecutive games against Sheffield Wednesday and West Brom. At home to The Wednesday on 23

S.T.D from
sketch by A.A.F.

TAYLOR WINS THE MATCH FOR EVERTON A FEW SECONDS FROM TIME

MASSEY SAVING A SHOT AT THE EXPENSE OF A CORNER

SHEFFIELD GOAL KEEPER FISTING BALL OUTSIDE

December Everton thrashed the Yorkshire side by eight goals to one, with Jack Southworth scoring four. A week later, as the year wound to an end, Southworth topped the previous week's feat by scoring six in Everton's 7–1 rout of West Brom. It was a club goalscoring record that stands even today. He hit 10 goals in two matches and ended the season with 27 from just 22 games.

Southworth had joined Everton from Blackburn Rovers, after a spell with those other aristocrats, Blackburn Olympic, in 1893, for what was then an astonishing fee of £400. He stayed just two seasons before injury forced him into retirement, but in his 32 appearances he hit an incredible 36 goals and was dubbed by one paper 'the prince of dribblers'. He won only three England caps, all with Blackburn Rovers, scoring three goals, and in a career total of 139 games struck 139 goals. When he retired he pursued his other interest in life – the violin – and became a professional musician, playing with a number of leading orchestras including the Manchester Hallé.

The following year Everton were again challenging for the title, but with Liverpool newly promoted from Division Two the most important fixture was the first League derby with their neighbours. On 13 October the Reds visited Everton, and before a crowd of 44,000, the biggest yet seen at a League game anywhere in the country, Liverpool were beaten 3–0. The Lord Mayor and other city dignitaries watched as Bell opened the scoring in the first half, with Latta and the former Third Lanark player McInnes adding further goals in the second half. The game finished in semi-darkness, but it was a scoreline which delighted the Goodison faithful, and when the two teams met again a month later 30,000 were at Anfield for what turned out to be an even more exciting clash. Everton led at half-time through Kelso, but Liverpool pulled back and the game ended with the honours even in a 2–2 draw.

Everton put up a brave fight for the title, but in the final three fixtures of the season threw away any hope of the championship. First against bottom-of-the-table Derby they lost 3–2 at Goodison, and then in the penultimate match of the season, against table-topping Sunderland at Roker Park, they went down 2–1 and so lost what slim chance remained of clinching the title. Sunderland finally took the honour by five points, with Everton in second place, while Liverpool in bottom spot promptly returned to the ignominy of Division Two.

The 1895/96 season brought problems Everton could well have done without. First the club was rocked by fraud, when it was discovered that some of the gatekeepers were helping themselves to the turnstile takings. As Everton was an extremely rich club, with a huge following, it was hardly surprising that some of their minor officials should be pocketing the gate-money.

That scandal was then followed by trouble with the fans. Riotous behaviour at the ground was not unknown and was often sparked off by bad refereeing decisions or poor play. On one such occasion torrential rain had brought a halt to the game with Small Heath, and with the referee in two minds as to whether or not to postpone it the players themselves stormed off the field, annoyed at his indecision. When he did decide to continue with the game, some of the players were already in the bath, so he finally called it off again. The crowd did not like his decision and made their displeasure known. As they trooped out of Goodison they went in search of the referee, throwing mud and stones at the club's windows and breaking some. As a result the club was reported to the Football League.

Aston Villa won the title, with Everton six points adrift in third place, while Derby, who had so narrowly missed relegation the previous season, were sandwiched in between, thanks to their new discovery, Steve Bloomer.

There was little to shout about in the League the following year other than for the return of the derby matches which brought a victory for Everton and a draw at Anfield. Instead, it was in the Cup where Everton shone as they fought their way through to their second final.

FA Cup Final 1897 Everton v Aston Villa

Everton's Cup exploits in 1897 began at home to Burton Wanderers, then lying in the lower depths of the Second Division, and it came as no surprise when Everton knocked five goals past them. Coincidentally, Wanderers' neighbours, Burton Swifts, were the visitors to Anfield in the first round, although they gave Liverpool a much tougher game, losing by the odd goal in seven.

In the second round First Division Bury were the

PREVIOUS PAGE Everton drew 2–2 with Sunderland in October 1894 with goals from Boyle and McInnes.

LEFT Everton win 2–1 against Sheffield Wednesday at Goodison in September 1896.

visitors, but they caused few problems, going out by three goals to nil. The next round pitted Everton against their Lancashire rivals Blackburn Rovers, whose Cup-fighting pedigree was second to none. The Ewood Park side had already appeared in six finals, and had won five of them, the last only six years previously. More than 20,000 turned up at Goodison and enjoyed a thrilling Everton victory, as Hartley scored twice from John Bell's accurate centres.

The Blues were now into the semi-final and faced Steve Bloomer's Derby County at Stoke. Meanwhile Liverpool, after their shaky opening, had also reached the semi-finals and faced Aston Villa at Bramhall Lane. For the first time there was the prospect of an all-Merseyside final, but the afternoon had barely begun before Liverpool were trailing to Villa and on their way to a 3–0 defeat. Everton began as favourites, even though Derby were riding above them in the League. However, Derby soon began to show why they were the punters' favourite. Relying on their usual quality play, and with their half-back line in superb form, they quickly blotted the aristocratic Bloomer out of the game. They tore at Derby, and with goals from Chadwick, Hartley and Milward won an exciting game by three goals to two and were duly into their second final.

The final against Villa was never going to be an easy one. The Midlanders had appeared in three finals, winning the Cup twice. They were at the height of their success and would go on to win five League championships during the 1890s. Already they looked to be well on their way to clinching the League title that season, so that they entertained the prospect of a League and Cup double.

The Crystal Palace had now become the venue for the Cup Final, but before their trip south the team took a few days off at Lytham St Annes, where they quietly prepared for the grand occasion under trainer Jack Lewis. The game was now adopting all the trademarks of a major sporting occasion, such as the pre-game holiday, the huge crowd, excited fans, special editions of the local newspapers, excursion trains and the promise of bonuses and luxuries galore for the victors. Everton travelled direct from Lytham to their secret London headquarters, but had something of a shock when they arrived to discover that Villa had booked into the same hotel.

More than 65,000 made the long journey south, with thousands travelling down from Liverpool on the special excursions which pulled out of Lime Street station long before dawn broke. It was another record crowd. 'The greatest assemblage that ever attended a fixture of the kind,' commented the *Birmingham Daily Post*. And to cap it all, the morning rain cleared to make 10 April another glorious spring day, just as it had been when Everton last contested the final. Bell, Holt and Chadwick were no strangers to the Crystal Palace either – they had played there the previous Saturday for England against Scotland.

A classic encounter was in prospect, and neither team disappointed as they battled it out for the honour of being England's finest football team. The first 15 minutes produced some of the best soccer the capital had ever seen as both teams attacked each other relentlessly. Either side could have scored, but first blood went to the Villa after 18 minutes, when a 25-yard shot went stinging past Menham. But Everton soon retaliated when John Bell, playing as skilfully as ever, sidestepped the Villa defence to send the ball flying past the advancing keeper.

Everton now powered at the Midlanders and minutes later were in front when Richard Boyle's free kick shot into the net. Their supporters went wild. Caps were thrown into the air and the roar could be heard miles away. But it was to be short-lived. Villa immediately struck back, and from Crabtree's pass Weldon scored the equaliser. Now it was the turn of the Midland fans to shout, but almost before they had calmed down Crabtree, Villa's English international, had headed their third goal. When the half-time whistle went, everyone agreed that if the first 15 minutes had been outstanding, then the last 30 had been possibly the finest football ever seen anywhere.

The second half could never be as exciting. Both teams continued to play brilliant football, with Everton defending skilfully, but they could not find the extra touch that would bring an equaliser. And so, at the final whistle, Lord Rosebery handed the Cup to Villa, calling it a 'splendid and Olympic contest'. Everton had lost, but they had lost gallantly, and to the finest team of the era who completed the double a few weeks later. The *Liverpool Football Echo*, which had produced a special edition with photos and pen pictures of all 22 players, ran the headline: 'GREAT BATTLE AT THE CRYSTAL PALACE', while *Association Football* called it 'The finest Final that has yet been fought'. And in John Bell Everton arguably had the most talented player on the field. In his 199 games for the club the former Dumbarton player scored 70 goals, delighting the crowds with the skilful and daring runs down the right wing that also won him his 10 Scottish caps.

ABOVE John Bell thrilled Everton supporters for more than a decade with his skilful running down the right wing.

ABOVE Smart Arridge, one of the most fearsome defenders left after only 56 appearances.

LEFT Goalscorer Jimmy Settle whose arrival transformed Everton's fortunes.

On the Tuesday after the final the *Liverpool Echo* carried an editorial praising the team for its endeavours, yet when the team arrived back at Lime Street there was only a small cordial gathering of friends to welcome them home. The next time they returned from a Cup Final it would be quite different.

Everton Menham, Meecham, Storrier, Boyle, Holt, Stewart, Taylor, Bell, Hartley, Chadwick, Milward.
Aston Villa Whitehouse, Spencer, Evans, Reynolds, James Cowan, Crabtree, Athersmith, Devey, Campbell, Weldon, John Cowan.

For the remainder of the century Everton promised much but delivered little. The year after their Cup Final defeat they were back on the glory trail but failed at the penultimate hurdle. This time their semi-final opponents were Derby County, but Everton were unlucky enough to catch Steve Bloomer at the height of his skills. Bloomer ran rings around them, scoring twice in their 3–1 win.

Everton ended the season in fourth place, but it was quite clear where their weakness lay. Only 48 goals had been scored in 30 League games. Bell was top scorer with a mere 12 goals, and only one other player managed more than eight. The following season was similar as they again wound up in fourth spot with 48 goals. Many of the great stars of the 1890s were now past their best. Chadwick would play only until the end of the century, while Richard Boyle was also nearing the end of his illustrious career. The former captain finally left Everton in 1902 for Dundee.

Smart Arridge, the Welsh international fullback, had also moved on, signing for New Brighton Tower soon after being disappointingly left out of the 1897 Cup Final side. He had come to Goodison from Bootle in 1893 but had to wait some years before securing a regular spot. In all he played 56 games, scoring five goals, and won eight Welsh caps. Another Welsh international was Charlie Parry, who joined Everton from junior football in 1889. He began life

27

as a wing-half but found his greatest success as a fullback, where he became renowned for his adventurous sprints down the wing. He was possibly the first attacking fullback, a role which did not become popular until many years later. In seven years at Goodison he played 94 games, won six caps and then in 1895 signed for Ardwick, later to become Manchester City, where he joined another famous Welsh international, Billy Meredith.

Billy Stewart, who had been an integral part of the Everton halfback line alongside Campbell and John Holt, left for Bristol City in 1897 after 137 games and half a dozen goals. A Scotsman, Stewart had arrived from Preston in 1893 after the Deepdale side had bought him out of the army after seeing him play for the Black Watch team. Sometimes called 'Wallie', he captained Everton in the final against Aston Villa.

The 1899/1900 season ended with Everton dropping into eleventh place, their lowest position since League football had begun, and being dumped out of the Cup in the first round by the Southern League side Southampton. It was not even as if they lost unluckily: they were trounced 3–0 and returned to Merseyside shamefacedly. And the man who had done all the damage, scoring twice for the southerners, was none other than the one-time Goodison favourite Alf Milward. Southampton, however, were no ordinary side, having won the Southern League championship three years in succession between 1897 and 1899. They would go on to win it three more times during the early 1900s. Having beaten Everton they continued all the way to the final, only to lose to Bury, and in 1902 they again reached the final, forcing a draw with Sheffield United before losing the replay. At this stage the Football League was dominated by the Northern and Midland clubs, with Woolwich Arsenal the only southern representatives. The bulk of southern sides would not join the continually expanding Football League until the formation of the Third Division in 1920, although a handful came into Division Two around 1910.

For Everton the season may have been unsuccessful but some new names were beginning to appear on the team sheet, and as the old century ended, there was increasing optimism that the New Year might bring another great era of Everton football. Queen Victoria, now aged 80, still reigned supreme over her Empire with Lord Salisbury as her Prime Minister. The Labour Party had yet to be formed and, over at Anfield, Liverpool were still awaiting their first major trophy. Everton could at least look back on the first 12 years of the Football League with some satisfaction, having won the title once and made two appearances in the Cup Final, and could count themselves among the most distinguished soccer clubs in the land.

The first full season of the new century began with a flurry of wins against Preston, Wolves and Villa but soon deteriorated. Seven games had been lost before 1900 was over and the remainder of the season brought little improvement. By the time the final fixture arrived Everton had lost thirteen games and were lying in seventh spot, though surprisingly only eight points behind the eventual champions, Liverpool. Suddenly the limelight in the city had swung away from Goodison and towards Anfield, where Liverpool were recording their first championship triumph. It was an event Everton were going to have to get used to.

In the Cup Everton found themselves drawn against Southampton again, but this time they proved that they had learned a lesson and came away from the Dell 3–1 winners. But it was of little consequence, as they crashed 2–0 to the previous season's Cup-winners, Sheffield United, in the next round. By no stretch of the imagination could the 1900/01 season be described as successful.

Yet there were signs that Everton had replaced their old stars with a few useful-looking prospects. Tom Booth had been appointed captain after just one season at right-half. A Mancunian, he had joined the Goodison staff from Blackburn Rovers in 1900 and was to have an enormous influence on the team. Jack Sharp was another who had arrived at the club the previous season, this time from Aston Villa, and during the next 10 years would become not just one of Everton's foremost players but one of the finest in the Football League.

But the one player who was instantly to transform Everton's fortunes was centre-forward Jimmy Settle. He was signed from Bury, after a spell with Bolton, in April 1899 and hit 10 goals in his first full season. In the 1901/02 season he went further – he scored 18 goals and gave Everton the power up front they had been lacking since the days of Milward, Southworth and Latta.

Everton began the 1901/02 season by beating Manchester City 3–1 and then Wolves 6–1, with Settle hitting a hat-trick. In the next game they forced a draw with champions Liverpool at Anfield and then, with injuries mounting, threw away further points before hitting another winning streak. A home defeat to Aston Villa on Christmas Day, however, put paid to all the good work, and when they lost further home games to Blackburn, Grimsby and Notts County they waved goodbye to the title. Sunderland were the champions but only just – no more than three points separated them from Everton. Everton might have counted themselves unlucky – after all, they had gone to Roker Park and won 4–2, as well as beating the prospective champions 2–0 at Goodison. But in the end it was their own fault, for having dropped so many points at home. Settle was top scorer, with 18 goals, but received little help from his colleagues – Jack Taylor was second-highest scorer with only eight goals. Had Settle's team mates contributed more goals, then Everton would almost certainly have taken the title.

In the Cup, too, Everton struck unlucky, drawing neighbours Liverpool in the opening round. It was the first time the two teams had met in the Cup and Everton began as favourites, having won the bulk of their previous League encounters. They went off to Southport to prepare and must have been well pleased when they held the Reds to a 2–2 draw at Anfield, especially as they had twice been behind. Five days later, however, at Goodison, before a crowd of over 50,000, Balmer put into his own net and Everton never really recovered from the shock, with Liverpool adding a second before the final whistle.

During the close season Everton played Glasgow Rangers in a friendly at Goodison to raise money for the Ibrox disaster fund, following the deaths of 25 people in April 1902. Both Everton and Liverpool regularly played matches against Scottish opposition during this period, often as a means of assessing Scottish players they might be considering signing, but also to test their own abilities against what were generally reckoned to be the best sides in football.

A myth also developed during this period that Everton were the Catholic team and Liverpool the Protestant one. The story was possibly encouraged by the regular trips which both clubs made to Scotland, where sectarianism played a major role in everyday football. Yet Everton tended to play most of their Scottish friendlies against Glasgow Rangers, the staunch Protestant club, while Liverpool usually challenged the Catholic Celtic or Hibernian. The myth has varied in popularity over the years and some

ABOVE Jack Sharp, one of the few distinguished sportsmen to have played for England at both cricket and football, made more than 300 appearances for Everton.

RIGHT It took a semi-final replay before Aston Villa defeated Everton 2–1 in March 1905 at Trent Bridge, Nottingham. The game at Stoke was drawn 1–1.

crowd trouble has been recorded. However, there seems to be little evidence to suppose that either club had religious leanings one way or the other. Certainly John Houlding, a leading force behind Everton in the early days and the founder of Liverpool FC, was a staunch Protestant and Orangeman, which may account for Liverpool's link with Protestantism. But it was also the case that Everton during the early twentieth century primarily employed Protestants, although they did have a Catholic doctor. During the 1950s Everton forged strong links with Eire, boasting half a team of Irish international Catholic players. And the same has been true of Liverpool in more recent years, with its strong contingent of Irish Catholic internationals. The myth has been blown up from one or two snippets of information, fanned by those who wish to encourage sectarianism. Indeed the managements of both clubs have been on the friendliest of terms throughout their histories, from the time when players from the two sides carried John Houlding's coffin at his funeral to their sharing of a match programme for almost 50 years and the involvement of John Moores in both clubs.

From their close challenge for the title Everton slumped to twelfth place, their lowest yet. The problem again was goals. Settle missed 13 fixtures through injury and scored only five goals, while nobody else could manage more than seven. In all, the team scored a mere 45 goals in 34 games. In the Cup they began well, with a 5–0 home win over Southern League Portsmouth and then a 3–1 win at Goodison against Second Division Manchester United. They then faced Millwall Athletic, another Southern League side, away and lost by a single goal. But if the season had been a disappointment, the next few years would enliven and excite the Goodison faithful.

In 1903/04 they made a strong challenge for the title, putting in a fine run at the end of the season which saw them leap up the table. The highlight was a 5–2 win over Liverpool at Goodison in which Alex 'Sandy' Young, the former Falkirk player, scored four goals. This was followed by wins over Wolves and top-of-the-table Sheffield Wednesday before they surprisingly lost at home to lowly placed Stoke by a goal to nil. They soon recovered, winning the final three games of the season, but it was too late. Sheffield Wednesday were champions, four points ahead of Everton in third place.

With Jack Sharp and Harold Hardman in great form, Everton seemed to be the best team in the First Division for much of the 1904/05 season. And not only the League title but the FA Cup as well looked set to come to Goodison. But then, at the very end of the season, it all went disastrously wrong. A tremendous winning run in the New Year shot Everton to the top of the League as they won six consecutive games, putting five goals past the previous season's champions, Sheffield Wednesday. Then they stumbled, drawing at Stoke and losing at Manchester City, and faced Woolwich Arsenal in a crucial game at Plumstead. The match was a rearranged fixture, the first game having been called off in November because of fog when Everton were leading 3–1 with just fifteen minutes remaining. And, of course, the inevitable happened. Everton lost by two goals to one and Newcastle leapt sensationally into the top spot. Everything then hinged on the final fixture of the season. Everton had to beat Nottingham Forest and then hope that Middlesbrough would defeat their north-east rivals. Everton won 2–0, but so did Newcastle, and the title went to St James's Park by a single point.

Everton had been going so well in mid-March that there seemed every prospect of a League and Cup double. They were topping the table and destroying all before them in the Cup. Their Cup exploits began at Anfield in early February, in front of 30,000 spectators, but by half-time an early exit seemed inevitable. Liverpool's lively centre-forward, Jack Parkinson, had put the Reds ahead and the Anfield side were giving Everton a difficult game. Then in the second half, as Everton began to exert pressure, Parkinson undid all his earlier work by tripping Sandy Young in the penalty area. Harry Makepeace converted the penalty and the Blues hung on for a replay. The two sides met again six days later at Goodison, where in front of another huge crowd McDermott shot Everton into the lead. But it did not last long, as Liverpool equalised to send the two teams into the dressing-room at half-time with one apiece. In the second half the game appeared to be heading for another draw when, with just five minutes remaining, the England amateur international Harold Hardman cut in from the right wing and hit the winner.

In the next round Everton travelled to First Division Stoke and won comfortably by four goals to nil before facing old favourites Southampton at Goodison. The Southern League champions, however, had passed their peak and would never be quite the same side again. At Goodison they went down by four goals to nil and returned south, little knowing that it would be 60 years before such success returned.

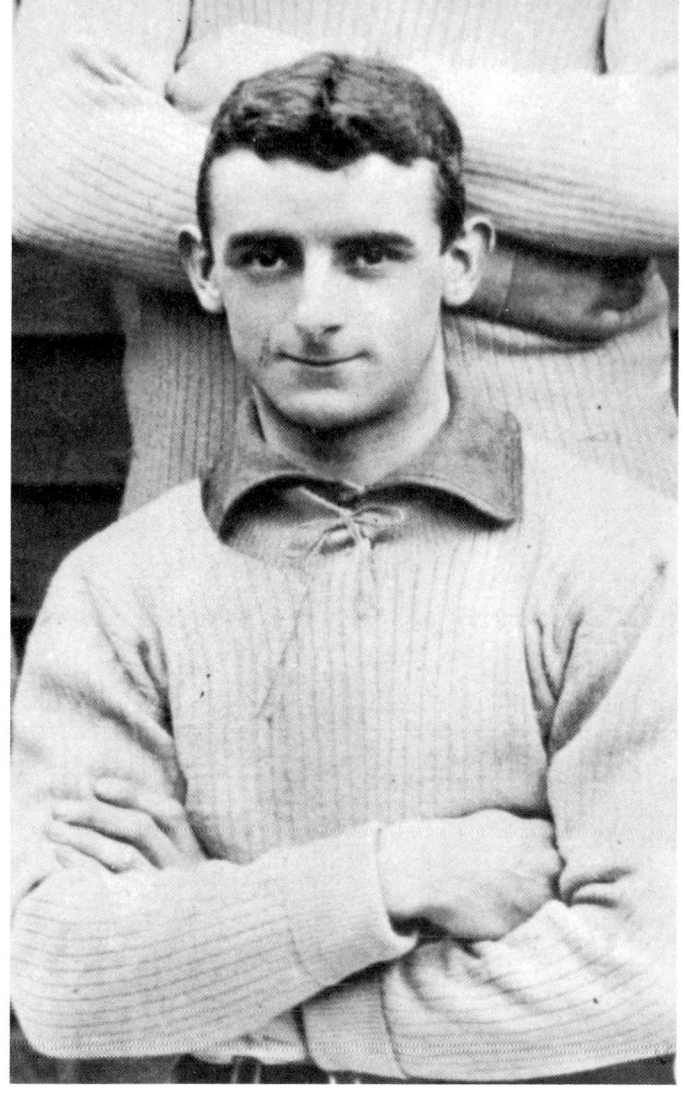

Olympic gold medallist and solicitor, Harold Hardman, left Everton to join Manchester United and later became chairman of his new club.

The draw for the semi-final pitted the Blues against Cup giants Aston Villa at Victoria Park and the double was beginning to look a serious possibility. The first game in front of 35,000 was drawn one each, and the two teams faced each other again at Trent Bridge the following Wednesday. This time Villa were by far the better side, going into a two-goal lead before Jack Sharp restored some respectability. Perhaps it was this defeat which left Everton so dispirited, for it marked the start of the three-week spell in which they managed to lose the championship as well.

There was bitter disappointment at Goodison after they had come so close to the double, but they need not have feared, as the following season would restore their dented pride. In Harold Hardman, Everton had discovered a player of outstanding quality. He joined the club from Blackpool in 1903 and over the next five seasons would make 156 appearances, scoring 29 goals. A winger, he left Everton in 1908 to join Manchester United, where he achieved even greater success, eventually becoming club chairman. He was an amateur in the finest traditions of sport, winning an Olympic gold medal with the England soccer team at the 1908 London games and also four full England caps while still finding time to ply his daily trade as a solicitor.

The double may have eluded Everton but they would be honoured in the 1905/06 season with a famous victory and another trophy. But first the team was rewarded with a close-season tour of Europe, taking in Hungary, Holland, Austria and Czechoslovakia, where they played a number of friendlies against both foreign and English clubs. It was the club's first trip abroad and was so successful that it soon became a regular feature.

The season, however, got off to a mixed start, with a couple of early defeats, and for most of the year the side lingered in the middle of the table, unable to make much headway, while Liverpool romped away with the championship. When the season closed, Everton lay in eleventh position, 14 points behind their neighbours.

Jack Sharp had now matured into a fine outside-right. He had been signed from Aston Villa in 1899, after making only 23 appearances for the Midlands club, but he immediately became a regular choice at Goodison. In a career that spanned 10 years on Merseyside he made a total of 342 appearances, scoring 81 goals and winning two England caps. But Sharp was renowned not just as a footballer but as a cricketer as well. Between 1899 and 1925 he scored more than 22,000 runs for Lancashire, including 38 centuries, and as a fast-medium-paced bowler captured 440 wickets. He also played in three Tests, scoring 105 against the Australians in 1909 at the Oval, and topped that by winning an FA Cup-winners' medal. After his retirement he opened a sports shop on Whitechapel in Liverpool that still exists today and became a distinguished director of his former club.

Coincidentally, playing just behind Jack Sharp was another England cricketer, Harry Makepeace. He had joined Everton in 1902, making his debut a year later, initially as a forward and then as a halfback. It was in the latter position that he won fame and his four England caps. In all, he played 336 games for Everton before retiring on the outbreak of the First World War and joining the coaching staff. Like Sharp, he played for Lancashire, and opened the England batting in four Test matches, scoring 117 runs in the 1921 Melbourne Test against Australia.

Everton's Cup run began with a home tie against West Bromwich Albion, of the Second Division, and

an easy 3–1 victory, thanks to goals from Hardman, Makepeace and Sharp. In the second round they were drawn away to Chesterfield, but the Second Division club foolishly allowed themselves to be tempted by Everton's seemingly generous offer to play the game at Goodison, where the financial rewards would be greater. In the event, not only did they lose by three goals to nil but only 8,000 people turned up. At home to another Second Division side, Bradford City, in the next round, Everton scraped through somewhat luckily with a goal from Harry Makepeace in the final minute that sent the Yorkshire side back across the Pennines cursing their ill-luck.

Another Yorkshire team, Sheffield Wednesday, appeared at Goodison for the quarter-finals, as Everton's luck with home draws continued. Wednesday were a useful side. League champions only two seasons before, they boasted internationals such as Frank Bradshaw and James Stewart among their ranks. Everton, however, were not impressed and tore at the Yorkshiremen from the whistle. Sharp opened the scoring after just three minutes, with Jack Taylor adding another five minutes later. Booth and Bolton added two more before half-time, and Everton went into their dressing-room 4–1 ahead. But the second half was a different proposition, as Wednesday fought their way back, scoring twice to give Everton a fright before the final whistle brought an end to what had been a classic Cup contest.

The previous season Merseyside had been the focus of football attention as Everton came close to a possible double, but this season it was Liverpool's turn. Top of the League, they were now into the semi-finals of the Cup, but who should they draw but Everton. The game was scheduled for Villa Park, and on the last day of March 1906 the two teams faced each other in what was the most important derby they had yet played.

The *Liverpool Echo* ran competitions and there were daily reports from the two camps as football fever gripped the city. The two teams decided to get away from it all – Liverpool went to Tamworth for a week's training, while Everton went off to Stafford and Northwich for 'hard brine baths'. More than 50,000 made the journey to the Midlands, with the first excursions pulling out of Lime Street station shortly after 10 a.m. The *Liverpool Echo* reported that 'the hardware capital was astonished' at so many football supporters and that the 'roads were congested and the ground full by 2.00 p.m.'.

Liverpool had an injury crisis shortly before kick-off, and compounded their problems by leaving their star striker, Sam Raybould, on the sidelines. Everton had no such worries and began at full strength, soon pressing Liverpool onto the defensive. But the Anfield side was a hard nut to crack, and in the end it was luck which told as Walter Abbott's long-range shot took a deflection that left Sam Hardy in the Liverpool goal helpless. Minutes later Harold Hardman volleyed a fierce shot that Hardy could do no more than parry out to Sharp, who neatly played the ball back to Hardman for Everton's second. Just as Everton had been thwarted the season before, so now it was Liverpool's turn. But there was some consolation for the Reds, as they wound up League champions for the second time.

FA Cup Final 1906 Everton v Newcastle United
Everton were into their third final and faced Newcastle United at the Crystal Palace on Saturday, 21 April 1906. Newcastle had reached the final via victories over Blackpool, Birmingham and Woolwich Arsenal and were the current Football League champions, although with two weeks of the season still remaining it was already clear that they would not retain their title. They would, however, win the championship the next two seasons. And, while Everton had come close to the double the previous year, the Geordies had come even closer by winning the League and then appearing in the Cup Final, only to lose 2–0 to Aston Villa. Newcastle had never won the Cup and were making only their second appearance in a final, but they were determined to improve on the previous year's disappointing performance.

Everton had at last welded together an outstanding team, but in Newcastle United they were facing probably the best side in the country, and also one of the

LEFT Harold Makepeace was another Everton player to represent his country at both cricket and football.

BELOW Everton attack the Newcastle United goal during the 1906 Cup final at Crystal Palace. Everton won by a single goal scored by Sandy Young with just 15 minutes remaining to bring the FA Cup home for the first time.

tallest. In John Carr, John Rutherford, and Colin Veitch, Newcastle had some of the finest English internationals of the day, while Andy McCombie, Peter McWilliam and James Lawrence had all been capped by Scotland. Everyone anticipated a classic encounter between these two Corinthian sides, with one newspaper dubbing it 'The Match of the Century'. Given that the century was only six years old, the claim was perhaps a little exaggerated.

The Everton supporters were now accustomed to the long journey south after their previous two trips and, as usual, more than 20,000 of them left Liverpool before dawn broke over the city. Sporting their colours, rattles, buttonholes, ribbons, hats and even umbrellas, they invaded London to the delight of the capital's population. The *Liverpool Football Echo* even carried a photograph of them gathered outside St Paul's Cathedral. 'CRYSTAL PALACE BESIEGED' read the headline on an early edition as the great crowd made its way across London towards the Crystal Palace.

Everton's only doubt was Makepeace, who was finally declared fit on the morning of the match. Everton, it has to be said, ensured that all their players would be fit by leaving most of them out of the club's pre-Cup fixtures and in doing so encountered the wrath of the Football League, who fined them £50. Newcastle were also fined for a similar misdemeanour.

More than 75,000 were crammed into the ground, though this was down considerably on the previous season's 101,000 attendance. Everton dominated for much of the first half, with Sandy Young and Jimmy Settle going close, before Newcastle began to display their talents. At half-time there was still no score but Everton looked the better side. With 20 minutes of the second half gone Young put the ball in the net; Sharp and Settle had contrived a neat move to put the Scottish international through for what appeared a perfectly legitimate goal, but the referee ruled him offside, and Everton had to begin their steady build-

up yet again. Finally, with Everton's attack well on top, and with only 15 minutes remaining, Sandy Young floated the ball out to Jack Sharp on the wing who swerved sensationally past McWilliam and Carr to return the ball to Young. The Everton centre-forward made no mistake, slamming the ball past Lawrence in the United goal. 'At last a goal,' read the *Liverpool Football Echo* report that evening. 'Sandy Young a hero. Fireworks and miniature earthquakes galore – shades of San Francisco,' it continued, referring to that week's horrendous earthquake in America. Newcastle piled on the pressure in a brave attempt to equalise, but with Everton pulling all 11 men back into their penalty area the Geordies could find no way to goal. Everton had won the Cup for the first time in their history, and Lord Kinnaird proudly presented the trophy to a beaming Everton captain, Jack Taylor.

Sandy Young had been the star of the match, highlighting the difference between the two sides. He had joined Everton from Falkirk in 1901 after a spell with St Mirren and soon made his debut, although it took him some months to hit his first goal for the club. Over the next ten years, however, he scored 125 goals in 314 games before moving to Tottenham and then Burslem Port Vale. He won two Scottish caps against England and Wales but was not always so highly regarded. After his winning Cup Final goal the *Liverpool Football Echo* somewhat ungraciously described him as 'a variable sort who plays one good game in three matches ... and determination makes up for lack of skill at times'. The *Athletic News* was more generous in its praise, offering a poem for the Everton hero:

O Evertonians, such a day
So fought, so sweetly won,
Hath ne'er inspired a roundelay
Since ever time begun;
As sweet as toffee to the tongue
Was that one splendid goal by Young.

But the final had not been a thrilling encounter and had fallen well below expectations. In the end Everton had, as the *Athletic News* put it, won by 'English muscle, English skill, English pluck'. But for the thousands of Evertonians the quality of the football hardly mattered. They had won the Cup and it was coming to Merseyside for the first time.

That evening the team went to the Alhambra Theatre in London, where they were given an ovation, and the next day they visited Hampton

ABOVE LEFT The victorious Everton Cup-winning side of 1906. Back row (left to right): Elliott (trainer), Makepeace, W. Balmer, Taylor (captain), Scott, Crelley, Abbott. Front row: Sharp, Bolton, Young, Settle, Hardman.

BELOW LEFT A year later Everton were back at the Crystal Palace but this time they were surprisingly beaten 2–1 in the final by Sheffield Wednesday.

Court. On the Monday they journeyed to Sheffield, where they lost 3–1 to Wednesday, and later that evening they boarded a special train decked out in blue flags for the journey to Central station. This time it was not a cordial gathering of friends but an enormous crowd of over 150,000 which greeted them. 'Cup Mafficking' reported the *Liverpool Echo*, adding 'Extraordinary scene in the City Streets'. The Lord Mayor and the club directors, as well as those from Liverpool, were waiting on the platform as the train pulled into the station, and after a few brief speeches the team boarded a coach and four to begin the long drive to Goodison. All along the route Sandy Young was the hero as the crowd made up a song about 'Sandy scoring a goal' that spread like wildfire among the fans. When they arrived at the ground, hundreds of fire torches were lit to illuminate the scene spectacularly, and an enormous cheer went up as Jack Taylor proudly lifted the trophy high above his head. It was 'the most remarkable popular demonstration that has ever taken place within the city boundaries', reported a local journalist. It had been a long wait to see the coveted trophy, but it would be an even longer wait before the Cup appeared in the City again.

Everton Scott, Crelley, Walter Balmer, Makepeace, Taylor, Abbott, Sharp, Bolton, Young, Settle, Hardman.
Newcastle Lawrence, McCombie, Carr, Gardner, Aitken, McWilliam, Rutherford, Howie, Orr, Veitch, Gosnell.

After their famous Cup victory Everton had become one of the most feared sides in the land. They began the new season in style, winning six successive games in October, and shot to the top of the table. In only their second game they clocked up their biggest League win by beating Manchester City 9–1 at Goodison, with Sandy Young hitting four goals. The Scottish centre-forward, inspired perhaps by his Cup Final exploits, was in dazzling form – he scored a dozen goals before October was out and hit a season's total of 29 goals.

Everton were regularly fielding eight or more internationals. Besides Young, there was Billy Scott, their Irish goalkeeper, as well as Walter Balmer, Makepeace, Abbott, Sharp, Settle and Hardman of England. Walter Abbott had been in the heart of the Everton defence for seven years or more, and even though he was nearing the end of his career was as fine a left-half as any in the country. He had joined the Blues from Small Heath in 1899 as a centre-

forward, but was soon shifted to left-half, where he played the bulk of his 291 appearances. He won his only international cap against Wales in 1902, although he represented the Football League as well. He was a strong, determined and forceful player who also had a fierce shot, and he contributed 37 goals before moving back to Birmingham in 1908.

Behind Abbott were the Balmer brothers, Robert and Walter. Walter had joined Everton as a 20-year-old in 1897 and came straight into the team, making over 300 appearances during the next 10 years. He was rugged and strong and not one for fancy footwork. If there was danger, the ball was belted straight upfield. He made just one appearance for his country, against Ireland in 1905, and moved on to Southern League Croydon Common in 1907. After the First World War he became coach at Huddersfield Town. He was uncle to Jack Balmer, later to be one of Liverpool's most notable centre-forwards. Robert Balmer was Walter's younger brother and for some years formed an effective partnership with him in front of Billy Scott. He was not as stocky as Walter but had the same no-nonsense style that made Everton's defence one of the toughest in the League. He retired in 1911 after 188 games.

Towards Christmas Everton's campaign began to falter as they lost to Woolwich Arsenal and Manchester City. Then, in the New Year, their League form fell away completely as they won only six of their final 16 fixtures. Seven of these were lost and Everton slipped from their perch at the top of the table to third place, six points behind the champions, Newcastle United.

The decisive factor was almost certainly their growing Cup commitments. In the opening round they had been drawn at home to Sheffield United and struggled against the competitive Yorkshire side. In the end it was an own-goal that saw Everton into the next round to face the Southern League side West Ham United. Everton did not relish the trip to London, but they had little need to fear, even though West Ham shot into an early lead. Everton always looked comfortable, and goals from Settle and Sharp ensured victory and a place in the fifth round against Bolton. The Lancashire side, however, were a different proposition. They were sturdy Cup-fighters, enjoying one of their best seasons in years, and attracted a record gate of 52,455 to Goodison. In the event, Everton could not prise Bolton's locked defence apart and, with the Bolton keeper, Edmundson, outstanding, a replay was necessary after a goalless draw. Another 50,000 turned up at Burden Park expecting to see not just as exciting a game, but the certain defeat of the Cup-holders. That inspired Everton, who even before the half-time whistle had blown had surprised everyone by going into a three-goal lead that was good enough to assure them a place in the sixth round.

The draw for the quarter-final did not favour the Merseyside team, who found themselves pitted against another Southern League side, Crystal Palace. The Palace were new to football, only having been formed in 1905, but did have the privilege of playing on the famous Cup ground. Everton did not take their task too seriously and soon paid for the mistake as Palace went into an early lead. After a bruising struggle the Blues equalised through Jack Taylor but could not force a winner, and the two teams were obliged to meet again at Goodison. This time Everton made no mistakes, dismissing the southerners by four goals to nil to win a place in the semi-final.

Everton found themselves making a return trip to Burnden Park for the semi-final, although this time the opposition was West Bromwich Albion, of the Second Division. Everton had been fortunate in the draw, avoiding Sheffield Wednesday and Woolwich Arsenal, and started the game clear favourites. No semi-final is easy, but Everton showed the marked difference between First and Second Division as they ran out 2–1 winners and into the Cup final for the second year running.

FA Cup Final 1907 Everton v Sheffield Wednesday

Sheffield Wednesday had reached the final the hard way, with victories over Sunderland, Liverpool and Woolwich Arsenal. Nobody doubted their ability, already twice champions since the turn of the century and winners of the Cup in 1896, but Everton had beaten them at Goodison early in the season and started as firm favourites.

Saturday 20 April 1907 was a chilly, wind-swept day in London, but the weather did not deter the thousands who travelled down from the north. As usual, the trains were streaming out of Merseyside the day before, with the final exodus at dawn on the morning of the match. More than 84,000 packed into the wide-open spaces of the Crystal Palace to await the Roses battle, paying over £7,000 for the pleasure.

From the outset it was clear that the swirling wind

BELOW LEFT Jack Taylor made three Cup final appearances for Everton and captained the 1906 winning side.

BELOW CENTRE Robert Balmer, who with his elder brother Walter, formed an effective last line of defence for Everton during the first ten years of this century.

BELOW RIGHT Edgar Chadwick, the former Blackburn Rovers inside-forward, joined Everton in 1888 and over the next 10 years played more than 300 games for the club.

would play a decisive part in the game. Wednesday were soon into their stride, and before Everton had even had time to settle the ball was in the back of their net. But fortunately for the Blues the goal was judged offside. Sheffield had looked the better side from the start, stringing their passes together and pressing the Everton defence to its limits. The Balmer brothers stood out splendidly and were even able to initiate some daring attacks. Sandy Young, looking to repeat his previous year's achievements, shot over the bar, while Harold Hardman missed an open goal. Everton were just beginning to impress when the England international James Stewart struck for Sheffield. The Yorkshiremen were deservedly in front but Everton did not panic. They simply continued to play their way back into the game, and with two minutes of the first half remaining Jack Sharp hit a timely equaliser.

The second half was a dour affair as the wind caught the high balls, making accurate passing difficult. Sheffield continued doggedly and should have gone ahead, but the longer the game went on, the more skilful Everton looked. Then, just as the match seemed to be petering towards extra time, and with the Cup-holders appearing the better side, George Simpson, Sheffield's 5ft 6in winger, scored against the run of play. Everton were justifiably dispirited, and in the remaining two minutes there was little they could do, so the Cup travelled north to the eastern side of the Pennines. It would be almost

Southampton won a stirring FA Cup quarter-final replay against Everton at The Dell in 1908 by three goals to two.

60 years before Everton would take their Cup Final revenge on Sheffield Wednesday.

Everton Scott, Walter Balmer, Robert Balmer, Makepeace, Taylor, Abbott, Sharp, Bolton, Young, Settle, Hardman.
Sheffield Wednesday Lyall, Layton, Burton, Brittleton, Crawshaw, Bartlett, Chapman, Bradshaw, Wilson, Stewart, Simpson.

That Cup defeat, so unexpected, stunned Everton. It seemed that a golden age, short-lived though it had had been, was over. In fact, it would prove but a temporary setback, as two years later the Blues would be back at their best, challenging for the title. But the 1907/08 season would awaken few fond memories.

On the field there were major changes. Tom Booth and Jack Crelly were both phased out, while Jimmy Settle and Walter Balmer had also disappeared from the line-up by the end of the season. Manchester-born Booth had first caught the eye of Blackburn Rovers in 1896 playing for Lancashire against Nelson and soon joined the Ewood Park club. He had already been capped by England when Everton signed him in April 1900, and over the next nine years he played

185 games at centre-half and won another international cap. He was captain of Everton during the early 1900s and left the club shortly after he had been dropped, moving on to Preston. But before he had even played a League game for them, he was on the move again, this time further north to Carlisle United, where after a short spell he retired.

Although he was a Liverpool lad, Jack Crelley arrived at Goodison from Southern Leaguers Millwall Athletic. Before Robert Balmer's arrival he had partnered his brother, Walter Balmer, at the back of the Everton defence and was in the victorious Cup-winning side of 1906. He played 127 games for the Blues before joining Exeter City in 1907.

If these defenders were great losses, then the loss of their diminutive inside-forward Jimmy Settle was catastrophic. He had come to the club after spells with Bolton and Bury and over the next 10 years scored almost 100 goals in 269 appearances. He was renowned for his speed and could outsprint any defence over twenty yards, making him one of the most dangerous strikers in the First Division. He won six England caps, appeared in two Cup Finals but never won the championship medal he so richly deserved. At the end of the 1907/08 season he was transferred to Stockport County and retired a year later.

Into their boots stepped John Maconnachie, a full-back signed from Hibernian, and Adamson, from the Scottish non-league side Lochgelly; but finding a goalscorer in the mould of Jimmy Settle was a far harder proposition. Everton ended the season in eleventh spot, without distinguishing themselves at any stage. The highlight of their League programme was a 6–1 win over Bury in late September; otherwise they managed to score more than two goals in a League game on just three occasions. Sandy Young, still as robust as ever, led the scoring with 16 goals.

In the Cup, Everton had more luck, beating Tottenham at home by a single goal in a rousing opening tie before drawing away to Oldham. Back at Goodison, the Second Division side were thrashed 6–1 with Hugh Bolton scoring four. Their reward was an away tie, appropriately at Bolton. In what was probably Everton's pluckiest performance all season they pulled themselves three times from the brink of defeat to end an exciting contest 3–3. And in the replay they were rewarded with a 3–1 win. Southampton also took them to a replay in the quarter-finals with a stirring 0–0 draw at Goodison. More than 20,000 crammed into Southampton's homely ground for the replay, hopeful of seeing a major upset on the same

lines as their great 1900 victory over Everton. They were not to be disappointed as the Southern League side gave the First Division giants a lesson. Everton began well enough, going into the lead after just four minutes, thanks to Sandy Young, but Southampton soon equalised and then added a second before half-time. In the second half Southampton took control and went 3–1 ahead with 20 minutes remaining. Young pulled back another but, although Everton tore at the southerners, they doggedly held on to win the tie 3–2. And that was the end of Everton's season.

During the close season they paid another visit to the Continent, playing games in Copenhagen and Gothenburg before returning to confront Woolwich Arsenal at the Manor Ground. Everton were in sparkling form, winning 4–0, with Bertie Freeman and Tim Coleman scoring two apiece. Freeman and Coleman had both joined Everton from Arsenal in 1907 but had not found it easy to break into the team. But with Sandy Young and Hugh Bolton now left out of the line-up they had finally secured their places and were quickly repaying the faith Everton had shown in them. With Harold Hardman also departed to Manchester United, the Everton team sheet was beginning to look dramatically different from that of a season or two past.

A memorable era of Everton stars had ended. It had been a period when moustached Corinthian footballers had led by their honest endeavours. Now a new age of professionalism was creeping in, when football would cease being an amateur game and would become a business. The new breed of players was more dedicated and dependent on the game and would nurture the sport into maturity.

Five days after Everton's victory over Arsenal, the London team visited Goodison and walked off with a startling 3–0 win that had everyone wondering what to make of this new Everton side. After the Blues had lost their next game to Preston, the supporters were looking back nostalgically to the old days of Hardman, Young and Settle. But it was a mere hiccup, as Everton then strung eight consecutive wins together, equalling their best record since joining the Football League. The goals were flying in – six against Manchester City, four against Bury, five at Sheffield United, four against Sunderland. Then after that run they drew 3–3 with Chelsea and 4–4 with Blackburn Rovers, a total of 35 goals in 10 matches. Freeman and Coleman were dynamic, the best scoring duo Goodison had seen in years. They had scored 32 goals between them in the first 17 games and Everton had rocketed to the top of the division. Then, just as dramatically, the goals dried up, and they failed to score in three Christmas fixtures. Coleman and Freeman never scored quite so freely for the rest of the season, as Everton threw away their lead at the top of the division and stumbled through a series of draws and defeats. But five goals still went past Bristol City, Sheffield United and, of all teams, Liverpool. In their final four fixtures the Blues dropped five points but still wound up the 1908/09 season in second place, seven points behind Newcastle United.

Bertie Freeman had hit 36 league goals in 37 games, making him the top marksman so far in First Division history, while his former Arsenal partner Tim Coleman struck 20 in 33 games. Altogether 51 goals had been scored at Goodison, a total bettered only once, in 1894, while 31 had been scored away from home.

The club directors rewarded their players by taking them on the most adventurous close-season tour yet, a trip to South America, where they played a series of successful exhibition matches against Spurs and the Argentinian and Uruguayan leagues. The tour led some to suggest later that it was thanks to Everton that the South Americans developed such wondrous footballing skills!

There had been worries that the long sea voyage and tiring tour of South America – a 14,000 mile round journey – might leave Everton exhausted for the opening of the 1909/10 season. But such fears were soon cast aside as Everton stormed to the top of the table. Of their first seven games they won five, taking 11 points out of a possible 14, and were already being talked of as prospective champions. Freeman had netted nine goals and looked set for a repeat of the previous season. But then, as the nights grew shorter and chillier, their long summer caught up with them. The rot set in with a home defeat by Liverpool, and they could win only four more games before the year was out. After the New Year the team fared little better, with a further six defeats and five draws out of 18 fixtures. The problem was up front. After beginning the season so well, Freeman was finding it difficult to score and his partner, Tim Coleman, ended the season with only five goals, compared to his 20 the previous year. Freeman himself managed 22 goals, well below his previous mark, while the second highest goalscorer Walter White, hit only six as Everton wound up in tenth place.

The FA Cup, however, proved to be more rewarding though after their first-round draw with Middlesbrough at Goodison it looked likely that it would be the north-eastern club making their way into the second round. But the odds were upset as Everton won handsomely by five goals to three. In the next round Woolwich Arsenal came to Goodison and within five minutes were on their way out as Everton hit the first of five goals. Sunderland were the visitors in the third round and were dismissed comfortably 2–0 before the Blues were obliged to travel to the Midlands for their quarter-final tie with non-leaguers Coventry. It was the biggest occasion Coventry had seen on their new ground, Highfield Road, but their performance hardly lived up to the event as Everton won 2–0, with both goals coming from Bertie Freeman. That win put Everton into the semi-final, where they fortunately avoided their old rivals, Newcastle, and instead found themselves challenging gritty Yorkshire competitors Barnsley, who were hovering in the middle of the Second Division. Everton began as favourites but, as ever, the Cup provided a shock. The first game, at Elland Road, ended in a goalless draw, with Everton's performance described in the local paper as 'miserable'. In the replay, at Old Trafford, they were said to be even worse, as they allowed the less skilful side to teach them a lesson in determination. Barnsley ran out 3–0 winners and Everton had been unceremoniously dumped out of the Cup.

Everton's defeat was compounded by a serious injury to Jack Taylor that led to the versatile half-back's premature retirement. Taylor had been struck in the throat by a ball which severely damaged his larynx and he never recovered sufficiently to play professional football again. He had been an outstanding servant to Everton, having joined the club from St Mirren in 1896. He began as a right-winger, playing in their first Cup Final in 1897, as well as in their two subsequent finals when he had reverted to centre-half. He made 456 appearances over 14 seasons, scored 80 goals and was rarely absent other than when injured. He was capped four times at Dumbarton and St Mirren, though he failed to win any further honours while at Goodison.

The next season, after 342 games, the great Jack Sharp also bowed out to pursue his career at the crease, while Tim Coleman went off to Sunderland after contributing 31 goals in 71 games, figures which any forward could be proud of. Coleman's disappearance from the Everton forward line had a profound effect not only on his long-standing partner from Arsenal days, Bertie Freeman, but on the team as a whole. His chirpy influence was greatly missed, and Freeman scored only two goals all season. No player managed to hit more than eight goals and Everton ended the 1910/11 season with just 50 goals. It was all the more surprising that they should finish in fourth spot, only seven points behind champions Manchester United. Changes were inevitable and the Everton directors did not hesitate to implement them.

Without his partner Bertie Freeman was lost, and in the summer of 1911 he was transferred to Burnley. Three years later he performed Everton one lasting favour by scoring the winning goal for his new club in the Cup Final against Liverpool. He had been a brilliant acquisition, playing 94 games in three seasons and scoring 65 goals, breaking the First Division goalscoring record with 36 goals during the 1908/09 season. Indeed, during that season and the following one he played 79 games and hit 62 goals. He won five caps, two of them with Everton in 1909, and scored three goals for his country, as well as playing once for the Football League against the Irish League, when he scored four goals.

Freeman's number nine shirt swapped backs for several weeks as Everton tried out various combinations before it finally settled on Tom Browell. The promising youngster had arrived from Hull in January 1912 and at the tender age of 19, as a desperate measure, was thrust into First Division action against champions Manchester United at Goodison. He was an instant success, scoring twice in Everton's 4–0 win. Inspired by the young lad who struck 12 goals in 17 appearances, Everton had soared to the top of the League by early April. But just as soon as they arrived, they were dislodged after a 4–0 drubbing from Sunderland. A week later they faced championship-chasing Blackburn Rovers at Goodison and went down disappointingly by three goals to one to allow the Lancashire side to sneak ahead of them and clinch the title by three points.

After seven seasons as Everton's regular goalkeeper, Billy Scott left for Second Division Leeds City during the summer of 1912. He had been a regular fixture between the posts, playing 289 games, including two Cup Finals, and had won three First Division runners-up medals. The six-foot Irishman took his final tally of international caps to 25 while at Leeds, in a career that spanned more than 10 years. The Scott tradition of goalkeeping on Merseyside continued after the war when his younger brother, Elisha, signed for Liverpool to become one of the best goalkeepers of all time. The pity was that Billy never recommended him to Everton, who were left with a desperate problem of finding a replacement. James Caldwell came from Reading as his successor

for the 1912/13 season but never seemed very happy behind a leaky defence, and before the season was over had given way to Hodge, who managed an even shorter career at Goodison, making a mere 10 appearances.

By Everton's standards it was a miserable season. They slumped from being near champions the previous season to eleventh, conceding 54 goals in the process. When Newcastle United won 6–0 at Goodison in October, it was Everton's worst-ever home defeat, made all the more painful by the fact that Sheffield United only the previous week had put four goals past them. The Cup brought only momentary cheer as well.

The only players who could hold their heads up high were Thomas Browell, who hit 16 goals, and Frank Jefferis, the regular number eight. Jefferis had joined Southampton in 1905, just as they went into decline, and came to Everton six years later, in March 1911. He immediately stepped into the forward line, acting as a goalmaker for Browell and Bradshaw, and won two England caps for his endeavours. He played until the war and then returned to the side in 1919 before moving on to Preston. His final game was for Southport in 1927, after 22 years of professional football.

If 1912/13 had been a miserable season, then the following year would be a near-disaster, as Everton progressively declined. In October, Blackburn put six goals past them and a week later, at Goodison, they were beaten 5–1 by Sunderland. As if that was not bad enough, Tottenham hit another four the week after that. The following week Hodge pulled on his goalkeeper's jersey for the final time, giving way to the former Lincoln City man, Tom Fern. By the end of the season Everton had dropped to fifteenth spot, their lowest ever in the First Division, although they could perhaps be content that Liverpool were in sixteenth place. Their defence had conceded 55 goals and, but for new buy Bobby Parker scoring 17 goals, they might well have found themselves heading for Division Two. Parker had been signed from Glasgow Rangers in November 1913 and immediately hit target, striking 17 times in just 24 games. Fern also quickly established himself and went on to wear the goalkeeper's jersey with distinction for another 10 years.

In the Cup, Everton drew Glossop North End, then languishing near the bottom of the Second Division, and were promptly dismissed 2–1. It was a defeat which convinced the chairman that the club needed to plunge expensively into the transfer market if they were to be a power in the land again.

5

THE WAR YEARS

In the 24 years since their one and only championship win, Everton had been runners-up on five occasions and in third spot four times. It was a proud record, but even the most ardent Blues' supporter had to admit that a second title win was long overdue.

Away from the insular world of football, events were occurring that would eventually reshape the map of Europe and rob so many nations of their flowering youth. On 28 June 1914, as Everton calmly contemplated the forthcoming season, a gun was raised on a street corner in Sarajevo in Bosnia and with the click of a trigger Grand Duke Franz-Ferdinand of Austria and his wife lay dying in a pool of blood. It was an incident that was to spark off a brutal World War. Even before the new football season had kicked off, Germany had marched on Belgium and on 4 August Britain declared war on the German nation.

The footballing authorities met to discuss the crisis, but at this stage there seemed little cause for panic and it was agreed that the forthcoming season should go ahead as planned. At first there were few signs of war, except for the posters and the advertisements, which even appeared in the Everton programme, urging young men to enlist in Lord Kitchener's army.

After two of the poorest seasons in the club's history there were signs that Everton at last might have something to look forward to. Bobby Parker had been an exciting discovery, while inside-forward Joe Clennell, a £1,500 buy from Blackburn, and centre-half Jimmy Galt from Glasgow Rangers gave the team a more forceful look. To make way for these new faces, Tom Browell moved on after scoring 37 goals in his 60 appearances. He had been an instant success when he arrived from Hull in December 1911, but had only managed two goals in his final season and Everton decided to capitalise on a tempting offer from Manchester City. Towards the end of the 1913/14 season a young Sam Chedgzoy, from over the Mersey in Ellesmere Port, finally made his breakthrough into the first team. He had made a handful of appearances in earlier seasons but had never managed to hold on to the number seven shirt. Once Chedgzoy had made the shirt his own it never left his back until 1926.

Everton began their season with a couple of useful wins against Tottenham and Newcastle, but then dropped seven points from a possible eight in their next four fixtures, and it began to look as if they were in for another gloomy season. But in their next game, away to Liverpool, they notched up one of their finest victories against the Anfielders, winning 5–0. Bobby Parker hit a hat-trick, while Joe Clennell added the other two. The game seemed to pump new confidence into them as they began a fine run. The goals were now coming with ease. Seven went past Sunderland, while in the New Year both Aston Villa and Bolton were hit for five. And the architect of all the damage was Bobby Parker, though with more than a little help from Clennell.

As the season wound to its climax, it seemed that Everton's Cup successes might damage their chances in the League. Oldham led with Everton just one point behind. Their Cup run had begun with an easy home victory against Barnsley, followed by the visit of Bristol City, who were disposed of just as easily by four goals to nil. Queens Park Rangers of the Southern League faced Everton next at Stamford Bridge, and it took an own-goal to help Everton struggle through to the quarter-final. First Division Bradford City were the visitors for that tie, and although they battled hard the Yorkshiremen went down by two goals to nil. Everton were now into their eighth semi-final and faced relegation candidates Chelsea at Villa Park. The Goodison men were hot favourites and a good bet for the double. But bad luck struck when goalkeeper Tom Fern and left-back John Maconnachie were sidelined through injury. To make matters worse, Harry Makepeace was injured early in the game and Everton struggled against a spirited Chelsea who had little else to play for that season. The Londoners won 2–0 and Everton's hopes of a double had been shattered. But at least that meant they could now concentrate on their final few League fixtures and hopefully wrest the title from threatening Oldham.

As they went into their final game, Everton were on top, a point ahead of Oldham but having played one more match. And while Everton were drawing at home to Chelsea, Oldham were also at home, facing Liverpool. As it was, Liverpool did their neighbours an enormous favour by winning 2–0 and Everton were champions for only the second time.

Bobby Parker had been the star who had made it all possible. His 36 goals, including six hat-tricks, scored in 35 games, equalled Bertie Freeman's First Division record. He had played 65 games since joining Everton and had scored 55 goals at a time when the offside law made it far more difficult to score than it is today. It was cruel luck that the war should intervene and rob him of first-class football when he was at the height of his goalscoring fortunes. He did return briefly five years later, at the end of the war, and although he could still score a dozen goals it was clear that his finest days were gone. His emergence as a goalscorer of international quality at a time when international football was suspended also sadly meant that there was no opportunity for him to be rewarded by his country.

Everton's title win was overshadowed, however, by events elsewhere. Even the *Liverpool Football Echo* could barely raise any enthusiasm. The front page was instead dominated by drawings of the battlefront at Ypres, with Everton's championship win forced onto the back pages. Many clubs were already losing players to the armed forces, while supporters had either deserted the terraces for the battlefields or were pressed into important activities at home in the munitions factories and shipyards. It was hardly a time for leisure and fruitless entertainments such as football. Men were dying by their thousands on the battlefronts of France and Belgium, and with the 1914/15 season barely over the Football League announced what had long been expected: that there would be no more League football until hostilities ceased.

The war marked a watershed for many Everton players. The Edwardian era of soccer was over and the long break during hostilities meant that many never returned to the First Division. Centre-half Jimmy Galt, who had captained Everton to their second title, played just one season for his new club. He had joined the Blues from Glasgow Rangers after eight highly successful years in Scotland that had brought him three Scottish championship medals and two caps. He rarely played during the war years and finally left for Third Lanark once League soccer resumed.

But the greatest loss was probably Harold Makepeace, who was already nearing the end of his illustrious career. After 12 glorious years war brought his footballing days to a premature end. He had played 336 games in a blue shirt, scoring 23 goals, with most of those arriving while he was still an inside-forward. He later dropped back into defence as a halfback,

Centre-half Hunter Hart made 300 appearances for Everton and was a vital member of the 1927/28 championship winning team.

where he won even greater fame, playing in two Cup Finals and on four occasions for England. Fortunately his services were not entirely lost as he returned to Goodison after the war as a coach while continuing his breathtaking exploits on the cricket field.

Nobody knew quite how long the war would last but everyone expected it to be over within a year. But the year had come and gone and on the Western Front there was stalemate as confronting armies lay encamped just yards away from each other in their respective trenches. Gradually the news filtered home of carnage and horror and every family was soon to become acquainted with the tragic meaning of war.

In place of the League system an *ad hoc* Lancashire League was established, but it was of little importance. The idea was to keep travel to a minimum while still providing some entertainment. Everton played fixtures at home and away against a variety of Lancashire clubs such as Bury, Preston, Southport, Bolton, Liverpool and the Manchester clubs. Many of their regular players were absent, either serving abroad or finding alternative employment to aid the war effort.

Joe Clennell had a particularly memorable period, scoring 114 goals in 104 games over four years to make many people wonder what a combination of Clennell and Parker would have done to First Division defences. Billy Gault, who had joined Everton in 1912, also hit the target with 93 goals in three years but never showed quite the same touch when League fixtures returned.

Everton acknowledged their uneasy position by contributing £500 to the War Fund and organising regular collections at games. Even the players dug into their pockets, giving a weekly remittance to the fund, and received training in case they should need to serve on the front. It was not a happy period, and when the Armistice was signed in November 1918 it brought immense relief to all. Meanwhile 15 million men and women had died and many millions more at home mourned their loss.

The war was 10 months over when Billy Gault kicked off the new season at Goodison. It was the first League game Everton had played since 26 April 1915, when, coincidentally, Chelsea had also been the visitors. On that anxious, war-depressed day Everton had forced a draw, to be heralded as the new League champions, but on a fresh summer's day in late August 1919 it was Chelsea who got the better of Everton with a 3–2 win.

It had been a long painful war and now everyone was ready to enjoy their rewards. Britain was about to enter a new era, football was set to become the national sport and Everton would be decorated as one of Britain's finest teams, while one man in particular would be honoured as the greatest goalscorer of all time.

The war had delivered a particularly telling blow to Everton, with so many of the club's leading players stepping down at the outbreak or seeing their careers peak while the guns flashed across the trenches. It was a makeshift team which took the field against Chelsea and a bewildered club which was forced to field 31 players during the season. As a consequence Everton struggled in the newly extended League of 21 sides, ending the season in sixteenth spot, their lowest yet. Two points fewer and they might well have found themselves heading for Division Two. Both West Bromwich and Burnley managed to put five goals past them, while Liverpool got the better of the derbies. Gault and Clennell headed the goal-scoring list with a dozen each, while in the Cup there was a first round exit at Birmingham.

The results may have been atrocious, but the crowds were pouring into Goodison. Gate receipts were up from a pre-war total of £12,000 to over £40,000, and the picture was much the same elsewhere. This prompted the Players' Union to demand an increase in wages to £10 a week that brought an unexpected response from the League, which suggested a cut to £9. After much bitter wrangling the players were forced to accept the reduction before the League became even tougher and reduced it further.

Everton desperately needed new talent but, with football having been disrupted for so long and with so many young men killed, it was not the easiest of tasks. Nevertheless, George Brewster from Aberdeen and Scottish 'Victory' international John McDonald from Airdrie arrived to help stave off relegation. McDonald's sojourn was far happier than Brewster's, who left within a couple of years to join Wolves. Left-back McDonald, however, remained for the next seven seasons, playing 224 games before joining New Brighton, where he played for several more years. After just one season at Goodison, McDonald had been appointed club captain and was said to be a major influence in the dressing-room, but his stay unhappily coincided with one of the bleaker chapters in Everton's history.

The changes in the line-up had the desired effect of improving performances. By the end of the 1920/21 season Everton had leapt up the table to a creditable seventh, 12 points behind champions Burnley. Indeed, had it not been for a disastrous end of season when they dropped seven points out of 10, they might well have been runners-up. Charlie Crossley, signed from Sunderland in 1920, was the best of the new players. In his first season he scored 18 goals, forming a productive link on the left with George Harrison, but the following season he was never able to reproduce the same form and managed only three goals. In June 1922 an exasperated Everton sold him to West Ham, where his form returned as he helped their successful push towards Division One. Bobby Parker, who had done so well before the war, hit 11 goals, but at the end of the season the curly-haired Scot decided on a change of scene and moved to Nottingham Forest, having scored 71 goals in 92 appearances.

In the Cup, Everton enjoyed a useful run, winning some stirring matches against Sheffield Wednesday and Newcastle before going out to the only goal of the game against Wolves at Goodison in the fourth round.

After such an impressive season there was every hope that Everton might improve on their League position and make a genuine bid for the title. But it was not to be. In fact, it was quite the contrary. After a breathtaking 5–0 win against Manchester United they managed only four more wins that year, with little improvement in the latter half of the season. During the late autumn they went a record 11 games without a win and found themselves propping up the division. Without Parker, and the experienced Kirsopp and Thompson, who had also been transferred, Everton struggled against even the most mediocre opposition. They reached a nadir in January, when Second Division Crystal Palace came to Goodison in the first round of the FA Cup and thrashed their First Division opponents 6–0. While Tom Fern in the Everton goal was besieged, the Palace goalkeeper was seen quietly eating oranges down at the other end of the pitch. Long before the final whistle the terraces had emptied. It was the blackest day any Everton supporter could remember, but at least it prompted the board into action. Within a week they had paid Airdrie £4,000 for halfback Hunter Hart and had begun the search for new talent. If ever £4,000 was well spent, it was on Hart, whose strength in defence saved Everton from the clutches of Division Two. At the end of the season they had avoided the drop by only four points, as Bradford City and Manchester United plunged into the lower reaches. Liverpool were champions, but at least Everton had saved themselves the embarrassment of

relegation in the same season that their neighbours clinched the title.

The early twenties did not belong to Everton. The following season, 1922/23, Liverpool again topped the League, but Everton at least made a spirited showing, ending the season in fifth spot, 13 points behind their neighbours. They began much as they had left off but gradually improved as the season wore on, losing only one of their last 11 fixtures. The cheque book had been out during the close season, though much to the disgust of some commentators, but it had paid dividends. The England centre-forward Jack Cock was signed from Chelsea, while winger Alec Troup and fullback David Raitt arrived from Dundee, and defender Neil McBain came from Manchester United. McBain's transfer caused a storm back at Old Trafford, with thousands packing a meeting to protest. They clearly recognised the man's talents even if their own club failed to, for McBain was a gifted wing-half who would enjoy four fruitful seasons at Goodison and win three Scottish international caps. He later managed Watford, New Brighton, Luton, Leyton Orient and Estudiantes of Argentina. He also holds the distinction of being the oldest player ever to appear in a League match, turning out for New Brighton – in goal – at the grand old age of 52. For the record, New Brighton won 3–0.

As if these new Scots were not enough, another had arrived from Celtic in April 1921 in the shape of Duggie Livingstone. He was a fullback who won early praise but soon encountered much bitterness from the Everton hierarchy and left for Plymouth Argyle in February 1926. He later enjoyed great success as a manager, taking Newcastle to a victorious Cup Final in 1955. Another forward, Billy Williams, came from Darwen, and centre-forward Fred Forbes arrived from Hearts to play just 14 games before moving on to Plymouth.

The new signings blended well, and although Everton made an early exit from the Cup, knocked out by Bradford, their League form offered much promise and was a considerable improvement on the disgrace of the previous year. The next season, 1923/24, presented a similar pattern as Everton finished in seventh place. Alec Troup, on the left wing, was superb, feeding delicate centres to the tall Wilf

The diminutive Alec Troup whose delicate crosses from the left wing helped make Dixie Dean the league's leading goalscorer.

45

Cornishman Jack Cock, who wore the number nine shirt before Dean, was said to be one of the snappiest dressers off the playing field.

Chadwick in the number 10 shirt, who consequently ended the campaign with 28 League goals. Jack Cock, at centre-forward, also benefited, hitting 15, while Everton began to acquire a reputation for their fine aggressive football. Manchester City were hit for six, with Chadwick scoring four, and Tottenham also suffered the indignity of five goals as the Everton forwards pulled out all the stops. By the end of the season Everton had bagged 62 goals, two more than champions Huddersfield Town, who finished eight points ahead of the Blues. But it was their defence that had let Everton down, by conceding 53 goals, 20 more than Huddersfield. Everton began well in the Cup, with a 3–1 win against Preston, but then, on a miserable Saturday in February, slumped to a shock 5–2 defeat at Brighton, from the Third Division South. It was the sensation of the round but spurred Everton into losing only two more of their remaining 13 League fixtures.

After a couple of good seasons Everton dramatically slumped. The close season had found them in Spain, playing Barcelona in a series of friendlies, one of which they won 2–1 while the other was lost by the same score. But the effects of that tour could hardly be blamed for the forthcoming season's debacle. 1924/25 began with one win in the first 10 fixtures and only seven goals scored. On just two occasions did the Blues manage to string two wins together as they tumbled towards the bottom of the table, contemplating the prospect of relegation yet again. But at the end of the season they had just avoided the drop, finishing seventeenth, nine points from relegation. They had managed to score a mere 40 goals in 42 matches, with not one player hitting more than eight League goals. It was a dire performance and the explanation for it was hard to pinpoint.

Wilf Chadwick had been injured, missing 15 games, and had lost the form that had brought him so many goals in previous years. He scored only six and played a mere two games the following winter before Everton transferred him to Leeds United in November 1925. The Bury-born forward had made 109 appearances over four seasons and scored 55 goals, and although the goals had dried up towards his final days he had still been scoring at the useful rate of a goal every other game. Cornishman Jack Cock also moved on in March 1925 to Plymouth Argyle after an eventful career. He had played for Brentford and Huddersfield before the war, and although he was presumed to have been killed during the hostilities he dramatically reappeared to play for Chelsea after the war before joining Everton in January 1923. He was capped twice for England, though never while at Goodison, where he was regarded as a rather dapper gentleman and a smart dresser who would not have looked amiss in today's dressing-room.

Duggie Livingstone was another who signed for Plymouth, joining the Devon club early in 1926. The former Celtic fullback had played 100 games for Everton, but after a row with the club's officials in 1925 became disenchanted and sought a move. He was back on Merseyside four years later, joining Tranmere, but wound up as coach at Sheffield Wednesday. He later managed Sparta of Holland, the Belgian national side and Newcastle United, where he remained until 1956. But, despite these losses, before the season was over another young man would step into forward line who during the years ahead would prove to be a most lethal goalscorer.

6

ENTER DIXIE

William Ralph Dean had been born on the other side of the River Mersey in Birkenhead in 1907 and had soon graduated through schoolboy football into the professional ranks of soccer with local favourites Tranmere Rovers, of the Third Division North. He made his debut for Tranmere during the 1923/24 season, when he played just two games, but the next season the 17-year-old played 27 matches, scored 27 goals and gave notice that he was about to become a major force in League football. Everton were quick to spot his talents, but even they found a queue was already forming outside Prenton Park, headed by Newcastle United and Arsenal. Everton, however, were fastest off the mark, and in the early spring of 1925 sent the club secretary, Tom McIntosh, over the water to sign the young man. Dean was delighted when he arrived home to be told by his mother that an Everton official had been around wanting to talk with him. He was so excited that he ran the three miles to the Woodside Hotel where he met McIntosh and without any hesitation signed there and then. Five days later at Highbury, on 21 March, he pulled on the famous number nine shirt for the first time. Everton lost 3–1 but Dean had arrived. A week later Goodison got its first glimpse of the young man as he made his home debut. Dean did not let them down, scoring in Everton's 2–0 win over Aston Villa. It was to be the first of 379.

He added a further goal that season, but it made little difference to Everton's overall position. Huddersfield, managed by the legendary Herbert Chapman, were champions again, while Liverpool wound up in fifth place. As Dean looked up the table at the 16 teams above Everton it might have crossed his mind, particularly as he saw Newcastle in sixth place, that he had perhaps been a little hasty in signing for the Goodison team. For the following couple of seasons those doubts would linger, as Newcastle succeeded Huddersfield as champions while Everton continued to struggle in the lower half of the division.

William Ralph Dean, the finest goalscorer of all time, arrived at Goodison in 1925 after just one season with Tranmere Rovers. His signing would transform Everton into the finest side in the league.

RIGHT Sam Chedgzoy was another arrival from across the Mersey. An outside-right, he played 300 games for Everton and won eight England caps before retiring in 1926 to America.

FAR RIGHT The Everton team during the 1926/27 season. A year later they would be champions.
Back row (left to right): Kennedy, O'Donnell, Brown, Hardy, Hart (captain), McDonald, Cooke (trainer).
Front row: Millington, Irvine, Dean, Dominy, Troup, Virr.

The 1925/26 season was not a particularly happy one for the Blues. They were dismissed from the Cup in the first round by low-lying Second Division Fulham, who held them to a draw at Goodison before winning by a single goal at Craven Cottage. For a club with such renown as Cup-fighters, Everton were having a lean period, not having appeared in a semi-final since 1915.

In the League they fared slightly better, pulling themselves up to eleventh place, but there were a couple of heavy defeats. The most embarrassing came at Anfield, where Liverpool put five goals past them, while Sunderland, up at Roker Park, thrashed the Goodison men by seven goals to three. The goalkeepers took the brunt of the blame as Everton swapped the men between the posts every few weeks before they finally settled on the former Stockport keeper, Hardy. The problem was that since Tom Fern had left for Port Vale in June 1924 they had never found an adequate replacement. Fern had been a fine keeper and a firm fixture for over 10 years, making 231 appearances. In the championship-winning team of 1914/15, it was Fern who regularly saved the team's skin and helped bring the title back to Merseyside.

Huddersfield were the first team to win the League three years in succession, but their manager, Herbert Chapman, had now moved on to Arsenal, where he would weave similar magical spells. But there was no doubting the star of the season, W.R. Dean, who struck 32 goals in 38 games including four hat-tricks. He missed the first four games of the season, in which Everton preferred Broad and relegated Dean to the reserves. But when he hit seven goals against Brad-

ford City there was little option but to reintroduce him to first-team football. He never looked back.

At the end of the season Sam Chedgzoy, who had helped create so many of those goals for Dean, bowed out after 16 years in the top flight. The outside-right had played 300 games and scored 36 goals. He had been a firm favourite at Goodison, writing himself into the history books in 1924 when he took a corner and dribbled the ball past bemused defenders and straight into the goal. Chedgzoy, an intelligent man, had carefully studied the rules of the game and realised that there was a loophole. So as an experiment, and as part of a bet, he decided to test the referee and the rulebook. Chedgzoy was right, of course, and the incident led to a swift change in the rules. He was capped eight times by England and won a championship medal with the 1914/1915 side before retiring to America in May 1926, just as Britain was plunged into the industrial chaos of the General Strike.

The goalkeeping problems continued into the following season, with three keepers again tested before the England goalkeeper, Ted Taylor, was purchased from champions Huddersfield Town. But Taylor was already approaching the twilight of his career and

survived only 42 games before joining Wrexham. Howard Baker, who played 13 games in goal, was transferred to Chelsea. An all-round sportsman, Baker competed in two Olympic games, winning a silver medal in the long jump. He also held the British high-jump record at 6ft 5in between 1921 and 1947, represented Lancashire at tennis and turned out for England at water polo.

Chedgzoy's powerful influence and experience were greatly missed, while the defence that had conceded 70 goals the previous season was creaking even more. There were too many players past their prime or simply not up to standard, and the result was that 90 goals were conceded in what was the worst season Everton had yet encountered.

The season began with an injury to Dean, who was thrown off his motorbike during the summer of 1926 and suffered a fractured skull. His jaw was also broken and he lay unconscious for 36 hours while anxious relatives and Everton officials wondered if their new goalscoring ace would ever play again. But they need not have feared, for Dean was back in action by the end of October, scoring with his head against Leeds United in his first game. It was rumoured that surgeons had inserted a steel plate into his skull, giving

him even greater heading ability, but of course this was completely untrue. He went on to score 21 League goals that season, but even his prowess in the penalty area was not enough to compensate for Everton's leaky defence. The Lancashire trio of Bury, Burnley and Bolton all hit five past them, while top of the table Newcastle went two better, winning 7–3.

At the end of the season, having courted relegation the entire year, Everton finished in twentieth place and avoided the drop by four points. But it had been a close shave, with a fortunate end of season run that brought only two defeats in their final nine fixtures rescuing them from their fate.

In the opening round of the Cup, Everton had a comfortable 3–1 win over non-leaguers Poole Town, but then went out to Second Division Hull City at the third attempt. It was clear that major surgery was necessary if Everton were to avoid crashing into Division Two the next season. By the end of the season the club's secretary, Tom McIntosh, and trainer Harry Cooke were scouring the League for new talent and experienced players.

The 1927/28 season was destined to be one of the greatest in the club's history, and for one man in particular it would have an historic outcome. After the previous year's near disaster nobody expected Everton to be title contenders. Instead the pundits were predicting that the Blues would probably wind up in the Second Division. They had not reckoned with the goalscoring machine of Dixie Dean. But before Dean could perform his wonders in front of goal, some new talent was desperately needed to supplement him, as well as to fill holes left by others. John McDonald was nearing the end of his days with Everton, and signed for New Brighton in August 1927. The fullback and former captain had played 224 games since 1920 but failed to lead the club to any honours. Another Scotsman, David Raitt, also bowed out, moving to Blackburn Rovers when Warney Cresswell secured his right-back position. He had played 131 games during his six seasons on Merseyside.

The most important acquisition was Warney Cresswell, signed from Sunderland in February 1927. Cresswell was an experienced and tough defender who knew how to organise and control a defence and was soon appointed captain. He was already an established England international, having won six caps with South Shields and Sunderland. Jerry Kelly had also arrived from Ayr United in the same month to play alongside him. Up front Everton signed an outside-right, Ted Critchley from Stockport County, for a small fee to take the place of Chedgzoy, and then surprised everyone on Merseyside in March 1926 by swooping on Anfield to sign Liverpool's prolific goalscorer Dick Forshaw. The former Middlesbrough man had spearheaded Liverpool's capture of two titles in the early twenties, scoring at the rate of a goal almost every other game in a distinguished career with the Reds. Many reckoned him at the end of his playing days and a waste of money, but under the guidance of secretary, Tom McIntosh, and trainer Harry Cooke he was to find a fresh lease of life with his new partner, Dean.

Everton kicked off the season with a good home win against Sheffield Wednesday, but then lost miserably by four goals to two at Middlesbrough. George Camsell, who had scored a record-breaking 59 goals for the Teesside club the previous season when they won the Second Division title, showed Dean a few tricks that day as he hit all four 'Boro goals. Everton then managed to win just one of their next five games, drawing the remainder, before knocking five goals past Manchester United. Dean, who had so far scored in every game, struck all Everton's goals that afternoon to take his tally to a remarkable 17 in just nine games.

In the derby at Goodison, before a 64,000 crowd, Liverpool and Everton scored one apiece, and then Everton faced West Ham at Goodison. The Hammers must have thanked their lucky stars that Dean was absent on international duty for England against Ireland that day, but Everton then demonstrated that the number nine's talents were rubbing off on his fellow players when they thrashed the Londoners by seven goals to nil. On Merseyside they still wonder what the score might have been with Dean in the line-up.

Dean returned for the next game and duly celebrated with a hat-trick and then struck another a week later as Everton destroyed Leicester City 7–1. Dixie, as he was fondly known on Merseyside, though much to his dislike, was now the talk of the Football League, and one or two statisticians were already reaching for their record books. Against Derby County in the next fixture he scored another two, but then against Sunderland dried up, failing to score for only the second time that season as the Rokermen ran out winners by a single goal at Goodison. It was mid-November and only Everton's second defeat, and Dean had scored 25 goals. His response was to hit two more in the next game as the Goodison club won a thriller against Bury by three goals to two. By the end of the year Dean had scored 35 goals and Everton sat happily at the top of the table, well clear of Cardiff City and Huddersfield Town, while the rest of the League wondered what they had to do to stop the man from scoring.

He began the New Year in much the same fashion as he had ended the old one, scoring a couple as Everton surprisingly went down to Blackburn Rovers, but they sprang back spiritedly in the following game with a 3–1 win over Middlesbrough. Two weeks later they visited Huddersfield Town and were hammered by four goals to one before 51,000 spectators. Dean scored in the classic confrontation, but the team's confidence had been shattered by the skills of the Leeds Road side and in particular by Alec Jackson's stunning hat-trick. That defeat narrowed the gap at the top of the table as Town crept to within one point of the Blues. The next match brought a further shock as Tottenham proceeded to put five goals past them at Goodison, and Everton suddenly looked like a side with the jitters. The next game brought a visit to Anfield, hardly an occasion to inspire confidence, and in one of their fiercest encounters Liverpool showed their mettle in a thrilling three-all draw with all Everton's goals coming from Dean. With those three goals Dean equalled

Eddie Harper's First Division haul of 43 goals for Blackburn, and as he turned from scoring he bowed gracefully, like a matador, in front of a less than enthusiastic Kop.

Everton and Dean then mysteriously went four games without scoring, during which they lost two and drew two. The title seemed to be drifting away as Everton slipped off the top of the table, but Dean, who had missed one of the fixtures, was back on the goal trail the following week with a couple against Derby County in a 2–2 draw, including the elusive forty-fourth goal to break Harper's tally.

To capture the title Everton would now need a storming finish, but when they journeyed to Roker Park on 31 March without Dean, who was again on international call, they must have suspected that their championship hopes were fading. Yet they produced a stirring performance, with local boys Albert Virr and William Easton helping them to a 2–0 victory. Everton then wreaked vengeance on Blackburn, to the glee of 60,000 Evertonians, as Dean returned to score twice in a 4–1 win. Everton shot back to the top of the table again, with Dean's goal tally at 47, but with just six games remaining it seemed that George Camsell's 59 goals was a safe record. Dixie, however, had other plans.

Against Bury he scored another as the Blues drew and then proceeded to add a further nine to his tally as Everton won four of their next five fixtures. Dean was back on form again but was injured as he hit four first-half goals against Burnley in the penultimate fixture of the season, and it looked as if he might miss the final game against Arsenal. The match against Burnley left Everton looking like champions, and they had only to beat Arsenal to clinch the title. Even before that game kicked off their nearest rivals Huddersfield Town lost, and it was Everton's championship, whatever the result against Arsenal. But that was not to say the Arsenal match did not matter, as Dean still had to score another three goals to break Camsell's record. Yet against the Arsenal, now under the tutelage of Herbert Chapman, it seemed an impossible task.

Saturday 5 May 1928 was a typical spring day. The sun shone with only occasional puffs of cloud drifting from the west to disturb the long shadows. The afternoon was all set for a fitting climax to a glorious season. More than 60,000 people from all over Merseyside crammed into the wide spaces of Goodison, hoping to see an exhibition of faultless football from two of the finest teams in the land. The match also marked the end of Charlie Buchan's illustrious career

TOP Warney Cresswell greeting the Chelsea captain in a Cup tie at Stamford Bridge in 1929.

ABOVE League Champions 1928.
Back row (left to right): McIntosh (secretary), Kelly, Hart, Davies, O'Donnell, Virr, Cooke (trainer).
Front row: Critchley, Martin, Dean, Cresswell, Weldon, Troup.

with Arsenal, as the former Sunderland and England star bowed out of football. In many ways it was a pity that the limelight did not shine on Buchan that day, for the Arsenal man was one of the greatest names in football history. But during the game he would see his mantle pass fittingly to a player of comparable skill and dedication.

Arsenal surprised everyone by opening the scoring in the first minute, when Arthur Davies, in the Everton goal, failed to hold a thunderous shot from Arsenal's Shaw, but Everton replied almost from the restart through Dean. It was the team's hundredth goal, and Dean's fifty-eighth, but the prospect of breaking the record still seemed remote. Then, just a few minutes later, Dean was bundled over in the penalty area and the referee unhesitatingly awarded a penalty. Dean stepped up to take the kick, and a deathly silence fell on Goodison as he carefully placed the ball on the spot and began his run-up. The ball rocketed into the back of the net and Everton were leading. But more importantly Dean had equalled George Camsell's record and now needed just one goal to make the record his own. By half-time Arsenal had equalised, and when the two teams emerged for the second half Goodison was at fever-pitch. Everton tore at Arsenal, creating chances, but nobody wanted to seize the opportunity. Instead, their only aim was for Dean to score. Then, with just five minutes remaining, Everton won a corner and the tiny Scottish winger Alec Troup stepped up to take the kick. The ball was lofted high into the area and seemed to hang for an eternity as Dean climbed above the Gunners' defence and with a flick of the neck sent the

ball soaring into the Arsenal net. Goodison erupted at what was and probably still remains its greatest moment. 'There has never been such a joyful shout at Everton,' reported the *Liverpool Football Echo*. Everyone rushed to congratulate Dean, who was suddenly swamped by red and blue shirts. The cheering was said to have continued for eight minutes. Only Charlie Buchan remained at a distance, annoyed that his passing from the game should have been upstaged by a curly-haired 21-year-old from Birkenhead.

With just seconds remaining Arsenal equalised, but nobody cared. When the final whistle blew Warney Cresswell was handed the glittering League trophy by the Liverpool chairman and Football League president, John McKenna, and Everton could boast the greatest goalscorer of all time. He had scored not only 60 League goals but had added a further three in the Cup, while in other representative games and internationals he had scored 35, bringing his season's aggregate to 100 goals in 56 games. In the League he had scored seven hat-tricks, with 31 of his total away from home, while Everton's tally for the season was a staggering 102 goals.

Everton's season had caught the imagination of the football world, while Dean's record attempt had captured the public's attention. A cartoon in the *Echo* simply showed a goalnet bulging with 60 footballs. Everton were now the most famous club in Britain, and nobody expected the next two seasons to bring anything but greater glory.

Everton's magnificent championship-winning team may have been inspired by Dean, but it nevertheless boasted other players of outstanding quality.

Ted Taylor, the former Huddersfield and England keeper, had kept goal for most of the season but had been replaced by Henry Hardy and Arthur Davies during the latter half of the season. At right-back the impeccable Warney Cresswell and at left-back Jack O'Donnell, the former Darlington man, kept a tight rein on a defence which conceded 66 goals, the lowest in the First Division. Scotsman Jerry Kelly, the robust Hunter Hart and Albert Virr stood steadfastly in front of them. Hart had joined Everton from Airdrie in 1922, usually filling the left-half slot, and for a time skippered the side. He was reckoned to be one of the strongest defenders in the division and was probably at the peak of his career during the championship season. The next season nine years of Division One football caught up with him and Everton slumped as he lost his form.

Up front Dean was ably assisted by Ted Critchley, the veteran Dick Forshaw, Alec Troup and Tony Weldon. Troup had come to Everton in 1923 via Forfar Athletic and Dundee, and more than any other player was responsible for creating so many of Dean's goals. The left-winger had an uncanny knack of floating the ball into the area, where it would hang tantalisingly waiting for Dean's head. Twenty of Dean's 60 goals were struck with the head that season, and usually thanks to Troup's efforts. Troup also won five Scottish caps, but, as with so many of the championship side, the season that followed was to prove his last. The other unsung hero was Tony Weldon, another one-time Airdrie player, who arrived in March 1927, but after 70 games he joined Hull City during the close season of 1930. George Martin, although he did not arrive at Goodison until March 1928, nonetheless made a major contribution in the number eight shirt. A versatile player, he made 86 appearances for the Blues and enjoyed five fruitful seasons before moving on to Middlesbrough and Luton Town. He later managed Luton before taking over the reins at Newcastle, where he guided them to promotion and fourth spot in Division One.

Much was expected of Everton as the new season kicked off in August 1928, the fiftieth anniversary of their founding. With Dean looking as fit and dangerous as ever, it was reckoned that Everton had every chance of retaining the title. They began well enough with a win at Bolton, a draw with Sheffield Wednesday and a win against Portsmouth. Dean had netted six goals already in those three matches but when they faced Sheffield Wednesday again, in the fourth fixture of the season, they went down by a single goal. That defeat looked a mere hiccup, for the following

OPPOSITE Dixie Dean hits his famous third goal against Arsenal at Goodison Park in May 1928. It was his record-breaking 60th league goal that also helped Everton to clinch the league title. In all, he scored 100 goals in 56 matches during the season.

BELOW Local boy Albert Virr played more than 100 games at halfback and was an influential member in the championship side before injury led to his early retirement.

week they won comfortably at Birmingham City. But it was the next two weeks that brought home the truth. First they were thrashed 6–2 at Goodison by newly promoted Manchester City in one of the shocks of the season, and then they were beaten 3–1 by Huddersfield Town. From then on the season slid from bad to worse. At no point could they string more than two wins together, and when they journeyed to Maine Road to meet City again in the New Year, the Light Blues put five past them. Who would have thought a year earlier that any one team could possibly put 11 goals past Everton in a season? Suddenly the glory of the previous year seemed a long way away as they ended their campaign with six consecutive defeats that saw them slump miserably to eighteenth in the table.

Dean had managed a mere 26 goals, while nobody else had scored more than six. But Dean's poor strike rate must be put into perspective. He had missed 13 games through injury, so that his 26 goals in 29 games was more than respectable. It was the injury to Dean in particular, as well as an unfortunate series of injuries to others, that had led to the team's decline. Albert Virr, playing in a Cup tie against Chelsea, sustained a serious knee injury and played only a handful more games for the Blues again before retiring. He had played just 126 games. Alec Troup, who had to strap a weak collarbone before every game, also missed a few fixtures and seemed well below his best. The next season he played just four times before rejoining Dundee. Tony Weldon also missed more than 20 games through injuries, while the great Dick Forshaw, now boasting three championship medals from his Merseyside clubs, played just eight times. What this meant was that the outstanding forward line of the previous season rarely played together all season. Consequently Everton struck only 63 goals compared with 102 the previous year.

Sadly, 1929/30 proved to be even worse, as Everton suffered the humiliation of relegation for the first time in their 51-year history. Life in Liverpool offered few pleasures during the 1930s. The Depression had led to mass unemployment, with one in every three men without work in the city. Unemployment benefit was barely enough to live on and the Means Test ensured that nobody out of work enjoyed any luxuries. For most it meant there was not enough money to squander on football matches, and for those who could afford the price of a ticket it seemed like money ill spent when your team lost. Things were not much better at Anfield either, though at least they held on to their First Division place.

The season began optimistically enough with a couple of draws followed by a 3–0 defeat of the Reds at Anfield. Dean was looking sharp again, but it was not long before Everton hit a lean patch of three consecutive defeats. The rot had now set in and between the beginning of October and the end of March they managed only six wins. Aston Villa, Bolton and Leicester City each put five goals past them as they crashed to the foot of the table. Relegation was soon a foregone conclusion, and their season might have been even grimmer had it not been for victories in their final three fixtures. When the points were totted up, they had a mere 35 and were duly relegated with Burnley. They had won only 12 games, scoring 80 goals with 92 against. It was a miserable record. Dean netted 23 goals but, as in the previous season, he had missed games through injury, so 23 in 25 games could still be regarded as a proud achievement. George Martin struck 15 goals, while Jimmy Stein, signed from Dunfermline to replace Alec Troup, hit 10. But without Hunter Hart, Virr and Kelly, Everton were a soft touch for any attacking team. Hart's playing days came to an end shortly after Christmas, when age finally caught up with him. The centre-half had joined Everton from Airdrie in 1922; he made 300 appearances and had captained Everton for a spell. He was a strong, spirited player whose very presence at the centre of Everton's defence was usually enough to overawe the opposition.

Everton had fielded 29 players during the season, with only five of them making more than 30 appearances. There was too much chopping and changing, and some of the expensive new purchases proved to be poor buys. At the Annual General Meeting a vote of confidence in the board was only narrowly carried, and with another poor Cup run ending with Everton's dismissal in the fourth round the club faced life in Division Two with little enthusiasm.

7

A HAT-TRICK OF HONOURS

On the weekend of 30 August 1930 Everton took the train from Lime Street and began the long journey to the West Country and unchartered territory as their sojourn in the Second Division started. Plymouth Argyle had won promotion to the division only that season, having topped the Third Division South, and more than 34,000 honoured the Blues by turning up to see the opening fixture of the new season. But Plymouth's youthful enthusiasm was no match for the subtle experience of the Blues, who won by three goals to two. Everton now found themselves visiting strange, cosy little football grounds where the players could almost touch the crowd at throw-ins. Millwall, Reading, Port Vale and Southampton were all teams unknown to most of them. But Everton were determined that their stay in the lower division would be a short one and quickly strung five wins together to send themselves shooting to the top of the League.

By March they had lost only three games, one of those a 5–2 thrashing at Burnley, and there was no

Ted Sagar was possibly the finest goalkeeper in Everton's history, making almost 500 appearances in 16 years and winning four England caps

doubt that they would be rejoining the elite at the end of the season. In the New Year they put together a record-breaking run of 10 wins which saw them score 43 goals. They were devastating as they hit nine past Plymouth, seven past Charlton and five each against Swansea and Barnsley. Earlier on in the season Swansea and Stoke had been hit for five, Charlton for seven, and Oldham for six. On 8 November, against Wolves at Goodison, Dean scored to become the youngest player, at 23 years of age, to score 200 league goals, and he had achieved it in only 199 games.

The title was well wrapped up before spring had dawned and Everton eased up to lose three of their final five fixtures. But it hardly mattered. They had still captured promotion back to their rightful home by seven points. In the process they had scored a phenomenal 121 goals, with Dean scoring 39 in 37 games.

And for the first time in years Everton enjoyed a useful run in the Cup before being surprisingly beaten in the semi-finals. They began with another visit to Plymouth and a comfortable win before thrashing Crystal Palace by six goals to nil. Dean scored four and in the next round found the net again in an

exciting 5–3 win over Grimsby in front of a 65,000 crowd at Goodison. Neighbouring Southport entertained Everton in the quarter-finals in what was the seaside club's finest Cup run, but it all ended in disaster for them as Dean scored four more while his colleagues added another five in their 9–1 win. In the semi-final Everton avoided the First Division giants Sunderland and Birmingham City and instead faced West Brom, who were challenging for promotion not far behind Everton. Having already beaten the Midlands club at home and away that season, they were quietly confident that Wembley was beckoning. But it was not to be. West Brom's name was clearly etched on the trophy as Everton missed chances and then gave away a foolish goal, the only one of the game. More than 70,000, roared on by another 20,000 locked outside, watched in disbelief at Old Trafford, but no matter how near Everton came it was not close enough and West Brom went on to lift the Cup. The Cup had given Dean a further nine goals and the team another 22, making 143 goals in all, a tally unlikely ever to be bettered.

Everton returned to First Division football with a new goalkeeper. Billy Coggins, who had kept goal for most of the Second Division days, had arrived at Goodison from Bristol City in 1930 but was to be permanently replaced by a young teenager who had played just a handful of games in the lower division. Ted Sagar had joined Everton from Thorne Colliery in the Doncaster Senior League after Everton had cleverly beaten a hesitant Hull City to his signature. Within a season Coggins saw the writing on the wall and was on his way to Queen's Park Rangers after just 56 games for the Blues. Sagar quickly established himself between the posts and remained there until long after the Second World War, to set up the unique record of becoming the longest-serving player with any one club. And with Elisha Scott still keeping goal at Anfield, Merseyside could boast the two finest goalkeepers in the country.

Everton kicked off the season with a win against Birmingham and followed that up with confidence-boosting victories at Portsmouth and Sunderland. They then lost a couple of needless games and, with Dean still to score, journeyed anxiously across Stanley Park to Anfield. But there was no need for concern as Dixie suddenly struck form on his favourite away ground to hit a hat-trick that gave the Blues a 3–1 victory. In early October they began an astonishing run that was to see them net 59 goals in 13 games. Sheffield United were the first victims, beaten 5–1 away. This was followed by a 9–3 win against Sheffield Wednesday at Goodison, with Dean scoring five; an 8–1 win against Newcastle; a 7–2 win over Chelsea, with Dean scoring another five; a 9–2 win against Leicester, where Dean struck four; a 5–1 win over Middlesbrough; and another hat-trick for Dean in a 5–0 win against Blackburn. Dean had helped himself to 24 goals in the short spell and Everton had rocketed to the top of the League. And there they remained for the best part of the season. By early May they had clinched their fourth title, but owing to a couple of late defeats they finished only two points ahead of Arsenal, who had had the better of them twice that season.

In the process they had scored 116 goals, 26 more than Arsenal, and Dean had netted 45 of them. Goodison had witnessed 84 goals in 21 matches, a rate of four a game. It was hardly surprising that, even though there was little money around during the Depression, the crowds continued flocking to Goodison to watch Dean. Throughout the season the great centre-forward had been ably assisted by Tommy Johnson, enjoying his second full season at Goodison after his transfer from Manchester City in the spring of 1930. Johnson was no youngster, having played for the Manchester club during the First World War, as well as in the 1926 Cup Final. But, even though he was now into his early thirties, the skilful inside-left was still capable of scoring goals, and he helped himself to 22 to add to the 18 he had scored the previous season in the Second Division. When he left Everton in March 1934 he had scored 64 goals in 159 games and went on to score a few more with his new club, Liverpool.

The versatile Tommy White also had a superb season, contributing 18 goals in just 24 games. He had come from neighbouring Southport in 1927, and although he was recognised more as a centre-half he was so adaptable that he even donned Dean's shirt on occasion and liked nothing more than to be up in the forward line, having a crack at goal. He won just one England cap, wearing the number five shirt in Rome. Eventually he left Everton in October 1937 to join Northampton Town after 202 games and 66 goals.

In the Cup, Everton drew their rivals Liverpool out of the hat for the opening tie, and with the Reds winning 2–1 at Goodison it was a short-lived tournament. Over two seasons Everton had clocked up a phenomenal 260 goals in 90 games, a rate of almost three goals a match, and Dean himself had scored 94 of them.

The other stalwarts of the team had been Jimmy

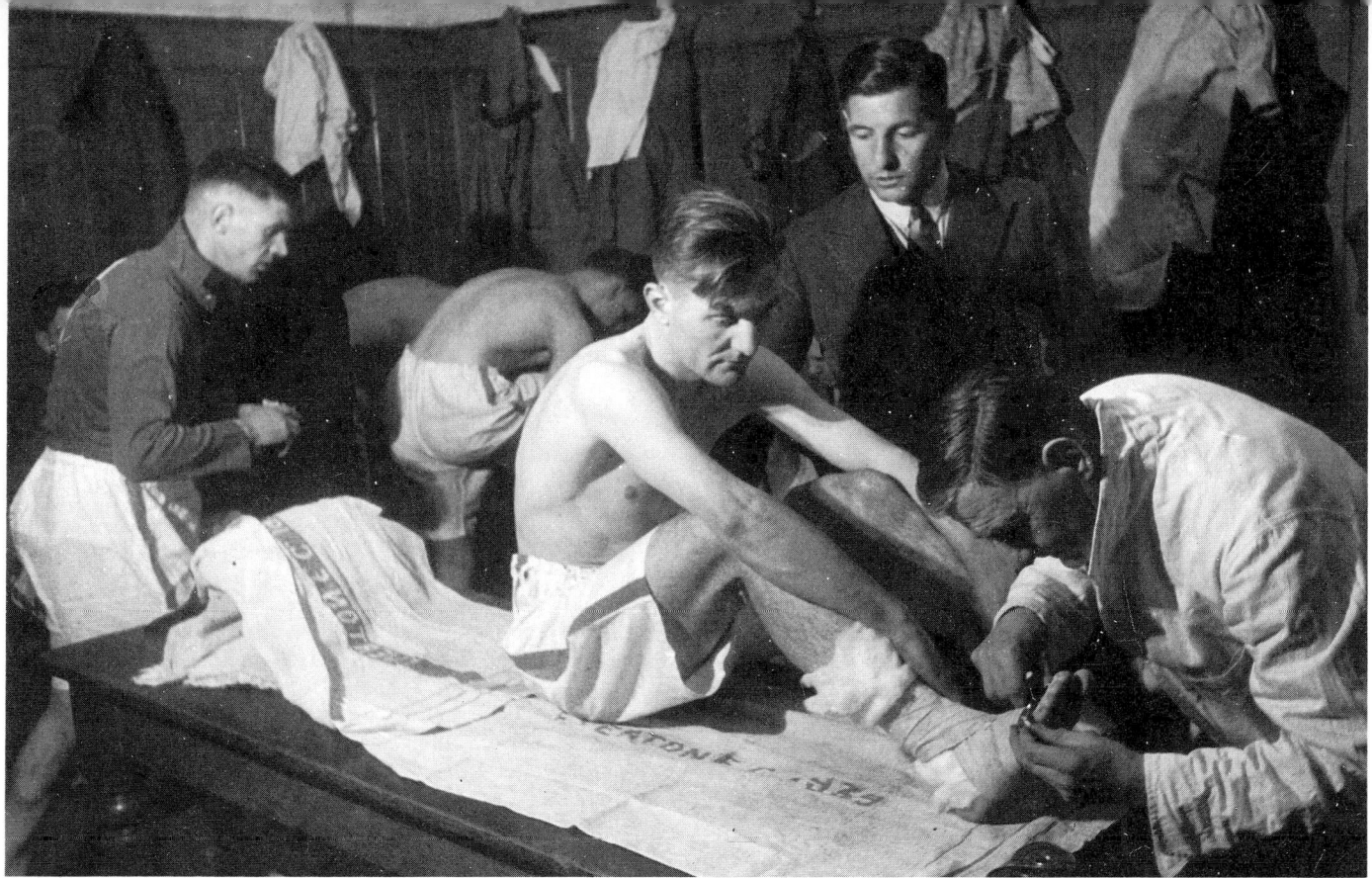

Scottish international Jock Thomson looks on anxiously as he receives treatment to a foot injury.

Stein, Ben Williams, Jock Thomson, Charlie Gee, Warney Cresswell, Archie Clark and William Brocking. Stein was one of a number of fine Scottish players the club had signed during the 1920s. He had come from Dunfermline in 1928 and remained for seven seasons before joining Burnley and later New Brighton. He was a clever winger who weaved his skills up and down the touchline, creating chances for Dean and others, as well as snatching more than a few himself. In a Goodison career of 215 games he managed a creditable 65 goals.

At left-half Jock Thomson was another useful Scot who had come south, from Dundee, in March 1930. He played a vital role in Everton's fortunes over the period, and when he retired in 1939 it was with a bagful of medals and a record of 294 appearances, but with only one Scottish international cap. After the Second World War he spent three years as manager of Manchester City but left when they were relegated to Division Two.

At fullback Everton could boast in Warney Cresswell and Ben Williams the best pair in the business. Williams, a Welsh international, had joined from Swansea shortly before Christmas 1929 and was soon partnering the England international, Cresswell. Known as Khyber, Cresswell played 139 games for the Blues before a serious cartilage injury ruined his First Division career. He was transferred to Newport County in 1936 after 139 games, but even Third Division football proved too much and within twelve months he was back at Goodison as a coach.

During the season centre-half Charlie Gee won the first of his three England international caps when he was chosen to represent his country against Wales. Less than a year previously he had still been awaiting his first-team debut after his transfer from Stockport County in 1928. He was only able to find his way into the team when Tommy Griffiths was injured, but once secure he refused to budge and became a permanent fixture until a cartilage injury interrupted his career in 1932.

It was as fine a team as Everton had ever known, a combination of strength in defence and flair up front, with the greatest goalscorer of all time leading the attack. With such players it was little wonder that Everton were so dominant. What is more, their dominance came at a time when there were other excellent teams around. Arsenal, for instance, beginning their period of success, could boast names such as Alex James, Eddie Hapgood, Cliff Bastin and a host of other international players.

After their magnificent title win Everton turned their attentions to the FA Cup. They had not won the coveted trophy since 1906, when they had beaten Newcastle United 1–0 at the Crystal Palace, and it was high time the Cup made a reappearance on Merseyside.

In the League they finished in mid-table, with Dean failing to score as consistently as he had in previous seasons. At the end of the 1932/33 season his tally totalled 24, with Stein adding a further 16. There were a few respectable wins, notably the six-goal victories against Sunderland and Leicester, and one disastrous defeat by seven goals to four against Liverpool at Anfield. The Liverpool fans regarded it as their finest victory during what was for them a dismal period, with the Evertonians forced to suffer for some considerable time.

In October, Everton faced the previous season's Cup-winners, Newcastle, at St James's Park in the Charity Shield. Everton won a thrilling game by five goals to three, but not before Newcastle had staged an exciting comeback which almost rubbed out Dean's hat-trick.

Everton's problem lay generally with the introduction of several new players, all of whom took some time to settle in. Cliff Britton pulled on the number

League champions 1931/32. Back row (left to right): Cooke (trainer), Clark, Williams, Sagar, Gee, Cresswell, Britton. Front row: Critchley, White, Dean, Johnson, Stein, Thomson.

four shirt for the first time early that season, some two years and numerous Central League games after his arrival at Goodison from Bristol Rovers. But he matured and established himself not just as a regular but also as an England wing-half.

Billy Cook was another new face, signed from Celtic for £3,000 in December 1932. An Irish international, he slotted into the right-back position and served the club until the outbreak of war. The other newcomer was Albert Geldard, the Bradford boy wonder who had set a record by playing his first League game at the tender age of 15 years and 156 days for Bradford against Millwall in September 1929. When he signed for Everton as an 18-year-old, in November 1932, he already boasted three years' League experience. He was spotted by Jack Sharp, who recommended him to the club, predicting a rich international future for the lad.

The championship went to Arsenal, who finished some 17 points ahead of the Blues as they began their record-equalling three consecutive titles under the managership of Herbert Chapman. But it was in the Cup where Everton's fortunes lay. They began with an away tie at Leicester City, and although they were trailing 2–1 at half-time gave a spirited second-half

performance to win by three goals to two. In the fourth round they faced Bury at Goodison and had little trouble in beating the Second Division side by three goals to one, with Tommy Johnson netting two and Dean the other. The next round brought a visit to Goodison from Leeds United, who had just scalped Tranmere after a replay in the fourth round. Dean took some revenge for his old club by scoring one of Everton's goals in a comfortable 2–0 victory.

Luton Town of the Third Division South must have quaked when they heard the draw for the quarter-finals, for they had drawn none other than the League champions at Goodison. Luton had been enjoying their best-ever run in the FA Cup and now they were travelling to Merseyside, suspecting they were in for a drubbing. And that was precisely how it turned out as Everton rattled in six goals without reply. That put Everton into the semi-final along with Manchester City, Derby County and West Ham United. The latter, hovering near the bottom of the Second Division, were by far the easiest proposition on paper, and Everton must have felt that luck was on their side as they drew the London team out of the famous bag.

The game was played at Molineux before 50,000 spectators in mid-March. But West Ham were determined not to be the proverbial pushovers. Instead they fought for every ball, giving the First Division side some early frights. Everton eventually took the lead as Jimmy Dunn headed home a Stein corner, but shortly before half-time West Ham equalised. In the second half the game swayed each way, and it took a West Ham error in defence to allow Ted Critchley, deputising for the injured Geldard, to sneak the winner for Everton's first trip to Wembley.

FA Cup Final 1933 Everton v Manchester City
Their opponents in the final were Manchester City, who had won an exciting semi-final encounter with Derby County by three goals to two. City had been semi-finalists the previous season and would appear in another Wembley final the following year. In Matt Busby, Sammy Cowan and Jackie Bray they boasted one of the finest halfback lines in the League, while Alex Herd and Jimmy McMullen in attack would be more than a handful for most defences. But even before the two teams kicked off there were a few surprises, while a footnote in soccer history was also written. For the first time in a final it was decided that numbers would be worn, and the two teams lined up from 1 to 22, with Everton taking the first 11 numbers. The clash of colours also meant a change

ABOVE Wing-half Cliff Britton made his debut in 1933 and went on to establish himself as an England regular.

OVERLEAF ABOVE An unusual sight as Everton and Manchester City take the field for the 1933 Cup final with the players numbered from one to 22. Everton played in white shirts with their opponents wearing red.

OVERLEAF BELOW Jimmy Stein scores Everton's first in their 3–0 Cup win over Manchester City. Dunn and Dean added the others.

ABOVE The incomparable Alan Ball.

LEFT Howard Kendall.

TOP Kevin Richardson and Kenny Dalglish battle for
possession during the 1984 Milk Cup final.

ABOVE FA Cup winners 1984.

LEFT Kevin Ratcliffe.

BELOW Dave Watson clears from Liverpool's Craig Johnston.

ABOVE The cup comes back to Merseyside held triumphantly aloft by captain Dean as the team parades through the city.

in strip, with the Football Association offering the two teams the choice of either red or white. City chose red and Everton found themselves unusually sporting white shirts and black shorts for the big occasion. But Dean was perfectly happy, arguing that City playing in red would give Everton an added incentive to win. A further surprise came when the teams were announced. Everton shocked even their most ardent supporters by dropping Ted Critchley in favour of Albert Geldard, who had returned to fitness. Dean admitted to having a say in the decision, and it turned out to have been a wise move.

It was the first time Everton had graced the hallowed turf of Wembley, and their fans turned out in force, pouring down Wembley Way towards the twin towers in their thousands. It was City's second appearance at the stadium, having lost there to Bolton Wanderers in 1926, when Tommy Johnson, now in the Everton side, had collected a loser's medal. The

fans began the long trek out of Liverpool in the early hours of the morning on 29 April 1933, boarding the 40 special trains of the LMS that steamed out of Lime Street station en route for Euston. Others undertook the journey by coach, which may have taken longer but at 20 shillings was somewhat cheaper. The supporters started arriving at Euston at 5.00 a.m. with their bells, rattles, buzzers and kazoos deafening the London crowds. Everton had spent the week in Buxton in Derbyshire having, as the *Liverpool Echo* fondly put it, 'a sprint or two or playing golf'.

A few days before the final a horrific earthquake hit the Greek island of Kos, and those with long memories recalled that the San Francisco earthquake had struck in 1906, a few days before Everton last won the Cup, and wondered if this was an omen. On the day of the big occasion City arrived at Wembley early, quickly changed and then hung around in the cold dressing-room as the tension mounted and their nerves got the better of them. Everton, meanwhile, held up in the crowds around the stadium, arrived later, and after a comfortable change were striding into the sunlight to be greeted with a roar from the 93,000 crowd.

The first attack went to City, but Sagar, by now one of the safest keepers in the division, was equal to it and soon had the Everton forwards racing after his long kick. Everton were confident, and it showed as they strolled about the wide acres of Wembley with Stein and Britton running at the defence to send in short threatening crosses towards Dean. There was really only one team in it and Everton's monopoly eventually paid off shortly before half-time, when Langford in the City goal dropped the ball under pressure from Dean, and Stein scored the simplest of goals. Early in the second half Everton went two up as Cliff Britton sent in a high cross for Dean to head home. The rout was completed ten minutes before the end, when Jimmy Dunn headed in a centre from the young Albert Geldard. The weary City defence had found Dean more than a handful, while Britton and Cresswell at the heart of the Everton defence had coped comfortably with the Manchester attack. It was the clearest margin of victory Wembley had ever seen in a final and there was no doubt that Dean had been the inspiration behind Everton's classy performance. Fittingly it was Dean, as captain, who climbed Wembley's 39 steps ahead of his team-mates to receive the trophy from the Duke of York, the last-minute replacement for King George V, who had been taken ill. The *Liverpool Football Echo* recorded the triumph with a front-page headline, 'EVERTON WIN THE CUP AND CREATE A RECORD'.

After a weekend of celebration Everton returned to Liverpool by train on the Monday afternoon, arriving at Lime Street in the early evening to be greeted by a vast crowd. More than 50,000 people were estimated to be crammed around the station, with another 50,000 outside St George's Hall. Boarding the same coach and four that had carried the victorious 1906 Cup-winning team, the Everton players, clutching the glittering Cup, then began the short journey to the Town Hall. It was a journey that should have taken no more than ten minutes. Instead it took well over an hour, as the throng cheered them through the city centre. From the Town Hall they then drove to Goodison, where an estimated half a million lined the streets, while at the ground itself another 50,000 were already in their places ready to cheer the Cup and the team on to the pitch. Dean later described the triumphal homecoming as the most moving experience of his life. And it was right that the city of Liverpool should have given such a reception to the team that had completed a unique hat-trick of honours.

Everton Sagar, Cook, Cresswell, Britton, White, Thomson, Geldard, Dunn, Dean, Johnson, Stein.
Manchester City Langford, Cann, Dale, Busby, Cowan, Bray, Toseland, Marshall, Herd, McMullen, Brook.

After their magnificent run of success Everton surprisingly slumped and in a lean five-year period failed either to win or even to challenge for any trophies. The team had reached its peak and over the next few years would fall apart, as players retired or moved on to the lower, though not always easier, divisions.

The first casualty of their cup success was Ted Critchley, the nippy outside-right who had been dropped in favour of the young Albert Geldard. A year later, after 229 appearances for the Blues, he packed his bags and went off to Preston North End. He was sorely missed by Dean, who was nowhere near as explosive in the penalty area without the delicate crosses of the former Stockport player. Jimmy Stein, operating on the other wing, also departed in October 1936 for Burnley, after 215 games and 65 goals, leaving Dean without the two men who more than any others had contributed to his prodigious goalscoring feats. Albert Geldard remained a while longer, but in 1938 he moved on to Bolton Wanderers for £4,500. He had won four England caps while at Goodison and his dazzling pace down the right wing made him as exciting a player as any on Everton's books. It was little wonder that his other interest was conjuring.

But perhaps the most influential departure was that of Warney Cresswell, for so long the pillar of Everton's defence. He had joined the club from Sunderland as far back as 1927, just five years after the north-eastern club had paid South Shields a record British fee of £5,500 for his services, and when he retired in 1936 he had played 306 games, scoring just one goal. He had also added seven England caps to his name and had established a reputation as one of the finest ball-players in the game. Small for a defender, he was never one to charge in unnecessarily

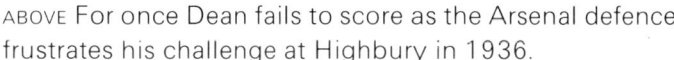

ABOVE For once Dean fails to score as the Arsenal defence frustrates his challenge at Highbury in 1936.

RIGHT New star Tommy Lawton settles in at Goodison, in a famous photograph by Bert Hardy.

at a tackle but instead would craftily hold off and force his opponent into a corner. And when he held the ball he could spray long accurate passes upfield that would send fullbacks scurrying nervously into defence. After Everton he became manager of Port Vale and later Northampton Town, before returning to his native north-east, where he died in 1973.

Jimmy Dunn, the Scottish international who had played for the famous 'Wembley Wizards' who trounced England 5–1, also moved on in 1935. He went off to Exeter City after 154 games and 49 goals, but later wound up back on Merseyside with Runcorn. In all, the skilful inside-forward won six Scottish caps, five of those while at his previous club, Hibernian, and was a leading part of one of the finest forward lines ever to grace a football field.

Although there was much retiring and departing from Goodison, the period also welcomed two young players who in the years ahead would become household names and play an important role in the team's next championship challenge. Joe Mercer signed on the dotted line as a junior in September 1932. He came from Ellesmere Port, across the River Mersey, as a budding halfback and was thrown somewhat prematurely into the First Division in 1933, playing only once. The following season he made eight appearances and finally broke into the first team during the 1935/36 season. He was a strong, cultured player with a superb understanding of the game and would go on to win more honours as both a player and a manager than possibly any other Everton player. Unfortunately most of his honours would not be won at Goodison.

The other new signing was Tommy Lawton, who came to Goodison from Burnley in March 1937 for £6,500. It was a considerable sum of money at the time but it was money well invested, for Lawton was to assume the mantle of Dean with astonishing ease. He had been born in Bolton, and as a schoolboy footballer had scored 570 goals in three seasons, quickly drawing him to the attention of an army of scouts, all eager for his signature. But it was Burnley, then a struggling Second Division club, who won the race, and on his League debut, just four days after his seventeenth birthday, Lawton scored a hat-trick, the first of many.

The 1933 Cup-winners made a dismal showing in the following year's tournament, going out to Tottenham by three goals to nil, and barely improved their performances in the League. Dean, after scoring his three-hundredth goal for the club in September 1933 – in 310 games – sprained an ankle and, although he returned to the team six weeks later, further damaged a knee and was forced to undergo a cartilage operation. He was out of the side for most of the season, playing just 12 games. Everton wound up in fourteenth spot, with little to recall of their exploits other than a 7–1 win over Blackburn. Less happily, Newcastle United came to Goodison and gave them a 7–3 drubbing that must have left the Goodison faithful wondering what had happened to their great team. With Dean injured, the club enterprisingly tried to sign the Chelsea and Scotland centre-forward Hughie Gallagher, but the deal fell through and Gallagher joined Derby County instead.

The next season, 1934/35, brought only minor improvements. In the League the club finished in eighth place, just behind Liverpool but well down on Arsenal, who clinched their third championship in a row. Dean was fit again and playing regularly, scoring 26 league goals in 39 appearances. He was ably supported by Alex Stevenson, regarded as one of the finest ball players of his generation, who knocked in a season's total of 18 goals. Stevenson had joined the Blues from Glasgow Rangers in 1934 but he was not a Scotsman. He had been born in Dublin and was already an Irish international long before he pulled on the blue jersey of Everton.

Everton fared much better in the Cup and at one point there were high hopes that they might again go all the way to Wembley. But in the end it was not to be. They began the competition with an impressive 6–3 win against Grimsby, who at the time were riding high in the First Division. In the fourth round they faced Sunderland, and after a tense 1–1 draw at Roker Park beat the north-easterners by six goals to four in front of 60,000 people in one of the most exciting games Goodison had seen in years. Everton went into a quick two-goal lead but shortly before the interval the Wearsiders pulled one back. When Stevenson restored Everton's advantage in the second half, it looked all over. Sunderland however, much to their

credit, threw everything into attack and mid-way through the half made it 3–2. Then, with just seconds remaining, they stole an equaliser that forced extra time. The two teams kicked off again, and when Coulter scored his third it seemed that Everton would again take the tie, but the cheers had barely died away when Sunderland again equalised. The match was finally settled with just eight minutes remaining, when Albert Geldard jinxed through the Sunderland defence to score; and then, with the referee poised to blow for full-time, he again tricked the tired Sunderland legs to make it 6–4.

In the fifth round Everton entertained Derby and won comfortably by three goals to one before drawing Bolton for the quarter-final. The Second Division side were pressing for promotion, but Everton, with all their pedigree and experience, were rated favourites, especially as the game was to be played at Goodison. But, as so often happens in the Cup, the favourites took a beating, going down by two goals to one.

A young, unknown shipping clerk, then working in Liverpool and regularly supporting Everton, by the name of Michael Foot, wrote a poem for the *Liverpool Daily Post* which captured the season's drama and misfortunes in verse:

Ode to Everton FC
When at thy call my weary feet I turn
The gates of paradise are opened wide
At Goodison I know a man may learn
Rapture more rich than Anfield can provide.
In Coulter's skill and Geldard's subtle speed
I see displayed in all its matchless bounty
The power of which the heavens decreed
The fall of Sunderland and Derby County.
The hands of Sagar, Dixie's priceless head
Made smooth the path to Wembley till that day
When Bolton came. Now hopes are fled
And all is sunk in bottomless dismay.
And so I watch with heart and temper cool.
God's lesser breed of men at Liverpool.

Everton's brief recovery met with a setback the following season when they could manage only sixteenth in the League. Dean was again injured, missing 13 games, but still helped himself to 17 goals. Mercer came into the team during October, but the damage had already been done. Early on in the season Liverpool had thrashed the Blues 6–0 at Anfield in one of their most humiliating derby defeats, while a few fixtures later Middlesbrough and then West

Brom also put six past Sagar. Mercer's presence eventually began to tell, and after Christmas they lost only five matches. In the Cup there was an early exit as Preston comfortably won by three goals to one.

The year 1936 was a watershed in international politics. Civil War raged in Spain, Hitler had risen to power in Germany, while Britain was gripped by a bitter abdication crisis. During the close season Everton were invited to Germany again following their successful tour in 1932, but the trip almost got off to a disastrous start when the liner on which they were travelling was in collision with a Dutch ship. Fortunately, although the Dutch ship sank, nobody was killed and the team proceeded slightly behind schedule to Hamburg. Unemployment was gradually beginning to fall as the 1936/37 season kicked off although it would still remain depressingly high until the outbreak of war.

Robert 'Bunny' Bell, who had scored a record nine goals for Tranmere against Oldham Athletic on Boxing Day 1935, had been imported from Everton's Third Division neighbours to help Dean, but it never really worked out and after a couple of years and only

Irish international Alex Stevenson joined Everton from Glasgow Rangers in 1934 and played until after the war.

14 appearances he moved on. The 1936/37 season was no better than the previous one, as Everton wound up in seventeenth place. Lawton, signed in December 1936, made his debut at Molineux and scored, but it did little good as Everton went down by seven goals to two. During the season Dean contributed 24 goals, while Stevenson hit 19 and winger Torry Gillick added 14 League goals to the nine he had scored in 1935/36. Another Scot, he had joined from Rangers in December 1935 for £8,000 but never really fulfilled his potential at Goodison. Nevertheless he won five Scottish caps while he was there, but it was always said that he never really took the game seriously enough. And by the time he had matured Britain was at war.

In only the second game of the season, against Sheffield Wednesday at Goodison, Dean finally broke Steve Bloomer's all-time goalscoring record by bringing his tally to 353 League goals. He had achieved this in 12 seasons, playing only 379 games, most of them in the First Division.

In the Cup, Bournemouth were the visitors in the opening round but were soon making the long journey back south after a 5–0 hiding. Sheffield Wednesday crossed the snow-ridden Pennines for the next round and went down 3–0. The fifth round brought another home tie, but Tottenham were equal to it and after a 1–1 draw beat the Blues by four goals to three in an exciting replay at White Hart Lane.

Tom McIntosh, the club's long-standing secretary and the man who had signed Dean, had died early in 1936, to be succeeded by Theo Kelly. Kelly, while being a superb administrator, was not a popular man with the players and especially not with Dean. As captain, Dean had to work closely with the secretary and directors and was usually involved in team selection. Niggling arguments began and when, during the early part of the 1937/38 season, Dean was dropped in favour of Tommy Lawton, the rift became unbreachable. Dean remained at Goodison until the end of the season, playing in the reserves and watching the young man whom he had taught so much wearing his coveted shirt. Sadly Dean's last game for the club went unnoticed when he took the field in a match against Grimsby Town on 23 October 1937. Nobody knew that this would be his farewell performance, but that was the way it turned out. Everton lost and Dean failed to score. When they totted up the statistics at the end of his illustrious Goodison career, he had worn the blue shirt on 431 occasions and scored 379 goals. He ended his days at Everton one match short of 400 League games, in which he had

ABOVE Seven members of the victorious Cup final side of 1933 returned to Wembley in 1966 to cheer another Everton triumph. Standing: Jimmy Stein, Albert Geldard, Billy Cook. Seated: Tommy White, Ted Sagar, Dixie Dean, Jock Thomson.

scored 349 goals. He had been capped 16 times by his country, scoring 18 goals, and had won every honour the game could bestow upon him. But it was with bitterness that he left Everton. On Friday 11 March 1938, in a short statement from the club, it was announced that Dean had been sold to Notts County for £3,000, the identical sum Everton had paid for him 13 years previously. Merseyside was stunned and the local press voiced the astonishment that everybody felt. But perhaps the saddest part was that, when he departed on the Friday afternoon,

Goodison was deserted, so he quietly packed his bags and left the ground with neither players nor officials to shake his hand and thank him for all his loyalty and services. Thirty-odd years later the club partly made up for their appalling behaviour when they organised a benefit game in his honour.

Dean's career with Notts County was short-lived, as a foot injury quickly put paid to his days in the Third Division. He later played for the Irish club Sligo, but the war interrupted and he went into retirement, running the Dublin Packet pub in Chester. In 1976 his right leg was amputated after a long illness, and four years later, at his beloved Goodison Park, just minutes before the final whistle in the local derby, he collapsed and died. It was perhaps fitting that Everton's most gifted son should have died while watching the club that he had made so famous.

8

PRE-WAR CHAMPIONS

To the more astute observer it was clear that war was inevitable. Everton, during their regular visits, and particularly on their 1936 trip, had witnessed at first hand the increasing power of the German state. Trade unions and all opposition parties had been brutally wiped out and a war machine, second to none, was being blatantly developed. Britain, too, was priming itself for the inevitable. The factories and shipyards were back to full production, churning out destroyers, planes and guns. For the first time in a decade there were jobs as the poverty of the Depression slowly began to wilt away. But it was all short-lived. As the 1938/39 season kicked off in the late summer sunshine, a few suspected, but nobody knew for certain, that this would be the final full season before war. For most it would be a season to forget, but for Everton it turned out to be a season to remember.

Before the season began, Albert Geldard waved goodbye to Goodison after six seasons and 179 appearances that had brought 37 goals. The right-winger had also won four England caps and had laid on countless goals for Dean before departing to Bolton Wanderers. A couple of new faces, however, did appear in the team early on in the campaign. Wally Boyes, a 5ft 3in winger from West Brom, had arrived in February 1938, playing a handful of games before the end of the previous season, but now found himself a permanent fixture on the left wing. With the diminutive Alex Stevenson operating alongside him, the Everton forward line was beginning to take on an exciting shape. Torry Gillick and the former Wigan Athletic inside-forward Stan Bentham operated on the right, while the incomparable Lawton hovered in the middle, feeding off their crosses. Boyes was a splendid discovery, skilful, enthusiastic and full of energy, although the war would sadly disrupt his playing days. Capped three times for England before hostilities, he made 73 appearances for Everton, and although he reappeared once peace had returned he made only 19 appearances before being transferred to Notts County in 1949.

Norman Greenhalgh was the other new face, stepping into Jack Jones's old position at left-back. Jones, another Ellesmere Port old boy, had moved on to Sunderland after five seasons and 108 appearances in the Everton defence. Greenhalgh, meanwhile, had

arrived at Goodison via Bolton Wanderers and New Brighton and quickly slotted into the defence alongside Billie Cook and in front of the now veteran Ted Sagar. Ahead of them were the aristocratic Mercer, Jock Thomson and Tommy G. Jones. The Welshman Jones had been signed from Wrexham in 1936, becoming the automatic choice at centre-forward not only for his club but for his country as well.

BELOW Tommy G. Jones challenges Arsenal's centre-forward Reg Lewis at Highbury in January 1938. Jones was reckoned by Dean to be the finest all-round player he had ever seen.

Altogether it was a sturdy and skilful team, with as solid a backbone as possible in Lawton, Mercer and Sagar. The season got off to a cracking start as Everton notched up six wins in a row and shot to the top of the League. They were then beaten 3–0 at Huddersfield and returned to Goodison the week after to face Liverpool, currently lying in third position. The Prime Minister, Neville Chamberlain, had just arrived back from his famous meeting in Munich with Herr Hitler, waving the piece of paper which he claimed guaranteed 'peace in our time'. At Goodison the 60,000 crowd celebrated the occasion by heartily singing the national anthem. Everton celebrated by winning 2–1 and for a brief moment everything looked perfect and peaceful.

Everton held on to their top spot until late October, when a 3–0 defeat at Leicester saw Derby County climb above them. That was the way it remained until February, when they visited Anfield and before a gate of 66,000 gave the Reds a lesson in skills. Lawton scored twice and Bentham added a third as they ran out 3–0 winners and fittingly returned to the top slot. A fortnight later they journeyed to Molineux without the injured Sagar. The result was disastrous, as high-riding Wolves thrashed them 7–0 with 16-year-old Jimmy Mullen in only his second league game scoring a hat-trick. Luckily Everton still hung on to their top place, and with Sagar recovered went ten games before they suffered defeat again. On that day, 22 April, against third-placed Charlton, they went down by two goals to one, but with Wolves drawing against Bolton the players returned to the dressing-room to learn that they had clinched the title, their fifth championship.

They ended the season four points clear of Wolves, with Lawton hitting 34 League goals. Gillick added another 14 and Stevenson 11 as the team totalled 88 goals. Nor were their fortunes restricted simply to the League. In the Cup they began with a superb 1–0 win at Derby, followed by an 8–0 drubbing of Doncaster and four goals for Lawton. Birmingham City proved more of a handful in the fifth round, but Everton forced a draw at St Andrew's before winning 2–1 at Goodison. The quarter-final draw could not have been more difficult, as they faced Wolves away, just one week after their 7–0 thrashing. Sagar was back this time, but it made little difference as a highly slick Wolves side won 2–0.

It had been seven lean years since Everton's last title challenge, and now that the reshaped team had captured the honour once more, it was sad that war should intervene to rob them of further successes. By

Billy Cook joined Everton from Celtic in 1932 and went on to play almost 250 games for the club. He later coached in Peru and Norway before returning to England where he managed Wigan Athletic and coached at Norwich.

the time the war was over the team had been destroyed, with the older players retiring and the younger ones seeking their fortunes elsewhere. The Irish international right-back, Billy Cook, was one casualty who after 249 appearances played briefly during the war and then moved on to Wrexham in 1945. He eventually wound up as Sunderland's coach and then followed in the footsteps of other former Evertonians by coaching in South America, this time in Peru. It would be another 24 years before the League championship trophy returned to the Goodison boardroom as Everton now settled into the most ignominious period in their history.

The 1939/40 season was only a few fixtures old when Germany invaded Poland and war was declared. Not surprisingly the footballing authorities quickly intervened to disband the League structure until hostilities had ceased. It was clear to everyone that this was going to be a long and bitter war, with little time for leisure or spectator sports, but nobody could have guessed that it would be six lengthy years before League soccer kicked off again. They did, however, agree to allow the game to continue on a regional basis, and with many of the younger players already enlisting in the services it was also agreed that a guesting system would be allowed.

Everton were drafted into a Northern League, along with teams such as Liverpool, Tranmere, New Brighton, Manchester United and Wrexham. In their first season they finished in fifth place, but the League system did not always work out satisfactorily. Sometimes teams could not fulfil their commitments because players were on duty or travel was difficult, and the games always tended to be treated as friendlies rather than taken too seriously. Some of the opposition was also ridiculously weak for a team like Everton, who hit nine goals against Tranmere and seven against Stockport. Everton also courted trouble with the Football Association when they refused to release Joe Mercer for the England–Wales international despite an order from the War Emergency Committee. Instead the club insisted he play against Liverpool in the Liverpool Senior Cup Final. Everton won their battle with the FA and Mercer helped them to a 4–1 win but two of the club's directors were suspended by the FA.

For the 1940/41 season the League was extended, and Everton again finished in fifth place, though with not all teams playing an equal number of fixtures placings were decided on goal average. Everton themselves were unable to field a team against Blackpool in May and the match had to be postponed. Poor Tranmere again bore the brunt of Everton's merciless attack, beaten 9–0 and 8–2 at Prenton Park, with Lawton winding up the campaign with 22 goals.

The next season became even more complicated, since it was split into two parts. In the pre-Christmas session Everton were thrashed in their opening fixture 8–3 by Stoke City but did score nine against Manchester City. In the second part of the season they fared even worse, beaten 11–1 at Wolves to end up in fifteenth place. The 1942/43 season was similarly divided, with results getting worse, including a 5–3 defeat by Tranmere at Goodison. Tranmere gave a debut that day to a 17-year-old goalkeeper and with four other players under 18 they fought back from a 3–1 deficit to win.

But none of these matches could be taken too seriously, as was highlighted by some of the astonishing results the following season. Liverpool won 6–4 at Goodison, 15 goals were put past Tranmere in two games, Manchester United were hit for six, and Chester for 16 over two matches, while Blackpool put seven past Everton. Again the Blues finished in midtable, but fared considerably better during the 1944/45 season, when they ended in fifth and later in second place. They equalled that the following season when, with the end of hostilities in sight, the League was extended to 22 clubs, bringing in the north-eastern and Yorkshire sides. Harry Catterick was the leading goalscorer, with 25 goals from 28 appearances. The FA Cup also resumed that season, although on a two-legged basis, but Everton could not progress beyond the opening round, dismissed by Preston North End.

The guesting system allowed a number of unusual faces to appear in Everton colours including Frank Soo and the Tranmere player Abe Rosenthal, while Everton also signed a Chinese graduate of Manchester University, J. Scott-Lee. But for many players the war brought a premature end to fine careers. Brian Atkiss and William Summer were both killed in action, while others like Lawton and Stevenson lost some of their most prolific years. Cliff Britton was one exception and enjoyed a brief resurrection, not only to first-team soccer but to the England team as well. Britton had joined Everton from Bristol Rovers in 1930, going on to win a Cup-winners' medal in 1933, but he appeared only once in the championship-winning season of 1938/39. He made a total of 240 appearances for Everton and was capped nine times before the war. During the war, however, he played a couple of seasons and collected 12 wartime international caps, combining with Joe Mercer and Stan Cullis to form one of the most effective halfback lines English soccer has known. As the war ended he moved on to Burnley, but within three years he would be back at Goodison, though this time in a very different capacity. The star of the Everton team throughout the war had been Tommy Lawton and, although he guested for a number of other clubs, he scored 64 goals during the 1944/45 season and 62 the following season to give him a war total of 301 goals.

Battle-weary Britain began the slow return to normality as soon as the war ended. In the General Election the wartime leader, Winston Churchill, was surprisingly ousted from office and the Labour leader, Clement Attlee, became Britain's new Prime Minister. The troops started the long trek home, at first those from Europe and later those stationed in the Far East. The job of reconstructing the bombed cities and factories began in earnest as the new government sought to create work for the millions of ex-servicemen returning from their duties. The nation wanted to forget the painful years of war. Sport and leisure, not surprisingly, were high on the agenda as everyone began to lap up the entertainment that had been denied them during the dark days of fighting. And football was soon attracting vast crowds as it enjoyed the most popular period in its history.

When Germany surrendered, it was already too late to think in terms of League football recommencing that year. Instead it was agreed that soccer would begin again on the last day of August 1946, with the teams that had been relegated and promoted the season before the war taking up their new positions in their respective leagues. It was as if war had never intervened.

As champions, Everton ironically received no special privilege; they simply learned that six years is a long time and that they were no longer championship material. The first major post-war shock for Merseyside football arrived in November 1945, when Tommy Lawton asked for a transfer. Without much hesitation the Goodison board surprisingly bowed to his request, and there was soon a queue outside the ground for his signature. Eventually he signed for Chelsea for £11,500 and later played with Notts County, Brentford and Arsenal. At Everton he had made just 95 appearances, scoring 70 goals, but he went on to clock up a career total of 231 goals in 390 League games, winning 23 England caps and scoring 22 goals for his country. Joe Mercer may have been the bedrock of Everton's pre-war championship team but Lawton had been the man who made it all possible, and there could be no argument that, in Lawton, Everton had found the one player in the country capable of stepping into Dean's boots without fear of embarrassment.

No sooner had the Lawton sensation died down

than Everton were rocked by yet another transfer request, this time from their other star player, Joe Mercer. Sergeant-Major Mercer returned from his wartime duties to discover that Everton had already appointed a captain in his absence, despite the fact that he was the current England captain. Mercer was angry and played 12 miserable games in his old position at left-half before Arsenal dramatically stepped in and whisked him away to Highbury for £7,000. It was a sad end, especially as Mercer went on to win a League championship and Cup-winners' medal with the Gunners before settling into a highly successful managerial career that climaxed with his taking charge of the England team. In a short space of time Dean, Lawton and Mercer, arguably the three finest players of their generation, had all departed from Goodison unhappily. Something was wrong. Many fingers pointed at Theo Kelly who, in line with new trends and as a reward for his part in their championship win in 1939, had been appointed team manager. It was Kelly who had upset Dean and as manager was responsible for selling Lawton and Mercer. Although he was a fine administrator, he was not popular with the players, who found him difficult and uncommunicative; in recognition of this, his term as manager came to an end in 1948, when he reverted to his former position of secretary. He never believed

in buying players either, arguing that they should be maturing through the club's nursery teams rather than arriving via the cheque book. On the one occasion when he did attempt a major signing, that of Newcastle's Albert Stubbins, he allowed neighbours Liverpool get the better of him. In his first season at Anfield, Stubbins went on to help Liverpool lift the title.

It was a strange team that took the field for much of the new season. Ted Sagar was still there, now aged 36, as were Norman Greenhalgh, Tommy G. Jones, Stan Bentham and Alex Stevenson. But there were also some new additions. Tommy Eglington and Peter Farrell were among the most impressive; they had arrived jointly at Goodison from Shamrock Rovers in 1946 for £10,000. Ten years later the pair of them would still be turning out regularly for the Blues. The whippet-like Eglington was small, skinny and fast and one of the most dangerous wingers in the business. Farrell, on the other hand, was strong and sturdy, a bulldog of a defender. Between them (nobody ever thought of them individually) they won 52 Irish caps and were both members of the famous 1949 Eire team that beat England 2–0 at Goodison, the first foreign side ever to win on English soil.

Wally Fielding was another useful acquisition; he signed professional forms in 1945 and wore the

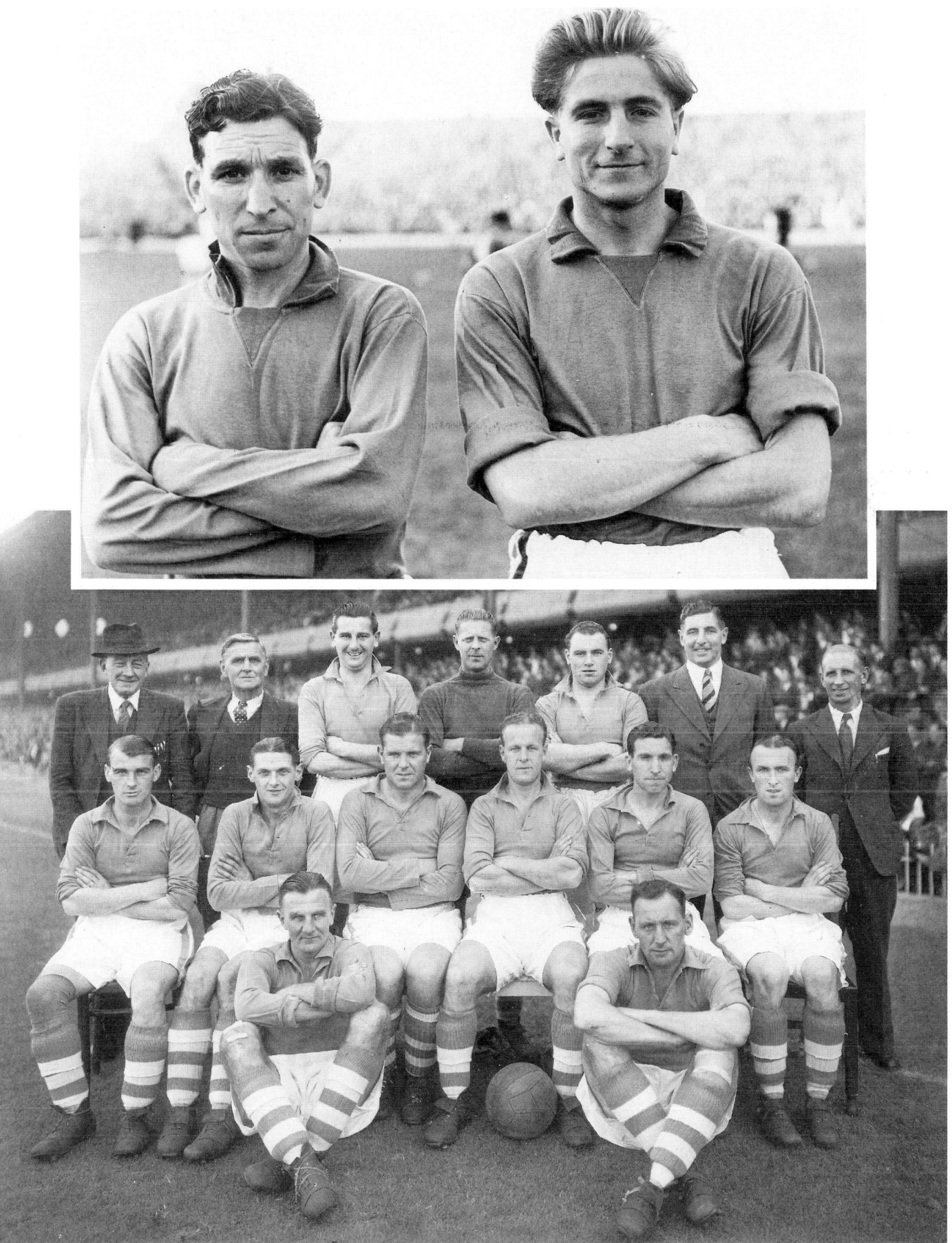

number ten shirt for the next 14 seasons. There were others, such as Ephraim Dodds, George Jackson (who had played for Everton before the war), George Saunders, Eddie Wainwright and Tommy Watson, who all turned out during the season. Another man who was to have an important influence on the club in later years also made his first league appearance in a blue shirt. He was a centre-forward called Harry Catterick, signed in 1937, who went on to make 71 appearances and score 24 goals before joining Crewe Alexandra.

The first season after the war was not a good one for Everton, who wound up near the middle of the table in tenth place, 14 points behind champions Liverpool. At one stage they had slipped anxiously into the relegation zone and it took a fortunate final run-in to pull themselves up the table. Dodds topped the goalscoring list with 17 goals, but nonetheless, having been purchased to replace Lawton, was a disappointment. The former Huddersfield, Sheffield United and Blackpool player was never in the same class, and although he played in eight wartime internationals for Scotland he lasted only three seasons at Goodison before moving to Lincoln City.

There was no improvement the following season, as Everton dropped further down the table and finished up fourteenth, a position they had hovered around for much of the season. There was a rare flourish in the Cup as they progressed to the fifth round before losing a replay with Fulham, but generally there was little to boast about. Dodds was again the top scorer, though this time he collected a mere 13 goals.

Before things could get any better, they had unfortunately to get worse. The next season began optimistically as Cliff Britton returned to Goodison to take charge of team affairs, while Theo Kelly reverted to his old job as secretary. Since leaving Everton in 1945 Britton had enjoyed a successful spell as manager of Burnley, taking them from the Second Division to third place in the First. But all his endeavours and hopes were of no avail as the 1948/49 season found Everton narrowly avoiding relegation in eighteenth place, just four points away from the Second Division. A catastrophic start to the campaign, in which they managed just two wins in the first 14 fixtures, put them firmly on the bottom until results picked up after Christmas. With Dodds departed, there was no one to score and Eddie Wainwright was the club's leading scorer with 10 goals. The highlight of the League season was the drawn derby with Liverpool, which attracted a record gate to Goodison of 78,299; with today's reduced attendances, the record will stand for ever. The skilful inside-forward Alex Stevenson parted company with the club after 15 years and 271 appearances that had brought 90 goals. The former Glasgow Rangers star was capped 17 times by Northern Ireland and seven times by Eire in an international career that spanned 17 years.

It was exactly the same the following year, 1949/50, when Everton finished in eighteenth place. The only light in what was to be a dark and dreary period for the club came in the Cup, when against all expectations they reached the semi-finals. The tournament opened at Queens Park Rangers, from the Second Division, with a 2–0 win. They then visited another Second Division ground in London, West Ham, and came away with a creditable 2–1 victory that put them into the fifth round. That tie pitted them against yet another London Second Division team, Tottenham. This time the match was at Goodison, but Spurs were running away with the Second Division title and under the guiding influence of Arthur Rowe had knitted together a very skilful side, with players like Ramsey, Ditchburn, Burgess, Medley and Duquemin. Everton played their hearts out that day, with Wainwright scoring the only goal to put Everton into the last eight. The quarter-final draw brought no luck, as they came out of the bag for an away tie with First Division Derby. County were hot favourites, yet Everton, with nothing to lose, gave a spirited performance and with good fortune going their way came out 2–1 winners.

Everton and Liverpool had not been in a semi-final together since 1906, so when Liverpool beat Blackpool to clinch a place in the last four there was tremendous anticipation in the city of an all-Merseyside final. But it was not to be, as the two teams faced each other at Maine Road for a place at Wembley. More than 72,000 were packed into City's ground to watch the contest, which turned out to be an enthralling encounter. Everton battled hard, and with a following wind might have gone one up in the first half, but instead it was Liverpool, through Bob Paisley, who went into the dressing-room a goal ahead. The second-half was much the same, with Eglington coming close to an equaliser, but in the end Billy Liddell squeezed in a lucky goal and Everton were denied a trip to Wembley. It was a bitter disappointment, especially considering that they had had so little to cheer about since before the war. It was Liverpool who made the journey to the capital, but they too came home dejected, beaten 2–0 by Arsenal, though there was some compensation for Evertonians in that Arsenal's captain was their old halfback Joe Mercer.

The slide into the Second Division was inevitable, and relegation duly arrived in May 1951 as the Blues ended the season with a 6–0 thrashing at Sheffield Wednesday. Even before September was out they had slipped into the relegation zone, and although they pulled themselves free for a short time during the spring, a disastrous run-in ensured a spell in the lower division. They managed to win only one of their final eleven fixtures and ended the season propping up the other 21 teams. Relegation was finally decided on goal average, with the bottom three teams all on 32 points, but Everton, having scored only 48 goals while conceding 86, were certainties for the big drop.

Life in the Second Division was not to the liking of a grand club like Everton. Gates fell, and the visiting teams and players were names unknown to the greater Merseyside public. They expected to see half a dozen internationals gracing Goodison each week, not the hardened stock of Barnsley or Rotherham. It took Everton some time to settle and after four games they found themselves in seventeenth place, wondering if the unbelievable could happen. By late October they had slipped even further and were third from bottom and staring the Third Division North full in the face. But fortunately results improved, thanks mainly to the young Dave Hickson. He had joined the Everton staff as an 18-year-old in May 1948 from Ellesmere Port, home of so many of the club's past stars, and broke into the team as their Second Division form slumped. He was a tall, powerful, old-fashioned centre-forward who scored more through aggression than skill. Nevertheless he was effective and soon became a great favourite with the crowd as he hit 14 goals in 31 games in his first season. Alongside Hickson was John Willie Parker, who had joined the club as an amateur. Although often derided, Parker was capable of scoring a goal or two and ended the season with 15 League goals of his own.

Everton finished the season in seventh place and waved farewell to Ted Sagar. The giant Everton keeper did manage one further game the next season, but 1951/52 was effectively his final campaign for the Blues. His record was as impressive as any player's who had donned an Everton shirt. Since 1929 – 16 seasons – he had played 495 games, not including wartime matches. He won four England caps, two championship medals and one Cup-winners' medal. He was generally regarded as the safest goalkeeper in

Former player Cliff Britton returned to Goodison in 1948 to take over the managerial chair.

the Football League and was not only brave but could judge a high ball with uncanny perception.

The following season brought no improvement. By September Everton were bottom, and the only autumnal highlight was a 7–1 drubbing of Doncaster Rovers, with Tommy Eglington hitting five. They soon climbed off the bottom but were always in danger of slipping back. After an 8–2 defeat by Huddersfield in early April there were more than a few who would have bet on them dropping another division, but somehow they clung on and finished sixteenth, five points clear of relegation.

In the Cup they surprised everyone by going all the way to the semi-final, before coming across a precocious Nat Lofthouse. In the opening round they faced Third Division Ipswich at home and needed all their experience and guile to pull off a 3–2 victory. The next round brought Second Division opponents Nottingham Forest to Merseyside, and they were dismissed comfortably by four goals to one. More than 60,000 people turned up for the fifth-round tie with League champions Manchester United, and for once the Evertonians really had something to cheer about as the Blues came out on top 2–1. And it was Dave Hickson, playing the game of his life with blood pouring out of an open head-wound caused by an earlier injury, who scored the winner with 15 minutes remaining, for the upset of the round. In the quarter-finals Everton travelled to Villa Park to meet an Aston Villa side led by Danny Blanchflower, and with time running out, and a goalless draw looking likely, Ted Buckle nonchalantly stroked Hickson's careful pass into the back of the Villa net.

Everton were into the semi-final, where they drew Bolton Wanderers for a match to be played at Maine Road. The Manchester ground had not proved to be a happy one for Everton over the years, and 1953 was to be no exception. At half-time they must have wondered why they had bothered turning up as Bolton ran into the dressing-room four goals up. Nat Lofthouse was at his deadliest, scoring twice and causing all kinds of problems for a nervous Everton defence. But the second half was a very different affair as Everton marshalled their troops into action. Within a minute John Willie Parker had pulled one back and Peter Farrell soon added a second, but Everton then had to wait until eight minutes from time before adding a third. Suddenly it was Bolton who were reeling chaotically, but, although Everton pressed furiously for an equaliser and cursed a first-half missed penalty, it remained Bolton's day.

Everton 1954. Back row (left to right): Britton (manager), Grant, Moore, T. Jones, O'Neill, Donovan, Lello, Leyfield (trainer). Front row: McNamara, Fielding, Wainwright, Farrell, Eglington, Hickson, Parker.

The Cup run did Everton's confidence a power of good, and it showed the following season. What they needed more than anything was a flourishing start, and that was precisely what came their way as they notched up eleven games without defeat. That put them up among the leaders and there they stayed for the remainder of the season. Hickson and Parker were now playing with some flair, feeding off Eglington's crosses and scoring regularly. In February Everton hit 20 goals in three games as the pair struck a dozen between them, and by the end of the season Parker had 31 goals and Hickson 25, making them the most formidable duo in the whole division. Everton finally squeezed their way back into Division One by holding on to second place by one point from Blackburn Rovers. It had been their longest spell outside the premier division.

When Everton had last won promotion, in 1931, they had followed it up by winning the First Division title. But there was to be no repeat of that achievement this time. Instead the fifties remained the years of mediocrity, when silverware was a scarce commodity around the Goodison boardroom. Not once did they finish in the top half of the table, their best season being the first back in the division, when they ended in eleventh spot.

It was not a star-studded team, and although it boasted a host of Irish internationals there was not one single England cap throughout the period. The Scots were also in short supply, and it was not until the late fifties that a couple of Scottish internationals appeared. Farrell and Eglington reflected the continuing association with the Republic of Ireland and had been joined by other Irishmen. Jimmy O'Neill,

a Dubliner, had stepped into Ted Sagar's position between the posts and had certainly not disgraced the memory of his predecessor. Making his debut in 1950, he went on to play 213 games over the next 10 years and won 17 Irish caps before moving on to Stoke City. Tall, lean and agile, he could count himself among the League's top goalkeepers.

Wing-half Don Donovan was another Irish import, spotted purely by chance when the Everton directors took a walk one evening in Cork where Everton were due to play a friendly. Stopping to watch a local kick-about, they were so impressed with the young defender, Donovan, that he was signed up before they had left town. He went on to win five Irish caps and between 1951 and 1958 made 187 appearances for the Blues. The Dundalk-born fullback Tommy Clinton was a regular choice for five seasons until 1953. He lasted a further two years at Goodison and was then transferred to Blackburn after 80 appearances and three Irish caps. Mick Meagan joined the Goodison staff in 1952 but did not make his debut until August 1957. He went on to make 176 appearances before joining Huddersfield Town, in a deal that brought Ray Wilson to Merseyside. Capped four times at Everton, he ended his international career in 1970 with a total of 17 caps.

The rest of the team was largely composed of local players. Brian Harris, Ken Birch and Jimmy Harris all came from Birkenhead, while George Kirby, Eric Moore, Tommy Jones and Eddie Wainwright all hailed from the northern shores of the Mersey. The Southport-born inside-forward Wainwright was the longest serving of these, having joined the club on amateur forms as far back as 1939. He made his debut during the war and went on to play 228 games before his career ended in 1956. He probably came closer than any other Everton player at the time to winning an England cap when he toured North America with an FA party, and also played for the Football League against the Irish League. Jimmy Harris managed an England Under-23 cap but never matured to full England honours, although he too played for the Football League. He had come directly from schoolboy football in Birkenhead and in 1955 pulled on the injured Dave Hickson's shirt for his debut. A month later Hickson moved to Aston Villa and Harris was the permanent replacement. There was also John Willie Parker, who had made his first appearance in 1951 in the number eleven shirt. A local lad, he played 176 times for the Blues and scored a respectable 89 goals before joining Bury in 1956.

Their first season back in the top division brought Everton up against Liverpool in the fourth round of the FA Cup. With Liverpool now wallowing in the Second Division, the result looked a foregone conclusion, but the Reds had something to prove and trounced Everton by four goals to nil at Goodison.

The season after, 1955/56, Everton's form declined and they wound up in fifteenth place, clearly missing the goalscoring feats of Hickson. The big centre-forward, disgruntled at Jimmy Harris's liking for his shirt, was sold to Villa for £17,500. Two months later, unable to settle, he was off to Huddersfield Town for £16,000, and in July 1957 he sensationally returned to Everton for £7,500. Harris meanwhile did well and scored 19 League goals in his first season, though that was to be his highest season's tally at Goodison. In the Cup the Blues reached the last eight before going out 2–1 to Manchester City, the eventual Cup-winners, at their unlucky Cup ground, Maine Road.

At the end of the season, while the team was on a summer tour with manager Cliff Britton, the club casually announced that it was appointing an acting-manager. Britton knew nothing of the decision and, interpreting it as a lack of confidence in himself, quit the club angrily. Whatever the reason behind the directors' decision, they made little attempt to persuade Britton to change his mind and appointed a three-man committee to take charge of the team until a suitable replacement was found. Two months later Ian Buchan, the one-time Scottish amateur international and former lecturer at Loughborough College, was appointed to take charge of team affairs. Buchan was a fitness fanatic and demanded the same commitment from his players. His aim was to make them the fittest in the League so that they could outrun any team. But football takes more than that, and unless you have the basic skills all the fitness in the world will not prove enough.

In his first game in charge he stopped the team coach two miles short of the Leeds United ground and made the players walk the rest of the way. Leeds won 5–1, and in the next three games of the 1956/57 campaign the club leaked 10 more goals and conceded five goals or more on five occasions that season. It was not a good start, and they quickly slipped into the relegation area.

A highlight, however, came at Old Trafford, when Everton visited champions Manchester United. The Busby Babes, then at the height of their success, had gone 26 League games without defeat. In Tommy Taylor, Roger Byrne, Duncan Edwards and Bobby Charlton, United had some of the finest players in

81

ABOVE Irishman Jimmy O'Neill succeeded the legendary Ted Sagar in goal and went on to make more than 200 appearances.

RIGHT Wee Bobby Collins joined Everton from Glasgow Celtic in 1958. Already a Scottish international Collins collected a further half dozen caps before joining Don Revie's Leeds United in 1962.

post-war football. But Everton refused to show them any respect and won an astonishing game by five goals to two. Four months later they returned to Old Trafford in the fourth round of the Cup, and United took their revenge by a single goal.

Everton ended the season in fifteenth place and signed the young Scot Jimmy Gauld from Charlton Athletic for a sizeable fee, but he proved to be a poor investment and a year later was on his way to Plymouth Argyle. But it was not the last Everton would hear of Gauld. Cyril Lello's career also came to an end after 254 games, when he was transferred to Rochdale. Signed from Shrewsbury Town in

September 1947 he spent nine years at Goodison, initially as an inside-forward but later as a halfback.

Tommy Eglington and the captain, Peter Farrell, both left Goodison, the pair of them joining Tranmere. Farrell became player-manager of the Third Division North club, but it was not the happiest of experiences and he eventually returned to Ireland. In his eleven seasons at Goodison he had played 453 games and had won 28 caps for Eire and seven for Northern Ireland. Eglington had played 428 games, scoring 82 goals, while making 24 appearances for Eire and six for Northern Ireland, and at his height was one of the most skilful left-wingers in the business.

After he had spent just two years in the managerial chair, the Everton board decided in October 1958 that Buchan was not going to lead them to glory. What was needed was a big name, and after some careful deliberation the board agreed that Johnny Carey was the man for the future. Carey, the former captain of Manchester United during its distinguished post-war days, had been managing Blackburn Rovers for five years and had just brought them back into the First Division. As a player he had been one of the finest fullbacks United had known, winning 29 Irish caps as well as League and Cup honours, and as a manager had the technical understanding and respect that would bring results.

His job was made considerably easier by a number of fine youngsters that Buchan had reared and who were now ready for first-team action, and by an important signing made during the managerless days between Buchan and Carey. While Theo Kelly had been manager at the club he had signed a small Scottish lad, by the name of Bobby Collins, but the 16-year-old had quickly grown homesick and had rushed back north, signing for Glasgow Celtic. In 1951 he had been capped for the first time by his country and in September 1958, now fully grown to 5ft 4in, he re-signed for Everton in a staggering £23,500 deal.

The deal was made possible thanks to the introduction of pools millionaire John Moores to the Everton boardroom. Moores, who had founded the football pools empire of Littlewoods, had long been an Everton supporter and began lending not just his financial advice but money as well, particularly for the purchase of floodlights and players. At this stage he was not on the board, but within two years he would be chairman and would be leading the club into a new era.

Carey immediately introduced new faces into the team. Brian Labone, a home-grown centre-half, was

given a vote of confidence, as was Albert Dunlop, who had succeeded Jimmy O'Neill in goal. Johnny King, Derek Temple and Eddie Thomas all stepped into the team, while another Scot was the subject of a major signing. He was Alex Parker, a defender with Falkirk, who was to become one of the finest fullbacks ever to wear an Everton shirt and one of the original attacking defenders. He signed in June 1958 but was immediately posted to Cyprus to complete his National Service and did not make his debut until November 1958. But it was worth waiting for, and Parker quickly became not just a Goodison favourite but a permanent fixture in the Scotland team.

The Goodison floodlights were switched on for a friendly against Second Division neighbours Liverpool on 9 October 1957 and, with undersoil heating also installed, Goodison began to prepare itself for a more eminent future.

But results were slow to pick up. Carey arrived with Everton propping up the rest of the division and just in time to see them suffer the biggest hiding in their history as Tottenham beat them 10–4 at White Hart Lane. Jimmy Harris scored a hat-trick and Everton's four goals were the highest away score in the League that day, but that was little consolation. After this, anything had to be an improvement.

Carey, however, did tighten up the defence, and by the end of the season Everton had managed to pull themselves up to sixteenth in the table.

In 1959/60, for the third season in succession, Everton finished in sixteenth spot after another battle against relegation. To give the attack the width it had lacked since Eglington's departure, they purchased Tommy Ring, the Scottish international outside-left, from Clyde, but after a disappointing couple of years he left for Barnsley. Bobby Collins was showing flashes of skill but needed support and above all lacked a partner who could turn his ability into goals. Hickson, who had been the club's top scorer with 17 goals the previous season, suddenly staggered the Everton supporters by signing for Liverpool in November 1960. Although he had his critics, he had managed 111 goals for Everton in 243 games and his departure left them without a recognised striker.

The search was now on to find a centre-forward and a halfback who could link up with the diminutive Collins. Finding a centre-forward was not easy. There were a number around but they were well established, and of course expensive, but with John Moores now encouraging the club to be more extravagant the possibilities opened up. At the top of their list was Roy Vernon, the Blackburn and Wales inter-national who had been spotted and groomed by Carey when he was managing the Lancashire club. Vernon duly arrived at Goodison in February 1960 in exchange for Eddie Thomas and £27,000. Weeks later Everton swooped on Dundee to end their search for a right-half when they signed the young Jimmy Gabriel. At £30,000, he was the most expensive teen-ager in British soccer, but after a nervous start he went on to become one of the most astute purchases Carey ever made. The two transfers quickly led to Everton being dubbed the 'millionaire club', but it showed they meant business and were determined to recapture the glory days of the past.

OPPOSITE The former Manchester United fullback Johnny Carey took over the managership from Ian Buchan in October 1958.

ABOVE The agile Albert Dunlop saves against Chelsea at Stamford Bridge.

OVERLEAF The Welsh international centre-forward, Roy Vernon, joined Everton from Blackburn Rovers in February 1960 and went on to score 110 goals in 199 games.

85

THE CATTERICK YEARS

The 1960s began with a flourish that was to herald better times. Under the tutorship of Johnny Carey an accomplished side was beginning to develop. The club had not been afraid to go out and purchase the best it could see and was adding to its ranks all the time. Billy Bingham, an Irish international outside-right, joined from Luton in October 1960 during a lean opening to the season and was to prove a more than useful asset over the years. He was no newcomer to the Football League, having joined Sunderland in 1950 from Glentoran and then eight years later moved south to Luton, playing for them in the 1959 Cup final. A small, skilful and cheeky winger, he was never afraid to attack, pushing the ball past defenders and beating them in the sprint. With Bobby Collins, Tommy Ring and Billy Bingham beavering away in the forward line, Everton soon became unflatteringly known as the 'team of midgets'.

Weeks after Bingham's arrival Carey made the most important signing of all when he swooped on the Scottish club Hearts and in a double deal signed a fullback, George Thomson, and a golden-haired forward by the name of Alex Young for £55,000. The spindly-legged Young was soon drafted into the team alongside Roy Vernon and by the end of the season was showing the graceful skills and vision that would make him the most revered Everton forward since the days of Dean and Lawton.

But there were also departures. The tireless centre-forward Jimmy Harris moved on to Birmingham City after 207 appearances and 72 goals in December 1960, while Wally Fielding had quit for Southport a year earlier after notching up more than 400 appearances since 1945.

After a hesitant start to the 1960/61 season Everton settled and began playing some impeccable football. By Christmas they were in second spot, behind Tottenham, but four successive defeats as a fierce winter gripped the country saw them tumble down the table. The frozen pitches and mud-clinging goalmouths were not to the liking of their delicate ball-playing skills. But results picked up as the weather improved and they concluded the season in fifth place, their best post-war position.

Roy Vernon in his first full season had been magnificent, knocking in 21 goals, while Bobby Collins, as effervescent as ever, had struck 16. But with League

champions Tottenham 16 points ahead there was no denying that a vast gulf existed between doing well and coming top. The new chairman, John Moores, recognised this and was not prepared to settle for second best. He wanted Everton back where they belonged and where he had known them in the thirties, and above all he wanted Goodison referred to as the 'School of Science' once more. And so Johnny Carey, for all his qualities, was the man who had to shoulder the blame. It came as a surprise to most for Carey had done well, pulling Everton out of their long post-war depression by building a team for the future. But Moores felt that he lacked the essential

BELOW The elegant Ray Wilson whose skills graced Goodison for five seasons and won him a World Cup winners' medal in 1966.

RIGHT It was the arrival of Harry Catterick as manager in 1961 that sparked off Everton's revival. Catterick, a former centre-forward with the club, had not enjoyed great success as a player but in his new role he would make Everton a name to respect once more.

OPPOSITE Gordon West was transferred from Blackpool as the most expensive goalkeeper in football history.

hunger and dedication to make Everton champions again. In the back of a London taxi Moores broke the news to a phlegmatic Carey. His short career at Goodison was over, but he went on successfully to manage Leyton Orient, taking them into the First Division, and had five thriving years at Nottingham Forest.

The search for a new manager was on and it did not take the board long to settle on a candidate. Harry Catterick, the former Everton centre-forward, had been managing Sheffield Wednesday for a couple of seasons, taking them impressively into Division One and second place within a year. He had first joined Everton as an apprentice in 1937 and had witnessed at first hand the unrivalled team of the thirties. He had played only a handful of matches before the war, enjoying his most fruitful days with the club after the hostilities. But he was an Everton man through and through and promised Moores that he would make the club the leading force in the land once again.

Under Catterick they began nervously, losing six games before September was out and plunging into the relegation zone. But he intelligently reorganised them, stiffening up the defence so that they lost only five more games the remainder of the campaign. By the end of the season he had taken them into fourth spot, just five points behind champions Ipswich, and had spotted the weaknesses in the side. Major surgery was necessary, and it was without hesitation that he took what seemed a surprising step when he sold favourite Bobby Collins to Leeds United. Collins had netted 48 goals in 147 games for Everton and had always given his best. He was a gifted player, skilful and brave, yet Catterick reckoned the team needed some muscle up front, rather than an abundance of skill. In March the new manager signed Dennis

Stevens from Bolton Wanderers and five days later Collins was sadly on his way. But Collins had no cause for anxiety. Joining Don Revie's lowly placed Second Division club, he helped them into the First Division and to a Cup Final before joining a succession of clubs at home and abroad.

In the same month Catterick paid Blackpool a record fee for a goalkeeper of £27,500 when he signed Gordon West. The tall, athletic West immediately stepped into the side, and Albert Dunlop, after a season lingering in the reserves and 231 games, was off to Wrexham and later Tranmere.

Roy Vernon was again the top marksman, with 26 League goals, while Alex Young hit 14, and Everton concluded their fixtures at Goodison with a rousing 8–3 win over Second Division-bound Cardiff City.

The 1962/63 campaign got off to just the start Goodison had hoped for, and as the club won their fourth successive fixture they went to the top of the League for the first time since May 1939. They would not drop below third place for the rest of the season. No sooner was the campaign under way than Johnny Morrisey, the Liverpool winger, was signed, crossing Stanley Park for £10,000, and immediately pulled on the number eleven shirt.

Within weeks of his arrival Morrisey was lining up against his old club as they faced each other in their first League derby since January 1951. More than

73,000 were crammed into Goodison and with the most ferocious noise whistling around the ground as the Everton fans copied the innovative chanting of the Liverpool supporters, Everton almost went a goal ahead in the first minute. Roy Vernon finally put Everton in front through a penalty, but Liverpool equalised shortly before half-time. In the second half it was Morrisey who out-manoeuvred his old club-mates to put Everton into the lead. Then, almost as the referee was poised to blow for full-time, the England international Roger Hunt stole an equaliser for the Reds.

Yet the two most important additions to the Blues' line-up were to come in the latter half of the season. Alex Scott, the Glasgow Rangers right-winger, came for £40,000, to take the place of Billy Bingham, who eventually moved to Port Vale. Bingham had played an important role in Everton's rise, making 98 appearances and scoring 26 goals, and would go on to win 56 caps for his country. Scott was top of everybody's wanted list and set off a ferocious battle for his signature when he became available. The outside-right, already a Scottish international and rated one of the finest in Britain, was soon displaying his abundance of talent across the First Division.

In December, Catterick returned to his old club, Sheffield Wednesday, and signed the young defender Tony Kay for £55,000. The red-haired Kay was a fierce yet polished halfback whom many would come to rate one of the finest ever to appear in a blue shirt, but who in time would be tragically caught up in one of the most notorious soccer scandals of all time. Although Kay had been signed in December, he was not to make his League debut until February, when he took over from Brian Harris, as the bitterest winter in living memory played havoc with the League programme. Everton in fact did not play a single League game between 22 December and 12 February, although they did manage to battle their way through to the fifth round of the Cup with wins at Barnsley and Swindon.

When their League programme recommenced they had slipped into second place, but with a backlog of fixtures to catch up on. To capture the title they simply had to win those games, but a couple of defeats at the end of March left them trailing behind Spurs. However, in a dazzling finale to their season they finished without a further defeat, drawing just four of their last dozen games and conceding only six goals. The title was wrapped up in the final fixture as Everton hammered Fulham before a full-house at Goodison by four goals to one, with Roy Vernon hitting a hat-trick. As the final whistle blew, the crowd went wild and the rhythmical chanting of 'Ev-er-ton!' echoed across Stanley Park for neighbours Liverpool to envy. The trophy was duly paraded

around the pitch in the bright sunshine, and for the first time in 24 years the cry of '*Champions!*' could be heard ringing around the rafters of Goodison.

The League title was a magnificent compliment to their defence, which had conceded a mere 42 goals throughout the campaign. In Tony Kay they had discovered the most combative halfback in the League, while alongside him Brian Labone was a tower of control and authority and Jimmy Gabriel was a refined technician. Behind them Alex Parker and George Thomson formed an almost impregnable Scottish wall, while Gordon West in goal provided a combination of experience and reliability.

Up front, Roy Vernon, with 24 League goals, and Alex Young, with 22, formed as effective a partnership as Goodison had seen since the days of the Depression. And in Dennis Stevens there was the ruggedness that had long been missing. Alex Scott and Johnny Morrisey on the flanks meanwhile were the principal architects of the attack, providing width and pace.

Alex Young was a revelation. He was an artist with the ball, capable of holding it for that extra second before slipping in the most delicate of passes. Yet at times, like so many first-class players, he could also be infuriatingly casual.

In the Cup, Everton finally went out in the fifth round to West Ham, who won by the only goal of the game at Upton Park. But there was also another Cup competition for Everton during the season, as their fourth spot in the previous season entitled them to a place in the Inter-Cities Fairs' Cup. Everton were inexperienced European competitors. Before the war they had made regular trips abroad, but the post-war era had seen only the occasional Continental visitor to Goodison. S.V. Sodingen, of Germany, played a friendly in 1955, while a year later Vasco Da Gama of Brazil were the first non-European club to grace Goodison. There had also been games against Banik Ostrava of Czechoslovakia, Red Star of Yugoslavia and Fortuna of Holland. But none of the crack European teams, such as Red Banner, Honved, Real Madrid or Moscow Dynamo, who had played friendlies against Wolves and Manchester United in the fifties, had ever appeared on Merseyside.

Fortunately Everton drew Scottish opposition for their opening game, in the shape of Dunfermline, but the Scots proved to be a stubborn obstacle. The Blues won the first leg by a single goal but mysteriously

The league championship returns to Goodison in 1963 after a 24-year absence.

contrived to lose the return game in Scotland by two goals to nil and were disappointingly out of Europe at the first hurdle. As champions of the English First Division, however, the following season would entitle them to a crack at the most coveted European trophy of them all, the European Cup.

The city of Liverpool had probably never had a more glamorous appeal than during the heady days of the 1960s. The Beatles topped the charts, swiftly followed by a succession of other Merseyside pop groups, and young people everywhere wanted to visit or live in the city. Liverpool was the place to be, but the success of the city was not restricted to music alone. Everton had just topped the League, and the following season Liverpool began their successful return to trophy winning when they captured their first League championship since 1947. And over the next 23 years some 30-odd football trophies would find their way back to Merseyside as the city established itself unquestionably as the soccer capital of Britain. Over at Anfield the massed choir on the Kop adopted 'You'll Never Walk Alone' as their anthem, while at Goodison the *Z Cars* theme became the supporters' favourite. Soon the rhythmical chanting and singing that had originated on Merseyside would spread to football grounds not just in Britain but throughout Europe.

The new season, 1963/64, began where the old had left off, with a comfortable home victory over Fulham. But the following fixture brought the champions firmly down to earth as Manchester United thrashed them 5–1 at Old Trafford. After a couple more defeats, including a 2–1 beating at Anfield, Everton slipped into the lower half of the table and spent much of the autumn and winter struggling to rise above mediocrity. In November there was a brief respite from these mishaps as they faced Glasgow Rangers for the newly created British championship, winning the home leg 3–1 and drawing a goal apiece at Ibrox to take the trophy.

Once into the New Year, however, their League form showed some improvement as they strung together a dozen games without defeat. By mid-March they had shot dramatically to the top of the table and looked set to capture the game's number one prize again, but in a dreadful end-of-season run they contrived to lose three matches and waved goodbye to their title chances. Instead the championship trophy wound up just a short distance across Stanley Park, with Everton in third place, just five points behind their neighbours.

There were probably two factors behind their early

season slump. The first was a loss of confidence that the team suffered after the United defeat. And the second was injuries to key players such as Jimmy Gabriel, Roy Vernon and Mick Meagan. Two weeks after the United game they faced Inter Milan in the first round of the European Cup at Goodison. It was also the baptism of Inter Milan in Europe's greatest competition and they arrived an unknown quantity. Yet in players like Suraez, Mazzola, Jair and Fachetti they boasted internationals capable of upsetting any team in Europe. Under the careful guidance of manager Helenio Herrara, the Italian champions in their blue and black striped shirts erected a defensive wall across Goodison, the likes of which neither Everton nor any of the 62,000 present had ever seen before. They were impregnable, and no matter how hard Everton tried to break the 11-man defence they could find no way through, and the game petered out into a disappointing goalless draw. So much had been expected, but instead of displaying their splendid Continental skills the Italians had made little effort at attack, preferring to sit back contentedly and soak up the pressure.

The return leg at the San Siro stadium in Milan, packed with 90,000 fanatical supporters, was always going to be a daunting prospect. With Jimmy Gabriel injured, manager Catterick was forced to give a debut to the home-grown 18-year-old Colin Harvey, who played years beyond his maturity and experience as Everton put up a spirited fight against the skilful Italians. But Everton could not afford simply to sit back and soak up pressure as Milan had done at Goodison. To win, they had to score, and in the end their counter-attacking left the gap which Milan exploited. The final result was a single-goal victory to Inter, who followed that up by marching on to defeat the famous Spanish champions, Real Madrid, 3–1 in the final. Everton had no need to feel ashamed for they had gone out, albeit at the first hurdle, to the champions of Europe, who would also go on to win the world championship. Everton had also witnessed at first hand the new European tactics of defending away from home and then piling on the pressure in the return home leg. In years to come this experience would prove useful. But their failure to progress beyond the opening round of the competition left them dispirited and further knocked their confidence for the domestic competitions.

On the morning of Sunday, 11 April 1964 Merseyside awoke to read in the *People* newspaper a sensational soccer-bribes story involving Tony Kay, the Everton captain. Kay, Peter Swan, the Sheffield Wednesday and England defender, and David 'Bronco' Layne, the Wednesday striker, were alleged to have thrown a game between Wednesday and Ipswich in December 1962. Kay was said to have won £100 in bets that had been laid on the result of the game. The newspaper investigations were part of a continuing probe by the *People* that had already revealed bribery in the lower divisions, but now the scandal hit the First Division and involved three of the country's finest players. The scandal also indirectly involved two former Everton players. Jimmy Gauld, who had moved to Plymouth in 1957, was the go-between who had organised the bribes but who had turned informer, providing the paper with its information. The other was the former Everton goalkeeper Jimmy O'Neill, who was approached to throw a game but refused and reported the approach.

As soon as the revelations broke, Kay was suspended by Everton, though there was no suggestion that he had ever attempted to fix a game while at Goodison. There was worse to come, however, as the *People* continued its probing and claimed, just as the new season was starting, that a number of Everton players had been taking pep pills to boost their performances. Goalkeeper Albert Dunlop admitted in the paper that he had been in a stupor throughout one game because of drugs. Dunlop also claimed that Everton players had contributed to a bribes kitty to be used for fixing crucial games during their championship run-in. The Everton directors immediately set up an inquiry but could find no evidence to support these allegations. In October 1964 Kay and others came to court where the Everton wing-half was sentenced to four months' imprisonment. He was later banned from football for life, with Everton losing out on the £55,000 record fee they had paid for him. It was tragic that so fine a player as Kay should have been tempted when a glittering career lay ahead of him. With one England cap to his credit, Kay had looked a strong possibility for the England World Cup team and would almost certainly have continued to lead Everton to further glory.

Towards the end of the season Everton, desperate to retain the title, invested heavily in the transfer market, signing Fred Pickering from Blackburn Rovers for £85,000. It was to prove a wise signing as the tall, dashing centre-forward threatened defences throughout the First Division. He began well by scoring a hat-trick on his home debut, yet it was in those final few games of the season that Everton lost the title. Pickering possibly upset the balance and rhythm of the side when it was at its height, but he

Local boy Colin Harvey made his debut at the age of 18 in 1963 and went on to play 380 games. He was appointed manager in June 1987.

Fred Pickering, an £85,000 purchase from Blackburn Rovers, scored 70 goals in 115 games.

still netted nine goals in nine matches. Vernon was top scorer with 18 goals from 31 games while the loyal Derek Temple contributed a dozen. In the FA Cup the club failed to make much headway, beating Hull and Leeds after replays but then losing by three goals to one at Sunderland.

The next season, 1964/65, again failed to see any trophies return to the Everton boardroom. Nevertheless it was by any standards a successful campaign as the team put up a useful challenge for the title and went further in a European competition than ever before.

During the summer of 1964 Everton had descended on Leeds Road, home of Huddersfield Town, and in a memorable deal signed the club's right-back, Ray Wilson. He had been with the Yorkshire side for 13 years, and at 30 years of age could hardly be described as a 'promising teenager'. But he was an experienced, solid technician, who over the next few years would mature into one of Britain's finest-ever defenders.

The season began with a flourish as three victories put the Blues out in front, but two defeats and three draws almost as quickly saw them slip to seventh spot. By the end of the season they were back in contention, however, with Fred Pickering proving to be worth every penny of his huge transfer fee as he collected 27 League goals. They finished in fourth place, a dozen points behind Manchester United, who had dominated the season with Best, Charlton and Law in devastating form.

The FA Cup again brought little cheer, and after a third-round draw at Goodison with Sheffield Wednesday an early exit looked the likely outcome. But Everton won a spirited replay 3–0 at Hillsborough and faced newly promoted Leeds at Elland Road in the next round. They returned from Yorkshire with a 1–1 draw, thanks to Fred Pickering, and looked set to win the replay at Goodison, but Don Revie had other plans and in a highly competitive match Everton went down 2–1.

Back in the Inter-Cities Fairs' Cup, Everton were

TOP The Everton team celebrate another famous Cup victory after defeating Sheffield Wednesday in 1966.

ABOVE Mike Trebilcock hits Everton's crucial equaliser in the Cup final.

able to put their recent experience to good use as they travelled to Spain to face Valerengen. But the Spanish side was quite unlike Inter Milan and folded with little fight as Everton rattled up a 5–2 victory. A fortnight later the Blues won 4–2 at Goodison and had successfully broken their European duck. In the second round they travelled north to Kilmarnock and had no trouble in establishing a 2–0 lead. Pickering was on form for the second leg, hitting two goals

in a 4–1 win that firmly put Scottish football into perspective. Of all the teams Everton should draw for the third round, it had to be Manchester United, then riding high in the League. More than 60,000 witnessed the clash at Old Trafford as Everton's defence stubbornly held out for a 1–1 draw. But unfortunately, in the assault on United at Goodison, the Blues forgot that Law, Best and Charlton were among three of the finest attackers in the world and quite capable of exploiting any gaps left by defenders. United won 2–1, and Everton would have to wait another year for the glamour of Europe.

The arrival of Fred Pickering heralded the exit of Roy Vernon in March 1965, when the tall striker left for Stoke. Vernon had performed his role well, scoring 110 goals in just under 200 games. He had notched up 24 League goals in the championship-winning season of 1962/63, had gone on to captain the side, and won a total of 32 Welsh caps. He was as dangerous as any striker prowling the First Division during the early sixties and had been a fine servant to the club during his six seasons.

Not since Dixie Dean had headed Everton into a winning lead over Manchester City at Wembley in 1933 had the Blues tasted Cup glory. And that was many years ago. On a grey day in 1950 at Maine Road they had come within 90 minutes of the final, only to be thwarted by a young Liverpool halfback called Paisley. And in Coronation year, in another Maine Road semi-final, Nat Lofthouse had almost single-handedly destroyed their dreams. But since then their Cup exploits had been a catalogue of misery and ineptitude.

John Moores had achieved his principal ambition of guiding Everton back to fame and respect. Under Harry Catterick they had won the League title and were now regular participants in European football. All that remained was for Everton to bring the FA Cup back home to Goodison for the new generation of supporters to cheer and admire.

In the League 1965/66 was hardly an outstanding season as Everton hovered in mid-table, rarely making any serious challenge to the leadership. They were humiliatingly thrashed 5–0 by Liverpool at Anfield and would be reminded of the result constantly over the next 20 years. But otherwise it was an unmemorable campaign as Cup distractions took their toll and they finished in eleventh place.

Europe brought little luck either, although they did at least travel outside Britain. They began with a trip to West Germany, where they secured a 1–1 draw with IFC Nuremberg, thanks to a vital Brian Harris goal, while in the second leg Jimmy Gabriel scored the only goal of the match. In the second round they journeyed to unknown territory, with a visit to Ujpest Dozsa of Yugoslavia. Although Yugoslav football was not renowned for its skill, their teams were well known for ruggedness and competitiveness, and on a bitterly cold East European November day Everton froze against the Slavs, losing by three goals to nil. In the return leg they wreaked some revenge, but a 2–1 win was not enough to put them into the next round.

The FA Cup opened with a visit by Sunderland who were soon travelling back north after a 3–0 defeat. In the fourth round Everton found themselves with the unenviable task of facing non-leaguers Bedford Town. Playing on small grounds, often with uneven or sloping pitches and fans just an arm's length away, is never to the liking of major First Division clubs and Everton, with their history and pride at stake, were no exception. But they stood up to their ordeal in style, with Derek Temple scoring twice in a 3–0 win. That victory brought them a home draw against the high-riding Second Division club Coventry City, but the gulf between the lower and higher division was too much for the Midlanders to overcome, and the goalscoring trio of Pickering, Temple and Young snuffed their ambitions.

So far nobody had managed a goal against Everton, but the draw for the sixth round did not augur well. Manchester City, on the verge of clinching promotion from the Second Division, were the opposition, with the game scheduled for Everton's jinxed Cup ground, Maine Road. But Everton stubbornly resisted a slick-looking City attack and came away with a goalless draw. The replay at Goodison produced the same result, so with still no goals after 210 minutes the two teams battled it out again a week later at Molineux. This time City looked the most likely to score as they threw everything into attack, but luck was on Everton's side, with Fred Pickering making the vital breakthrough with a rare Everton chance. Derek Temple added a second, and they were flatteringly through to their third semi-final since the war, having capitalised on their only two openings.

The other Manchester team, United, provided the opposition for the Burden Park semi-final, but the previous season's champions were a far different proposition from their neighbours. A week before the game Everton fielded a reserve side in a League match at Leeds and were severely reprimanded by the Football League and fined £2,000. Catterick drew up a masterplan to contain the United attack, and with Everton sticking rigidly to his scheme they soaked up the champions' pressure and then counter-attacked, with Colin Harvey shooting them into the final.

FA Cup Final 1966 Everton v Sheffield Wednesday

Sheffield Wednesday had reached their fifth final with stirring victories over Reading, Newcastle, Huddersfield, Blackburn and, in the semi-final, Chelsea. And not one of their games had been at home. Everton, on the other hand, were the first club in 63 years to reach Wembley without conceding a goal. Yorkshire against Lancashire; it was to be a fitting battle of the Roses, with memories stirred of the 1907 final, when Sheffield Wednesday had sneaked victory over Everton in the dying seconds at the Crystal Palace. Every Cup game between these two famous sides seemed to be filled with incident, excitement and drama. And 1966 was to be no exception.

Catterick's biggest headache before the game lay in his choice of centre-forward. Fred Pickering had been injured, and although fit again was nowhere near as sharp as usual, not having scored in his last half-dozen outings. In the gamble of a lifetime Catterick instead nominated a young Mike Trebilcock, a relatively new signing from Plymouth Argyle who had made only a handful of appearances but had performed well enough in the semi-final, to wear the number nine shirt. The £20,000 Cornishman did not even have his name mentioned in the Cup Final programme, yet he was to have a dramatic impact on Wembley and before the afternoon was out would have written his name into the football history books. But at one minute to three on Saturday 14 May 1966 Catterick's decision hardly had the unanimous acclaim of the thousands of Everton supporters basking in the warmth of the Wembley sun.

Within four minutes they were shaking their heads, convinced their manager had made the wrong choice as Jim McCalliog's shot took a deflection off Ray Wilson to send Wednesday into the lead. In just 240 seconds he had done what no other footballer in the Cup had managed to do – score a goal against one of the finest defences in the land. Everton were rattled and struggled to settle as Sheffield piled on the pressure, attacking in wave after wave. Everton might have had a penalty in the nineteenth minute, when Springett brought down Alex Young, but the referee was having none of it, and that was all the Blues had to show for a first half in which they had been totally outclassed and outplayed.

In the fourth minute of the second half a remarkable one-handed save by the England international keeper, Springett, from the unlucky Young, kept Everton at bay once more, but then eight minutes later Wednesday struck again. Fantham, with the ball seemingly tied to his bootlaces, drifted past four Everton defenders before sending in a fierce shot which West could only half save for Ford to score off the rebound. It looked all over. Heads slumped on to chests and in despair many an Everton supporter turned and began to head for home.

But within a minute, and while Yorkshire hearts were still celebrating what seemed a famous victory, Mike Trebilcock, with his socks dangling around his ankles, drove a right-foot shot beyond Springett and

Everton were on the verge of a dramatic comeback. Hundreds came scurrying back on to the terraces as the famous Everton roar let rip at the sight of the bulging net. That goal pumped new confidence into the Merseysiders, and with the stadium now awash in blue they rediscovered their form and energy. Six minutes later Trebilcock again capitalised on a hesitant Wednesday defence, sending in a low shot after Alex Scott's free kick had been poorly cleared. Everton were suddenly back on level terms, while a dispirited Wednesday looked confused and tired. But it was not all over yet.

With just 10 minutes remaining and with Everton now powering at Sheffield, Gordon West kicked a high and harmless clearance upfield. Gerry Young, the Wednesday defender, waited unmarked to collect the ball as it fell. But instead of calmly trapping it as he would have done on 99 occasions out of a 100, the ball spun off his foot and raced into the gaping no-man's land in front of the penalty area. Derek Temple, casually watching from a distance, saw the ball moving in his direction and like a greyhound was on it, carefully controlling it as he sprinted alone towards the goal with only Springett to beat. Every heart in the stadium stopped – all, that is, except for Temple's, who simply carried on running and lashed the ball past the advancing keeper to put Everton into an astonishing lead. In the space of just 15 minutes Everton had won the Cup with three goals in the greatest turnabout Wembley had ever witnessed.

The scenes were almost indescribable. Fans leapt on to the pitch to be chased by police, and the chant of 'Ev-er-ton!' rang deafeningly around the famous stadium. Catterick was raised shoulder-high, and any doubts over Mike Trebilcock had evaporated in the euphoria of Cup glory.

When the Cup returned to Goodison after its 33-year absence, almost a quarter of a million turned out to greet Everton. It was an astonishing welcome, with Everton's triumph made the more rapturous after the dramatic final 20 minutes. All around Lime Street station and St George's plateau the crowds crammed to pay their tribute and to show their keenest rivals that they too knew how to welcome a Cup-winning side.

Everton West, Wright, Wilson, Gabriel, Labone, Harris, Scott, Trebilcock, Young, Harvey, Temple. **Sheffield Wednesday** Springett, Smith, Megson, Eustace, Ellis, Young, Pugh, Fantham, McCalliog, Ford, Quinn.

TOP Everton clinch their first European trophy.   ABOVE Blues' supporters invade Rotterdam.

PREVIOUS PAGE Gary Lineker outpaces Paul McGrath of Manchester United during 1986 Charity Shield.

ABOVE Neville Southall.

LEFT Everton celebrate another Wembley goal.

OVERLEAF Peter Reid in command.

OVERLEAF The 1987 Charity Shield.

Alan Ball's record £110,000 transfer from Blackpool after England's World Cup victory was one of Catterick's wisest investments.

Tony Kay might have gone on to establish himself as one of the country's finest halfbacks had it not been for his tragic involvement in the most sensational scandal in football history.

Everton's Cup win at Wembley was merely the prelude to another famous Wembley victory that glorious summer of 1966. And one Everton man played a major part in helping to make it a summer to remember. He was Ray Wilson, who as England's right-back helped transform his country's defence into one of the surest in the world, laying the foundation for England's magnificent World Cup victory. Another star of that England team whose breathtaking energy was applauded by all who watched would within a month of the World Cup be signing on the dotted line at Goodison and donning the blue shirt of Everton. He was Alan Ball, whose £110,000 record transfer from Blackpool sent a shiver of excitement down every Evertonian's back. The 5ft 6in, red-haired inside-forward would swiftly become the idol of Goodison and the fulcrum around which a dashing new team would turn.

Goodison itself had shared in the World Cup, with five games staged at the ground, while players such as Pelé, Eusebio, Albert and Beckenbauer delighted the Merseyside crowds with their skills. With Liverpool as League champions and the two trophies back on Merseyside for the first time since 1906, the season began with the novel experience of a Charity Shield played at Goodison between the old rivals. And before the two teams kicked off, Everton and Liverpool's World Cup heroes paraded the Jules Rimet trophy around the pitch, followed by the FA Cup and the League championship trophy. Goodison had never seen so much silverware before.

The arrival of Alan Ball was the first in a number of changes that would occur around Goodison as youngsters and newcomers were given their opportunities, though not always to the approval of the fans who remained loyal to the likes of Pickering, Young and Scott. But every good manager has to make changes before time forces them on him and the 1966/67 season would prove to be the turning point for a number of players. The popular Alex Scott, for five years the doyen of Everton wingers, made only 23 appearances that season and in September 1967 moved back north to Hibernian. Known as 'Chico' to the fans, he had played 176 games, scoring 26 goals, and over a 10-year period had won 16 Scottish caps.

Brian Harris, who had worn the Everton shirt longer than any of his colleagues, also stepped aside to make way for youth and moved on to Cardiff City. He had played regularly since 1955, making 358 appearances, and went on to achieve a career total of 541 games. His talents were not always acknowledged, but in his time only one man ever seriously challenged his place and that was Tony Kay. Local-born Derek Temple was also nearing the end of his Goodison days, and although he would see the season out he was on his way to Preston in September 1967. He enjoyed 11 seasons with the Blues, playing 272 games and scoring 82 goals, but of all those goals his winner in the Cup Final would be the most memorable.

Dennis Stevens, who had arrived from Bolton to add muscle to the midfield in 1962, lost his place to the promising Colin Harvey and was transferred to Oldham Athletic in December 1965. Two years later he wound up at Tranmere and ironically played his last game against Everton. The delightful Jimmy Gabriel was another on the move, signing for Southampton in July 1967. His Goodison career came to an end after he was sent off and suspended, thereby allowing a youngster called Howard Kendall to step up into the first team. Over eight years Gabriel played 300 matches, scoring 36 goals, but surprisingly won only two Scottish caps. He was a typical Scottish halfback – skilful, resilient and sharp – and would be remembered for the touch of class which he brought to the club.

A year after being omitted from the Cup Final team Fred Pickering decided to try his luck elsewhere and was transferred to Birmingham City for £50,000 in August 1967. The purchase of Alan Ball had effectively curtailed his chances and that season he made only eight appearances. Yet his strike record at Goodison was as impressive as almost any centre-forward's since Dean. In 97 League games he had scored 56 goals, while in a total of 115 appearances he had struck the net 70 times. He was an old-fashioned striker, tall, burly and powerful, to whom goalscoring was instinctive rather than scientific. He was popular with the fans, who complained bitterly when he was left out of the team. But with a promising youth called Joe Royle waiting in the wings Catterick had no hesitation in letting him go. And the man who had so brilliantly replaced Pickering at Wembley, Mike Trebilcock, did not survive much longer either. After just two years on Merseyside and 14 appearances he moved back south to Portsmouth, but his name would always be warmly recalled on Merseyside as the man who won the Cup for Everton.

To fill these gaps a variety of young players emerged, mostly from the club's nursery teams. Jimmy Husband, John Hurst, Howard Kendall, Joe

Royle and Tommy Wright all began to make their presence felt over the next couple of seasons. And with Alan Ball continuing to display the form that had won him a World Cup medal, Everton were developing the nucleus of a team for the future. Royle played four games and netted three goals, having made his debut at Blackpool in January 1966 at the tender age of 16, to become the youngest-ever player to represent the club. He was stocky and powerful even at that age, yet had all the energy, confidence and skill of youth. Within four years the local boy would have had earned himself the reputation as one of Everton's finest post-war strikers and a fitting successor to the traditions of Dean and Lawton.

In the League, Everton ended up in sixth spot, a commendable achievement considering the abundance of youth and inexperience in the team, while in the Cup they defended their trophy well, finally relinquishing it only after stubborn resistance in the quarter-finals to Nottingham Forest. The fifth round had produced a titanic tie with Liverpool, when the precocious Alan Ball stamped his personality and value on the game with his match-winner. It was the second time that season that he had destroyed Liverpool, and the more the Reds hated him, the more the Evertonians loved him.

Everton's FA Cup triumph of the previous season opened the way for their initiation into the European Cup-winners' Cup, but it was to be a short-lived experience. The first round brought a narrow victory over Aalbourg, the Danish Cup-winners, while Real Zaragoza were the opposition in the next round. The tough Spanish side notched up a 2–0 lead in the cathedral town of Zaragoza, and although Everton took their revenge at Goodison their one-goal victory was not sufficient and again they had disappointingly flopped in Europe.

The 1967/68 season, however, brought marginal improvements. In the League they finished one place higher, in fifth position, but this year there was no European campaign. Instead there was the newly created League Cup to contend for. But Sunderland soon put paid to any ambitions they may have nurtured in that direction.

Their concentration was again focused on the FA Cup. They began just a few miles up the road with a visit to Third Division Southport and a narrow one-goal victory, thanks to Joe Royle's first-ever Cup goal. The fourth round brought another away tie,

The Everton team inspect the Wembley pitch prior to their final with West Bromwich Albion in May 1968.

this time with Second Division Carlisle, who proved easier fodder. Tranmere Rovers, enjoying an unusual run of Cup success with the scalps of Huddersfield and Coventry to their credit, were the visitors for the fifth round. Goodison was packed for the occasion, with more than 62,000 spectators, but in a mediocre game Dixie Dean's old team went down by two goals to nil.

That result brought a tie at Leicester that produced a comfortable 3–1 victory and put the Blues into the semi-finals for the fourteenth time in their history. But the opposition was probably the toughest they could have wished for. Leeds United, under Don Revie, were an enterprising, combative side who had already experienced a number of bruising encounters with Everton. The semi-final proved to be no different, yet despite Ball and Hurst's absence through injury Everton still managed to shock the favourites, with Johnny Morrisey scoring the only goal of the match. And so Everton were into their seventh Cup Final and their second in three years.

FA Cup Final 1968 Everton v West Bromwich Albion

Everton were the hottest Cup Final favourites for years. They had thrashed West Brom by six goals to two at the Hawthorns only eight weeks previously, with Alan Ball scoring four goals. Nevertheless West Brom had ended their season a respectable eighth, only six points behind Everton, and in reaching the final had impressively disposed of Liverpool and Birmingham City. And in Jeff Astle they had a centre-forward of international calibre.

Their Cup Final pedigree was also superior to Everton's, with 10 appearances to their credit and four victories, whereas Everton could only boast seven appearances and three wins. Be that as it may, form suggested that the trophy would be travelling back up the motorway not to the Midlands but to Merseyside.

In the event, the final turned out to be one of the dreariest for years, with Everton, in a changed strip of amber shirts and blue shorts, matching West Brom's defensiveness ball for ball. Perhaps, with all their quality players, Everton had one too many youngsters whose inexperience inhibited adventurousness and ambition. Alex Young had by now lost his place, though with hindsight his inclusion may have inspired the resourcefulness that could have unlocked West Brom's defensive door. Jimmy Husband, an enterprising young Geordie, had stepped into his boots; otherwise the team lined up much as it had throughout the season.

For the first 90 minutes neither side made much headway as they sweated it out in the bright sunshine of Wembley. The towering Brian Labone at the

ABOVE Brian Labone thwarts the Stoke City attack. Labone was a pillar in the Everton defence for 15 seasons and was capped 26 times by England.

RIGHT Howard Kendall, flanked by Alan Ball, sets up another Everton attack.

PREVIOUS PAGE West Brom goalkeeper, John Osborne, saves from Joe Royle (left) and John Hurst. Yet despite all their attacks Everton lost the 1968 final by a single goal.

centre of Everton's defence comfortably controlled the rangy Astle, while Ball was, as ever, the motor that drove Everton onwards. But up front Everton could find little room as Husband frustratedly roamed the right wing, with Royle carefully policed by an ever-watchful Albion defence. Chances were few and far between and extra time was almost inevitable. Then with just minutes remaining Jimmy Husband, who had already missed a couple of half-chances, muffed the opportunity to clinch victory for Everton. As he stood unmarked in the penalty box, Morrisey lobbed a perfect centre towards him, and with only the goalkeeper to beat Husband headed well over the bar.

When the two teams kicked off for extra time, desperation to win and tired limbs began to play their part. Gaps suddenly appeared and players were slow to respond to the dangers. In the end it was Jeff Astle who settled matters just two minutes into extra time: he stumbled past Kendall and sent in a right-footed shot that was blocked by West, yet somehow he managed to hit the rebound with his other foot into the top corner of the net. It was a glorious goal and the one moment of genuine genius throughout the entire 120 minutes.

West Brom's name was clearly carved on the trophy from the outset, and there was little Everton could do to change their fate. To win championships and FA Cups you need a little luck, but on that painful summer's day at Wembley Everton and their fans found that luck was in short supply.

Everton West, Wright, Wilson, Kendall, Labone, Harvey, Husband, Ball, Royle, Hurst, Morrisey, sub. Kenyon.

West Bromwich Albion Osborne, Fraser, Williams, Brown, Talbot, Kaye (Clarke), Lovett, Collard, Astle, Hope, Clark.

Harry Catterick had welded together a new team capable of challenging for every honour in the game and, over the next few years, it would prove to be one of the most formidable sides the club had ever produced. The midfield of Kendall, Ball and Harvey had already established itself as the most effective and stylish in the League and would be the driving force behind the club's surge to success.

Howard Kendall, whose name in time would become synonymous with the success of Everton, had joined the club from Preston North End in March 1967 for £80,000. At the age of 18 he had become the youngest-ever player to appear in a Cup Final, when he was a member of the Preston team defeated by West Ham in 1964. He was a refined and accomplished left-half with an astute understanding of the game that would hold him in good stead in later years. Surprisingly, he never won any international honours, yet many rate him as the finest uncapped player of his generation. Colin Harvey was another classic halfback who had made his debut in the cauldron of the San Siro stadium at Milan as an 18-year-old. A Liverpool lad, he went on to play 380 games for the club over the next 12 years before joining Sheffield Wednesday in 1974, but like Kendall he was virtually ignored by his country, capped just once. Harvey's finest quality was his vision and ability to spray long accurate passes to his front-runners while at the same time effectively blocking any impending attacks by his brilliant positional play. The bubbling Ball alongside them completed the halfback line up, and together they dictated the pattern and pace of a game and would come to be remembered as possibly the most formidable midfield trio of all time.

Immediately behind them was another Liverpool-born lad, Brian Labone. The massive centre-half had made his first appearance back in 1957 and would still be donning the blue shirt 15 seasons later. In all, he made 530 appearances, scoring just two goals, and narrowly failed to overtake Ted Sagar's record number of League appearances. He led the club out for both Wembley finals and was capped 26 times by England; it was reckoned that there was no safer sight in football than to see Labone marshalling his defenders.

But two of Everton's post-war finest decided to hang up their boots. Ray Wilson, considered by many the most flawless fullback in England since the war, was forced to end his career in the summer of 1968 after a knee injury. He had made just 150 appearances since his transfer from Huddersfield but took with him a World Cup medal and 63 England caps. He battled back from injury and later played briefly for Oldham before joining Bradford City as player-coach. He now works back in Huddersfield as an undertaker.

Alex Young was possibly the most revered Everton player since Dean. He was idolised, drawing excited crowds whenever he played, and brought gasps of expectation from the terraces with almost every touch of the ball. A BBC television play, *The Golden Vision*, featured him and helped carry the hero worship to hysterical proportions. He was certainly a gifted player with a confidence and sway about him that has been typical of so many outstanding Scottish players throughout the years. Yet at the same time he could be temperamental, standing aside from bruising clashes and avoiding the graft and commitment that was sometimes necessary. But, for all that, anybody who ever witnessed his flash of genius around the box or skill on the ball would quickly forgive him his carefree moments. After 268 appearances and 87 goals the Golden Vision left Goodison in 1968, joining Glentoran as player-manager, but after a short spell he returned to the mainland and the north-west to play for Stockport County. In 1969 a knee injury forced his retirement and brought to an end the career of a man who remains a legend among Evertonians.

For much of the 1968/69 season Everton challenged vigorously for the League, but Leeds and Liverpool had the better of them as they wound up in third spot, ten points behind the Yorkshiremen. Goals came easily, with Royle the leading marksman on 22, while Jimmy Husband hit 19 and Alan Ball added a further 16. The FA Cup brought another

fine run as they reached their fifteenth semi-final, only to go down by a single goal to Manchester City. But it was a season that promised much for the future and the riches would not be long in arriving.

The first League table of the 1969/70 season showed Everton sitting proudly on top after three wins. And, save for a handful of weeks when they slipped into second place, they occupied that spot until the season ended eight months later in April. It was a magnificent campaign at the end of which they headed Leeds by nine points and had lost only five games. Everton could claim with every justification that they had won the title with style, and they gained countless admirers with their aristocratic midfield play. Joe Royle was leading scorer with 23 goals, while Alan Ball backed him up with a further 10 and newly signed Alan Whittle struck 11 in just 15 games.

It was their seventh championship and had been won with a club record of 66 points, 10 more than Dean's famous 1932 side. Harry Catterick and John Moores could be well satisfied that they had finally achieved their aim of producing a team to match any the 'School of Science' had ever produced.

Four Everton players – Ball, Labone, Newton and Wright – joined the England party in the summer of 1970 for the journey to Mexico to defend the World Cup. But it was a debilitating and depressing campaign that left the quartet in no fit state to confront the new domestic season. Consequently the sharpness of Everton's game was missing for much of the 1970/71 season, and once the team had settled into that rut escape became impossible.

Keith Newton had joined the club from Blackburn Rovers for £80,000 in December 1969. The England

Alan Whittle was an exciting attacking player, rated by Harry Catterick as potentially one of the finest he had ever seen. Sadly, Whittle never really lived up to his promise and was transferred to Crystal Palace in December 1972.

left-back was never quite the same after his trip to Mexico, even losing his place at Goodison. In June 1972, after only 57 games, he was sold to Burnley in a deal that recharged his batteries and he was soon back in the First Division, having inspired his new club to promotion. He won a total of 27 England caps and like one of his great predecessors, Alex Parker, he was a fullback always looking to attack down the flanks and take on defenders.

Alongside Newton was Tommy Wright, the man who actually took over from Parker. He may not have been quite so adventurous as Newton or Parker in his forays into the opposite half, but when the opportunity offered itself, he was not afraid to probe. A local lad, he had joined as a schoolboy, making his debut at the age of 19 in 1964, and when he retired in 1972 he had played 370 games for the club and collected 11 England caps.

A year after returning from Mexico, Brian Labone was forced to quit the game after an Achilles tendon injury. His was as distinguished a career as any player in Everton's history could boast, and but for injury would no doubt have continued for a few more years. Labone was a fine example of a man dedicated to his sport; he was booked only twice in his career yet was as tough and combative a defender as any. His loss was a shattering blow to the club that would be felt for another ten years.

After their championship-winning season Everton finished a disappointing fourteenth in the League. But there was some compensation as they reached the FA Cup semi-finals, only to be knocked out by neighbours Liverpool. In the opening round they defeated Blackburn Rovers 2–0 and then took on Middlesbrough. A 3–0 win brought them up against Derby, who were beaten 1–0. In the quarter-finals they were drawn at home for the fourth time against giant-killers Colchester United, winners over Leeds United in the previous round. But Everton were in no mood to be generous and thrashed the Fourth Division outfit by five goals to nil.

That brought them up against Liverpool in a semi-final played at Old Trafford in front of 63,000. But it was a day when Everton would be dogged by bad luck. First, Harry Catterick was taken ill and had to leave the side in charge of coach Wilf Dixon, and then, just as Everton were rediscovering their championship form, Brian Labone limped off the park with a pulled hamstring. Sandy Brown substituted, but the pattern had been disrupted and Everton went down by two goals to one.

The League championship triumph had brought European Cup football back to Goodison, though this time Everton were determined not to repeat their opening-round exit of 1963, when they were dismissed by Inter Milan. Fortunately the draw was favourable, although it meant a long journey north to face the Icelandic champions Keflavik, one of the weaker teams in the tournament. With a 6–2 win from the home leg, however, there was little doubt that they would go into the draw for the next round. In Iceland they added a further three goals, but faced far tougher opposition in the second round, when

The legendary Alex Young, whose skills have rarely been equalled at Goodison, seen here leaping over the Sheffield Wednesday goalkeeper, Ron Springett, during the 1966 Cup final.

they drew the accomplished German champions Borussia Mönchen-Gladbach. The first leg, in Mönchen-Gladbach's compact modern stadium, ended in a 1–1 draw, with Howard Kendall's vital away goal giving them more than a sporting chance for the return. But their opponents were not short of quality players, and in Berti Vogts, Gunter Netzer and Jupp Heynkes they had experienced German internationals who knew their way around Europe's great stadiums. On a rain-sodden November evening, in front of a 42,000 crowd, Everton sensationally opened the scoring after only 23 seconds, when an innocent-looking cross from Johnny Morrisey was fumbled into the goal by the German keeper, although he later compensated for that blunder with a series of world-class saves. In the thirty-fourth minute the Germans equalised, again as a result of a goalkeeping error, when Andy Rankin failed to hold the greasy ball, allowing Laumen to tap in the rebound. From then on it was end-to-end soccer, yet despite all the chances that was how the score remained after extra time and the two teams faced the drama of a penalty shoot-out.

It was probably the first-ever penalty shoot-out seen at Goodison, and those who suffered the unbearable tension would probably not wish to see it repeated. Joe Royle, the deadliest striker of a ball in the First Division, began by missing, and it was finally left to Andy Rankin to save Everton from another early exit. With the score at 4–3 in Everton's favour, Rankin flung himself full length to save magnificently from Müller, and Everton had earned themselves a tie with Panathinaikos.

The Greek champions arrived at Goodison an unknown quantity except for their manager, Ferenc Puskas, the great Hungarian who had led his country to a famous 6–3 victory over England in 1956 and had then gone on to help Real Madrid become the most famous club side in Europe. Now he was hoping to achieve similar honours with the Athens-based club. With Goodison packed, David Johnson shot the Blues into the lead, but Panathinaikos scored a vital equaliser, and with the second leg ending in a goalless draw that away goal was enough to put the Greek side on the road to a final with Ajax.

In the semi-final programme against Liverpool, Harry Catterick was reported as saying that he would expect a transfer fee of a million pounds for Alan Ball. 'We would consider it,' he added, 'and then we would say "no".' It came as something of a shock nine months later when the England international was dramatically sold to champions Arsenal for a mere, though record, fee of £220,000. Nobody could believe it. Ball had been the inspiration behind Everton's rise to glory, playing 249 games and contributing 78 goals. He was the most competitive player in football, sometimes pugnacious, but always sporting. Above all he was a worker, tirelessly attacking, defending and encouraging his team-mates to greater efforts. He was also skilled, able to drift past players and spray long accurate passes around the park. In Ball, Everton had a match-winner whose value could be quantified by the hatred he aroused among Liverpool supporters. The day he joined Arsenal, the Kop smiled.

The transfer of Ball brought nightmarish memories back to an older generation who could remember how a fine team had been broken up with the sale of Joe Mercer and Tommy Lawton to London clubs just after the war. And, as with the sale of those two players, Ball's move would have a similar effect, plunging the club into depression and anonymity for the next decade.

Ball was sold in December 1971, and with the

Keith Newton, the England fullback, joined Everton in 1969 and with Ray Wilson formed one of the most effective fullback partnerships in the club's history.

New Year only five days old Goodison slumped into further despair when manager Harry Catterick suffered a heart attack. Although he recovered and was back at work within three months, it marked the beginning of the end of his reign. In the meantime, in a desperate attempt to build a new team, Goodison became something of a railway station as players came and went, some remaining for only a brief stay. Out went goalkeepers Gordon West after 399 games and Andy Rankin after just 103 appearances, while in came Dai Davies from Swansea and David Lawson from Huddersfield for £80,000, a record fee for a keeper. Long-serving Johnny Morrisey moved on to Oldham in the summer of 1972 after 312 games and 50 goals. Often underrated, the tenacious Morrisey had been a bargain buy at £10,000 from Liverpool and played a crucial role in Everton's rise to fame and honours during the sixties.

The classy Henry Newton, purchased from Nottingham Forest for £150,000 plus Irish international Tommy Jackson in October 1970, stayed only three years and John McLaughlin, a £65,000 fullback, arrived from Falkirk along with John Connelly, a £75,000 winger from St Johnstone. Mike Bernard came from Stoke for £140,000 and was one of the better purchases, playing 161 games over five seasons.

Less successful was the sale of the budding David Johnson to Ipswich. The Liverpool-born player, after 55 games and 14 goals, was swapped along with £50,000 for Rod Belfitt. But after just fourteen matches Belfitt moved to Sunderland, while Johnson enjoyed a good spell at Ipswich and then a stunning career at Anfield, where he won every honour in the game. As if by way of apology, Everton surprisingly signed him again in 1982, but with equally disastrous consequences. At the tail-end of his career, he played just 37 games, and Everton had sadly missed out on a player who could have contributed much during a lean period. One promising buy was Joe Harper, the 5ft 6in Aberdeen striker who arrived for £180,000, but after 46 games and 14 goals he returned disillusioned to Scotland, never having really made the expected impact on English football.

Everton ended 1971/72 in fifteenth place and sank even lower, to seventeenth, the following year. There had also been poor runs in the Cup, and with Liverpool outperforming them every time it was clearly time for a change at the top. And so, as the season wound to an end, Harry Catterick stepped aside, moving into a consultancy position with the club, and the search was on for a new manager to revive Goodison's sagging fortunes.

David Johnson enjoyed two spells at Goodison but, sadly for Evertonians, his better days were with Ipswich and Liverpool.

In May 1973, another former Evertonian stepped into the managerial hot spot. He was the ever-popular, smiling Billy Bingham, who had enjoyed three successful seasons at Goodison during the early sixties, scoring 26 goals in 98 games as an outside-right. Since then he had played with Port Vale and followed that up with managerial experience at Southport, Plymouth and Linfield, as well as with the Northern Ireland and Greek national sides. He arrived eager to put into practice the ideas and styles he had learned on the Continent and soon dipped into the market, buying quality players who reflected his commitment to skill and free expression. Striker Bob Latchford arrived from Birmingham City for £350,000, making him the most expensive player in Britain, and the experienced Northern Ireland international defender Dave Clements moved from Sheffield Wednesday for a bargain £60,000.

In his first season in charge the new man at the helm took the Blues to an encouraging seventh spot, though they were rarely in contention for the title. Bingham had promised success, and during the close season the polished midfielder Martin Dobson was added to the squad after a £300,000 deal with Burnley. The team was beginning to take on the look of prospective champions and during the 1974/75 season made a serious challenge for the title. In mid-January they went top and by mid-April, with only four fixtures remaining, were still clinging on with half a dozen teams breathing down their necks. The title was theirs for the taking, but in a disastrous end to the season they lost two and drew one of those games and slumped to fourth, just three points behind champions Derby.

Starting the new season as potential champions, Everton could do no better than finish eleventh, well behind Liverpool, who captured the title for the first time under new manager Bob Paisley. His squad racked by injuries and still experimenting, Bingham was forced to use 27 players during his campaign. The problem remained up front, with Bob Latchford still not providing the goals for which he had been so expensively purchased. There were only 12 this season, and with Royle now at Manchester City nobody else managed double figures. Royle's career had been dogged by injury, yet he had proved to be as prolific a goalscorer as any other post-war striker at

Goodison. He collected 119 goals in 272 appearances, with his best performance being 23 League goals in 1968/69, the year they won the championship. He was powerful, with a clinical finish and an ability to head the ball not seen at the club since the days of Dixie Dean. He won a total of six England caps, only two of those while at Everton, and it was perhaps surprising that Bingham should have let him go when the club was so desperately short of goalscoring talent. Bryan Hamilton, the small, tenacious Ipswich midfielder, came in November 1975, bringing yet another Irish accent to the squad, but lasted only 47 games before moving to Millwall.

There was no fortune for Everton in the Cup either, as they tumbled at the first hurdle, beaten by Derby County, while in the UEFA Cup they were unfortunately drawn against the crack Italian club AC Milan. The first leg at Goodison ended in a goalless draw, and Everton made the long journey to Italy more in hope than with ambition. In the event, Milan won by a single goal, repeating the scoreline of their neighbours, Inter Milan, twelve years previously. Yet again Europe had proved to be a stumbling block.

Everton kicked off the following season showing some impressive form, but as the pitches grew muddy they began to slide. Duncan McKenzie, the mercurial striker who had fascinated football followers everywhere with his dazzling skills, was bought for £200,000 from the Belgian club Anderlecht. It was a gamble, for McKenzie, despite his skills, all too often allowed himself to be blotted out of games, spending long idle periods alone up front. Had he been surrounded by more talented midfielders, or played with the Harvey–Ball–Kendall midfield, he might well have been inspired to more consistent performances. As it was, he spent just two years at the club, playing 61 games and scoring 21 goals. Bruce Rioch, the Derby County and Brian Clough favourite, was another expensive Bingham signing at £200,000 and, like McKenzie, lasted only 39 games.

Bingham's signings, however, did little to arrest the slide and on 10 January 1977 the board of directors took an inevitable decision and sacked the genial Irishman. He had been there only three years. He had bought heavily, and although he had built the nucleus of a good side they still looked to be inferior to their neighbours Liverpool, whose winning ways

Joe Royle was one of the most prolific goalscorers since
the war, scoring 116 goals in 272 games and going on
to win six England caps.

had relegated Everton to second best. And for the 'School of Science' that was not good enough.

Gordon Lee had not enjoyed a particularly distinguished career as a player. After 11 years with Aston Villa and Shrewsbury the tall, lean defender had little to show for his endeavours. It was surprising therefore that he should have turned to coaching, first with Shrewsbury and then with Port Vale and Blackburn, where success landed him the manager's job at Newcastle. He steered the north-eastern club to the League Cup final and a place in Europe, and caught the eye of the Everton board. He looked just the man to sort out the chaos and depression that had beset the club, and a week after Bingham's departure in January 1977 he strode into Goodison and took over the managerial chair.

When he joined the club they were eighteenth in the League, but Lee had one helpful factor in his favour: they had just reached the semi-finals of the League Cup. It was a competition in which Everton had displayed little interest in the past, never having managed to progress much further than the early rounds. But with victories over Cambridge, Stockport, Coventry and Manchester United, they now faced a two-legged semi-final against Second Division Bolton Wanderers. Lee's first task was to ensure victory and a long-awaited Wembley final. In the first leg at Goodison, Everton had a miserable time, with Bolton equalising in the last minute to scrape a 1–1 draw. But in front of a 50,000 crowd at Bolton, the biggest Burnden Park had seen in years, Everton played their hearts out for the new manager, and rightly earned their one-goal win, thanks to Bob Latchford. For the second year in succession Gordon Lee would be leading a team out at Wembley.

It was nine years since the excursion trains had last pulled out of Lime Street station bound for Wembley carrying the blue and white colours of Everton. And the more than 30,000 making the journey south were determined to demonstrate that Liverpool were not the only outfit on Merseyside. Opponents Aston Villa had already appeared in four finals, winning the trophy twice, and in Andy Gray and John Gidman had two players whose talents would one day come Everton's way. Besides these two, there was Dennis Mortimer, Brian Little, Alex Cropley and captain Chris Nicholl to contend with in a team that would five years later be European champions.

Sadly, it was to be a dire final, ending in a goalless draw. Few chances fell either way, with Duncan McKenzie providing the only lasting memory when with his first touch he bamboozled the Villa defence

to set up a scoring opportunity that was wasted. After that he drifted out of the game. Everton had dominated for large parts of the game, but even extra time failed to prise open either defence, and 100,000 fans returned disappointed up Wembley Way to prepare for a replay.

The two teams met again at Hillsborough a few days later in front of another packed house of 55,000, with the injured Martin Dobson and David Jones making way for Roger Kenyon and Mike Bernard. But it was to be a night Kenyon would want to forget as he put one into his own goal to give Villa the lead. The minutes ticked agonisingly away as Everton piled on the pressure to find the equaliser, but then just one minute from normal time, and with all looking to be lost, up popped Bob Latchford to slam home Kenyon's cross to keep them in the hunt. Extra time brought no further goals and yet again the two teams were forced to replay. If nothing else, the two clubs

were certainly making some profit out of their meetings.

The venue for their third encounter a month later, was Old Trafford, in front of a crowd of 54,729, and if excitement and goals had been lacking in the first two matches, both arrived in abundance on a warm April evening in Manchester. Everton began the proceedings with Latchford putting them ahead for the first time, but Chris Nicholl soon equalised, and a minute later Brian Little had shot Villa into the lead. Everton again looked to be finished, but they battled away until Mick Lyons, drifting into the penalty area, hit an equaliser after Martin Dobson had headed against the bar. For the third time the two teams were level after 90 minutes and were forced into extra time yet again. Finally, with just 90 seconds remaining and another replay looking certain, Villa ended the long-drawn-out affair when Brian Little scored his second and won the trophy for the Midlanders.

Everton had given their all but still mustered the energy to salute their fans, who had followed them so loyally and at such expense.

Ten days later the same fans were back in Manchester, this time at Maine Road to face Liverpool in the semi-finals of the FA Cup. Everton's Cup campaign had begun with a 2–0 victory over Stoke, followed by a 2–1 win over Swindon after the Third Division side had held them to a draw at the County

ABOVE Duncan McKenzie was one of the most stylish players to wear an Everton shirt, yet he had a tendency to fade out of games.

OPPOSITE Trevor Ross was another expensive purchase by Gordon Lee who paid Arsenal £180,000 for his services.

Ground. In the fifth round they won at Cardiff and then faced Derby County at Goodison, where Latchford and Jim Pearson combined to give their team a creditable 2–0 win and a glamorous tie with Liverpool.

It was the fourth time the two Merseyside clubs had clashed in an FA Cup semi-final, with Liverpool having so far got the better of the tussles. Not since 1906 had Everton stopped their neighbours at this stage, and sadly 1977 was to prove no exception as the jinx of Maine Road struck again, even though it required two attempts. In the first game Liverpool took an early lead through Terry McDermott, but Duncan McKenzie pulled the teams level shortly before the half-time whistle. In the second half a

Jimmy Case header put Liverpool in front again, but Bruce Rioch equalised, and then with just minutes remaining Irishman Bryan Hamilton hit what looked to be the winner. But referee Clive Thomas ruled him offside and a replay was necessary. Four days later thousands of Evertonians were making their way along the much-travelled path back to Manchester and Maine Road. But luck was not on their side, and with an early penalty going Liverpool's way Everton's chins dropped and Liverpool added two more to clinch their place at Wembley.

When the club came to count the number of games played that season Everton had taken the field 58 times. In March, April and May alone they had played 23 games and it was little wonder they stumbled at the final hurdles. But with an end of season League place of ninth, a League Cup final contested three times and an FA Cup semi-final fought twice, Gordon Lee could look back with some satisfaction on his first five months in office.

During the close season he dipped into the transfer market, adding the nippy QPR winger Dave Thomas to the squad for £200,000 and the Blackpool and Scotland keeper George Wood for £150,000. There was also a clear-out, with Bruce Rioch, Bryan Hamilton and Ken McNaught parting company with the club. The new season, 1977/78, began with two surprising defeats, the first at home to newly promoted Nottingham Forest, managed by Brian Clough. But once those defeats were out of the way the Blues began a surge that took them into second place. Their next defeat was not until Boxing Day, 18 games later, when Manchester United hammered them 6–2 at Goodison. They recovered, and although they were in contention for the title they could never close the gap with Nottingham Forest and finished in third place, nine points behind.

Latchford was at last proving to be an effective goal-poacher, hitting 30 League goals. But with little back-up for him from elsewhere, manager Lee was forced to sign the Arsenal midfielder Trevor Ross for £180,000. With only half a dozen goals from the Eire international the following season, however, and a mere 11 League goals from Latchford, Everton could count themselves lucky to be in fourth place. In early February they had even topped the table, but by the end of the season there was a 17-point gap between themselves and champions Liverpool, who had also scored 33 more goals than their Merseyside rivals. Those statistics alone told the tale.

To supply Everton with those much needed goals, Brian Kidd arrived for £120,000 from Manchester

City. A proven goalscorer with Manchester United, Arsenal and City, he stayed only one year, scoring 20 in 51 appearances, never really producing the touch that had brought him so many goals elsewhere. Colin Todd, the rugged Derby County and England defender, was also purchased for around £180,000 to bring some bite to the defence. Todd, with 27 England caps to his credit as well as two League championship medals with Derby, was one of the most effective defenders in football. He was tough, but had the vision to spray long, accurate passes around the ground, and in many ways was similar to one of his predecessors, Tony Kay. Sadly, Todd clashed with Gordon Lee and after just one year and 35 games he moved on to Birmingham City. Martin Dobson also moved back to Burnley for £100,000 in August 1979, five years precisely after his £300,000 record transfer from the Lancashire club. Dobson had taken time to settle at Goodison, but once he had done so he began to show the skilful touches that made him one of the finest midfield players in the game. Yet even then, there was always a feeling that somehow he never quite realised his full potential. He won only one more England cap while with Everton to add to the three he had already collected at Burnley. In all he made 230 appearances in a blue shirt, scoring 40 goals.

Back in Europe after a three-year gap Everton drew the Irish club Finn Harps in the opening round of the UEFA Cup. They won both legs comfortably by five goals to nil, but then faced the formidable Czech side Dukla Prague in the next round, winning the first leg 2–1 at Goodison but then going down and out 1–0 in the Czech capital.

After two seasons in harness Lee had brought the club to respectable positions in the League, but in truth it was little more than his predecessor had achieved and considerably worse than the continuing success that was flowing Anfield's way. With transfer fees rocketing Lee recklessly brought out the cheque book again, adding further players to the squad in a desperate bid to bring glory back to Goodison. Peter Eastoe came from QPR in exchange for Mick Walsh,

OPPOSITE Asa Hartford, the Scottish international, was one of the club's more successful signings. After 98 games, however, he returned to Manchester City.

BELOW John Gidman was a tough, no-nonsense fullback who cost the club a record £650,000 from Aston Villa. In July 1981 he was transferred to Manchester United.

the one-time Blackpool player, but he managed only four seasons and 108 appearances before moving to West Brom. Gary Stanley, Asa Hartford, John Gidman and Gary Megson were all known names signed during the 1979/80 season. Stanley came from Chelsea, Hartford from Nottingham Forest in a £500,000 deal, Gidman from Aston Villa for a club record fee of £650,000, and Megson from Plymouth Argyle. Of these only Hartford and Gidman were quality players, and neither was probably worth the inflated price paid.

Hartford, the former West Brom, Leeds, Manchester City and Forest player, had already clocked up transfer fees worth a small fortune, and at the end of his Goodison career added another £350,000 to his name when he returned to Maine Road. A Scottish international, he was a wily character, quick of temper and determined, but also gifted and the kind of terrier-like midfielder every successful side needs. But it never really worked out for him at Goodison and after just two years, with 98 appearances and seven goals, he moved on. Fullback John Gidman arrived from Aston Villa with League championship and European Cup medals, but like Hartford was arguably at the wrong end of his career and susceptible to injury. He stayed less than two years, and made only 78 appearances before he was signed by Ron Atkinson at Manchester United.

Buying so many players, however, was not the solution to Everton's problems, as results quickly demonstrated. Their centenary year, 1979/80, turned out to be a disastrous season as they slumped to nineteenth in the table, only five points from relegation. After so much expenditure this was not what the supporters expected. But there was a fine run in the FA Cup as they reached their nineteenth semi-final, where they faced West Ham United. The game at Villa Park ended in a 1–1 draw, with the Hammers winning the Elland Road replay 2–1. In the UEFA Cup they again made an early exit, dismissed by the former European and world champions Feyenoord of Holland, beaten 1–0 home and away.

The next season, 1980/81, was just as bad and, although they held third place in early October, by April they had plunged to fifteenth and the terraces were displaying open hostility towards Lee and his team. The writing was on the wall, and two days after the season finished Gordon Lee was summarily dismissed by the chairman, Philip Carter.

12

KENDALL RETURNS

When the manager's seat at Everton became vacant, a number of well-known names were linked with the job, but Howard Kendall was always the favourite to succeed Lee. He had been managing Blackburn Rovers for a couple of seasons, taking them from the Third Division to within three points of promotion to the First. It was an impressive achievement, and one which had caught the attention of Phillip Carter, a long-time admirer of the former Everton player. And on 8 May 1981 Carter proudly presented Kendall to the waiting press as the new manager of Everton, their seventh since the war.

Kendall had enjoyed a distinguished career as a player at Goodison. Arriving at the club from Preston in March 1967 after being the youngest player in a Cup Final, he soon linked up with Alan Ball and Colin Harvey to form a brilliant midfield trio. In all, he had played 266 games for the club over eight years, scoring 29 goals, and winning most honours in the game except an England cap. In February 1974 he had been transferred to Birmingham in a deal that brought Bob Latchford to Goodison. Three years later he signed for Stoke City and eventually joined the coaching staff of the Potteries club under Alan Durban before moving to Blackburn in July 1979 as player-manager.

Goodison was in a depressed state when he took over. The achievements of Liverpool had become a haunting shadow as Everton supporters rightly demanded success on the same scale. They were tired of the jokes, of being labelled second-best, and living on memories. It was Kendall's task to change all that, but as the season kicked off it must have seemed an impossible dream. One of his first tasks, even before

The former Everton midfield star, Howard Kendall, became the club's eighth manager in 1981. Since leaving Everton he had played with Stoke before joining their coaching staff and becoming player-manager of Blackburn Rovers in 1979. An Evertonian through and through, Kendall would lead the club to new heights although his early managerial days at Goodison would not be so memorable.

a ball had been kicked, was to sell striker Bob Latchford to Swansea City for £125,000. The former Birmingham player had taken a little while to feel at home at Goodison, but once he did the goals flowed. In 286 games he hit 138 goals, to make him the most prolific goalscorer to wear a blue shirt since the war. He was strong and burly, a difficult man to shake off the ball and as fine a header of the ball as Dixie Dean or Joe Royle.

Kendall's first season could hardly have inspired him. By early January Everton were out of the League Cup and the FA Cup, and were just holding their own in the top half of the League table. It was not an auspicious start, even though they ended the campaign in eighth position, a long way behind champions Liverpool. But he did make a couple of signings that were to stand him in good stead over the next few years. The first was a young goalkeeper from Bury called Neville Southall. Kendall did not shirk

OPPOSITE Bob Latchford hits his 30th goal of the 1977/78 season. The former Birmingham striker scored more than 130 goals with the club to make him the club's leading goalscorer since the war.

ABOVE Neville Southall, seen here saving from Watford's John Barnes, was new manager Howard Kendall's first signing and arguably his best. The young Welsh goalkeeper cost £150,000 from Bury but proved to be a bargain as he helped Everton to a bagful of trophies.

125

ABOVE Adrian Heath was the most costly player in Everton's history when they paid Stoke City £800,000 for his talents.

OPPOSITE Gary Stevens emerged from Central League football to seize his opportunity in the first team when Kendall offered him his chance in late 1982.

at the asking price of £150,000 – expensive considering the young man had only had unproven spells in non-League football with a variety of Welsh clubs and the Cheshire League side Winsford. Yet Kendall had every confidence in him and soon gave the six-foot-plus keeper an opportunity.

The other inspired purchase was Adrian Heath, the 5ft 6in midfielder who arrived for a massive

£800,000 in January 1982, making him the most costly player in Everton's history. He initially looked out of place as Everton struggled to find any pattern to their play, but as time progressed he settled to become a major influence on the team.

Kendall's team of the eighties was now beginning to take shape. At the back of the defence was John Bailey, a local lad signed from Blackburn Rovers by Gordon Lee for £300,000 in July 1979. He was a rugged, no-nonsense fullback who inspired confidence in those around him and would battle until the final whistle. Alongside him as the 1982/83 season kicked off was Brian Borrows, who had progressed through the ranks of the club, but he was soon displaced by another apprentice, Gary Stevens. Stevens grabbed his opportunity and rewarded the manager's

vote of confidence by going on to wear the number two shirt for the next four years.

Many of the players who would shine in later years were to be found languishing in Everton's Central League team, awaiting their chance. Some were local lads, others had been signed as apprentices, but all were young, enthusiastic and longing to show what they could do in the First Division. Among them was Kevin Ratcliffe, who had been signed straight from school after winning a bagful of Welsh schoolboy honours. Twice over the next few years he would almost leave the club, but fortune kept him at Goodison, and within eighteen months he would be captain of his club and country. Also biding his time in the reserves was Mark Higgins, another apprentice who would force his way into the first team, eventually displacing central defender Mick Lyons when he moved on to Sheffield Wednesday.

Lyons had been a pillar of strength in the Everton defence for almost 12 years, playing 434 games, and his departure was greeted with dismay by many Evertonians. But at 30 he was at the tail-end of his career, although he went on to help the Yorkshire club win promotion back to the First Division. For a defender he scored a respectable 59 goals, most of them from corners, and there were few sights more encouraging than to see Lyons dashing upfield to take his place in the penalty area as a corner kick was lined up. Despite all his years at Goodison and Hillsborough the tall defender never won any honours or medals – not even

LEFT Kevin Ratcliffe was another apprentice to rise through the ranks. Club captain, he is now also a regular choice at fullback for Wales.

OVERLEAF LEFT Mick Lyons, with blood streaming down his face, was one of the toughest and most effective centre-halves to play for the club. After 434 games he joined Sheffield Wednesday but has now returned to join the club's backroom staff.

OVERLEAF RIGHT Kevin Sheedy was a surprise buy from Liverpool where he had been languishing in the reserves. Since joining Everton, however, he has proved to be a skilful and exciting midfielder who has gone on to win international honours.

an England cap – but he will go down as one of the most loyal and dependable centre-halves to have worn the blue of Everton.

In the summer of 1982 Kendall shocked Merseyside by crossing Stanley Park to sign two Liverpool players. The first, David Johnson, had actually begun his career at Goodison before joining Ipswich, and at Anfield had won every honour in the game. Kendall was short of firing power and hoped the former England international might contribute a dozen or more goals to their total, but it was not a particularly successful venture and within two years Johnson was off to Maine Road. Kevin Sheedy, on the other hand, turned out to be one of the bargains of the season. He had been playing in Liverpool's reserves, patiently awaiting his opportunity, but with a player of the quality of Graeme Souness ahead of him it looked as if he would be waiting for ever. Kendall spotted the young lad's frustration and jumped in with an offer that brought him to Goodison for £100,000 and an immediate first-team place. A year later Souness had moved to Italy, and with no ready replacement the Anfield backroom staff were kicking themselves for not holding on to the Irishman.

Although Kendall was not afraid to spend money, some of his more inspired signings came from the cheaper lower divisions. Derek Mountfield had been whiling away his time in the Fourth Division with Tranmere Rovers when Kendall signed him during that busy summer of 1982 for £30,000. A centre-back, he was forced to wait his opportunity, playing only once during his first season, but within two years he had established himself as one of the toughest defenders in the First Division. Later that year Kendall travelled to Bolton, where he signed the attacking midfielder Peter Reid for £60,000. Reid had been the subject of an Everton inquiry some years previously, but with the clubs haggling over a £600,000 asking price the deal had fallen through. It was another Kendall bargain, although with Reid's record of injury it hardly seemed so at the time.

Rounding off this complement of local and imported youth were Graeme Sharp and Steve McMahon. Sharp had arrived from Dumbarton in April 1980, signed by Gordon Lee for £120,000, but had yet to demonstrate his considerable goalscoring

Derek Mountfield came from fourth division Tranmere Rovers for a mere £30,000 but has now established himself as one of the most effective defenders in the first division.

Trevor Steven, a £300,000 signing from Burnley, has brought width and pace to Everton's midfield.

talent. The Liverpool-born McMahon, on the other hand, had quickly stepped into the first team under manager Lee, soon demonstrating his abundance of skill and drive, and Kendall continued to show faith in him. Unfortunately McMahon was desperate for honours, and before Kendall's team had hit the glory trail he had left for Aston Villa, turning down a similar offer from Liverpool.

Equipped with the nucleus of a championship team, Everton nonetheless soon found themselves battling at the wrong end of the table, and before autumn was out they were hovering in seventeenth place. Changes were made: Jim Arnold took over from the inexperienced Southall in goal and Stevens came in for Borrows, while Peter Reid arrived as an early Christmas present, and the defence that had already conceded far too many goals began to look more solid. A humiliating 5–0 defeat by Liverpool at Goodison had been the catalyst for change. In the second half of the season Everton looked a far tougher proposition, with Kevin Sheedy and Graeme Sharp hitting 26 goals between them, as the Blues clawed their way back into the top half of the table to finish in seventh spot.

In the League Cup they were dismissed in the second round by Arsenal, after beating Newport in the opening round. And in the FA Cup, Newport were again the opposition in the opening round, holding them to a 1–1 draw at a packed Somerton Park; but back on Merseyside Everton had the edge, winning by two goals to one. Shrewsbury Town were the visitors for the fourth round, but the Third Division side, after a plucky fight, were soon wending their way back to Shropshire. There was more formidable opposition for the fifth round, when Cup-holders Tottenham – most people's favourites to retain the trophy – provided the opposition. But Everton showed all their Cup-fighting qualities, with Andy King and Graeme Sharp firing them into the quarter-final for a lucrative tie with Manchester United. Just when they were beginning to look confident their luck deserted them, and United ran out winners with the only goal of the match.

In many ways that was the story of the season: much promise but a lack of experience. And at the end of the day there was nothing to show for it. For the Everton fans that was not good enough and their patience was being strained. Kendall had enjoyed two seasons at the helm and still there were no prizes on the sideboard. There were mutterings around the ground and in the press that the following season Kendall would have to deliver.

There was only one signing during the summer of 1983, that of Trevor Steven, a £300,000 buy from Burnley. Born in Berwick, Steven was a tenacious, buzzing midfielder, capable of taking on defenders,

beating them and then sending over those old-fashioned hanging crosses that Alec Troup had perfected for Dixie Dean in the thirties. What Steven needed was the kind of centre-forward who could thrive on his work rate and accurate centres, but that man would be some months in arriving.

The 1983/84 season kicked off with considerable optimism, but before September was out the crowds on the terraces were showing signs of restlessness. Even before the first dozen fixtures were past Everton had notched up five defeats, including two at home and a 3–0 drubbing at Anfield. There was a desperate shortage of goals, with only seven in those 12 games, and the prospects did not bode well for the remainder of the season.

To solve the problem Kendall dipped into the transfer market again, signing another injury-ridden player, who at the age of 28 was best described as a 'veteran' rather than 'promising'. He was Andy Gray, who arrived from Wolverhampton for £250,000 in November. But Gray was experienced as well as a proven goalscorer, and his maturity was just the ingredient needed to complement the youth and inexperience of his new colleagues. Gray had been around for some years: he had moved south to Aston Villa from Dundee United back in 1975, before teaming up with Wolves in a record-breaking deal of £1.5 million four years later, making his debut against Everton at Goodison and scoring for his new club in their 3–2 victory. A Scottish international with 18 caps to his credit when he arrived, he had played on most of the world's football stages, and without his injury problems would no doubt have collected many more caps, honours and accolades.

It took some weeks for Gray to make his presence felt, and as the old year ended the Blues lay in sixteenth place, having scored a mere 11 goals in 21 games. It was the worst opening half to a season anyone could remember, and the terraces were now openly calling for Kendall's dismissal. Goodison was not a friendly place to be. Gates had slumped to around 20,000, with only 8,000 turning up for the Milk Cup tie with Chesterfield, and there was an air of depression hanging over the old stadium. Everton had become a club of memories chasing the ever-elusive shadow of their neighbours Liverpool.

They say that managers can often pinpoint a precise moment or game when their careers have turned for either the better or the worse. And for Howard Kendall that moment arrived on the evening of Wednesday 18 January 1984 at the Manor Ground, home of Oxford United, in the fifth-round tie of

135

the Milk Cup. Everton had been going well in the competition, with wins over Chesterfield, Coventry and West Ham, and now faced the Third Division side at a packed Manor Ground for a place in the semi-final. Everton were never at their best against lower opposition and that bitterly cold January evening was no exception. The former non-League side had the best of the first half and shortly into the second half went a goal up. Everton looked dispirited and ragged and Oxford might well have gone two up but for some brave goalkeeping from Neville Southall, not long recalled from Port Vale where he had been on loan. Then with just ten minutes remaining the Oxford defender Kevin Brock made a foolish backpass to his goalkeeper and Adrian Heath, spotting the chance, raced for the ball, rounded the goalkeeper and Everton were saved. The game ended in a 1–1 draw, but that result pumped new life and confidence into Everton. The television cameras had been present to witness the funeral of Everton and Kendall but instead they had seen the rebirth of the Merseyside team. The replay was a mere formality, with Everton thrashing the Third Division side 4–1 after a snowstorm had engulfed Goodison. Suddenly there was a spirit about Everton that had been lacking for years; players began to believe in themselves, while the older hands were offering wise advice. Youth team coach Colin Harvey was promoted to first-team coach, and soon put his vast experience to good use as Kendall's number two. Chairman Philip Carter gave his unconditional support to the manager, and the terraces ceased their barracking.

A few days after ousting Oxford, Everton turned their attentions to the little matter of the FA Cup and the visit of Third Division Gillingham. In the third round the Blues had disposed of Stoke City by two goals to nil, but Gillingham, like Oxford, were tricky customers. They came to Goodison with nothing to lose and left with a goalless draw. It might have seemed that such a result would again spell despair for the club, but instead they cheerily made the long journey to Gillingham, and although they only managed another goalless draw they had battled spiritedly against the Third Division side. The third game was again played at Gillingham's quaintly named Priestfield Stadium, and this time Kevin Sheedy and Adrian Heath, in front of a full-house of over 17,000, combined to give the Blues a 3–0 victory.

The semi-final of the Milk Cup pitted Everton against Aston Villa, with the first leg at Goodison, while in the other semi-final neighbours Liverpool had the easier draw, against Walsall. With the two Merseyside clubs drawn apart for once, there was a real prospect for the first time in many years of an all-Merseyside final. And even before Everton kicked off they knew that Liverpool had already secured their place at Wembley. But first of all there was the matter of Andy Gray's former club, Aston Villa. Unfortunately the Everton man had been ineligible to play for his new club, having been Cup-tied following an appearance in the competition earlier in the season with Wolves.

More than 40,000 turned up at Goodison for the first game, and with the crowd firmly behind their fresh new hopefuls, Kevin Sheedy opened the scoring, with Kevin Richardson, playing with a broken wrist, adding a second to give them a two-goal lead to take to the Midlands. A week later, with 13,000 Evertonians making the journey and before another huge crowd, Everton dominated the first half, twice hitting the woodwork. And although Villa scored in the second half Everton battled bravely to hold out for a place in the final. When the final whistle went, Villa Park was invaded by blue as the Everton fans swept onto the pitch to celebrate their triumph. It was their first defeat of the year, ending a 14-game run, but it hardly mattered for they were back at Wembley after a seven-year gap.

In the League they were repeating their Cup form and finished the second half of the season with only three defeats, all away from home. Suddenly the goals had arrived, with 33 scored in 21 games, three times as many as in the first half of the season. It was an astonishing turnabout, and although their highest scorer was Adrian Heath, with only 12 goals, there were contributions from 13 other players. They ended the season having quietly climbed the table to seventh spot, but their thoughts were focused on the two Cup competitions.

Back in the FA Cup their victory over Gillingham had earned them a fifth-round tie at Goodison against Second Division Shrewsbury, but they made no mistake as they swept to a 3–0 win and a place in the quarter-final. First Division Notts County were their opponents, with Everton having to do the travelling, but goals from Gray and Richardson were enough to give them a 2–1 victory and put them just 90 minutes away from a second Wembley appearance. In the semi-final they faced Southampton at Highbury, while Watford played the season's giant-killers, Plymouth Argyle, at Villa Park. More than 20,000 Everton supporters made the trip to London and saw Adrian Heath snatch a spectacular winner for Everton in extra time.

The Milk Cup Final 1984 Everton v Liverpool

Everton against Liverpool in a Wembley Cup Final! It was the game all Merseyside had dreamed of for almost a century. Never before had the two teams met in such a showdown. There had been four semi-final meetings between them in the FA Cup, with Liverpool getting the edge in all but one of those clashes. The whole of Merseyside was agog at the prospect, with tickets impossible to obtain, even though more than 70,000 were shared between the two clubs.

So, on a wet Sunday in March, before a capacity crowd of 100,000 with millions more tuned in at home, the two teams lined up for their dramatic encounter. Liverpool, the League champions and already holders of the Milk Cup, were the most formidable team in Europe and were well on their way to winning their fourth European Cup. Everton could not have faced a more skilled and experienced team in Europe or possibly the world, but they were not to be overawed by either their famous neighbours or the occasion.

Everton began confidently and as early as the eighth minute should have taken the lead when Grobbelaar in the Liverpool goal failed to beat Adrian Heath to a pass from Graeme Sharp. Heath, seizing his chance even though lying on the ground, hooked the ball towards the gaping goal, but Liverpool's Alan Hansen, quick as a flash, appeared and seemed to scramble the ball away with his hand. A roar went up from the Everton end of Wembley and everyone expected the referee to point firmly towards the penalty spot, but instead he simply waved play on and refused to listen to Everton's pleas for a penalty. Everton probably enjoyed the best of the first half but were still unable to score, and as Liverpool began

ABOVE Andy Gray was an experienced Scottish international who, at 28, had already played with Dundee United, Aston Villa and Wolves when Everton signed him in November 1983. He was prone to injury and many also considered him too old but Gray arrived with a new zest for football and proved to be an important and exciting purchase.

Peter Reid brushes Liverpool's Alan Kennedy aside during the 1984 Milk Cup final.

to string their normal passing game together in the second half it looked as if the Blues were about to end up losers again. But they held out, and with two minutes of normal time remaining might have won the contest when Graeme Sharp shot wide.

Ninety minutes gone and still no goals. Extra time

to the shot, tipping it over the bar. Then, with the minutes ticking away, Everton made a final charge. Heath shot from close range, and with Grobbelaar beaten Phil Neal raced in to clear off the line.

The match was a draw, with neither side able to break down what were arguably the two best defences in Europe, but in the end it was probably a fair result. With the rain still pouring from the Wembley skies the two teams joined in a lap of honour while the crowd blessed the occasion with the chant of '*Mersey-side, Mer-sey-side, Mer-sey-side*'. It may not have been the most exciting final, but it was certainly the most passionate and sporting, with the two sets of supporters proving that you can be rivals and still be friendly. It had been a unique occasion.

From the final whistle the race was on to secure replay tickets, and with Maine Road capable of holding only 52,000 the black-market price was just as high as it had been for the Wembley game. The two clubs met again four days later beneath the floodlights at Manchester City, the same teams and no doubt many of the same spectators. Again there was little between the two sides, and only a fortuitous shot from Graeme Souness that skidded past Neville Southall settled the battle. Everton struggled to bring themselves level, but luck was not on their side, and it was Liverpool who held the trophy aloft for the fourth consecutive year. As a gallant Everton team trooped off the field, their supporters sang, to the tune of 'Che Sera Sera', "Tell me ma, me ma, keep the champagne on ice, on ice, we're going to Wembley twice, che sera sera.' Within three weeks the Everton players had responded to their chorus and booked themselves and their fans a return passage to Wembley, this time for the FA Cup Final.

Everton Southall, Stevens, Bailey, Ratcliffe, Mountfield, Reid, Irvine, Heath, Sharp, Richardson, Sheedy (Harper).
Liverpool Grobbelaar, Neal, Kennedy, Lawrenson, Whelan, Hansen, Dalglish, Lee, Rush, Johnston (Robinson), Souness.

FA Cup Final 1984 Everton v Watford

Just seven weeks after their Milk Cup Final appearance at Wembley, Everton were back in the old stadium, facing Watford for the most famous of all trophies, the FA Cup. It was a magnificent achievement to have reached the final of two competitions, and one which nobody would have guessed possible at Christmas. Yet in just a few months Everton's

was necessary, and as the two teams kicked off again it seemed a certainty that tired limbs and the open spaces of Wembley would combine to create more opportunities. But, surprisingly, there were again few chances to either side. Ian Rush might have scored from a fierce volley, but Neville Southall was equal

fortunes had dramatically turned, and from a team staring relegation in the face they were now reckoned one of the strongest in the League.

Their opponents in the final, Watford, had no Cup-fighting pedigree, never having reached this stage of the competition in their 93-year history. Indeed, their best performance had been to reach the semi-finals in 1970, and only six years had passed since they were in Division Four. Their climb to fame owed much to their chairman, the pop star Elton John, and their manager, the astute Graham Taylor, who had guided them through four divisions. Watford had reached the final with victories over Luton, Charlton, Brighton, Birmingham and Plymouth. They may not have been a team of household names, but in players like John Barnes, Keith Jackett and Mo Johnston they

ABOVE Everton prepare for their Wembley appearance with the now mandatory Cup final record.

OPPOSITE ABOVE Andy Gray scores Everton's second goal against Watford in the 1984 Cup final to win the Cup for the Blues.

OPPOSITE BELOW Scottish international Graeme Sharp scores from the penalty spot against Ipswich. A £120,000 buy from Dumbarton, he proved to be an effective foil for Andy Gray and later for Gary Lineker.

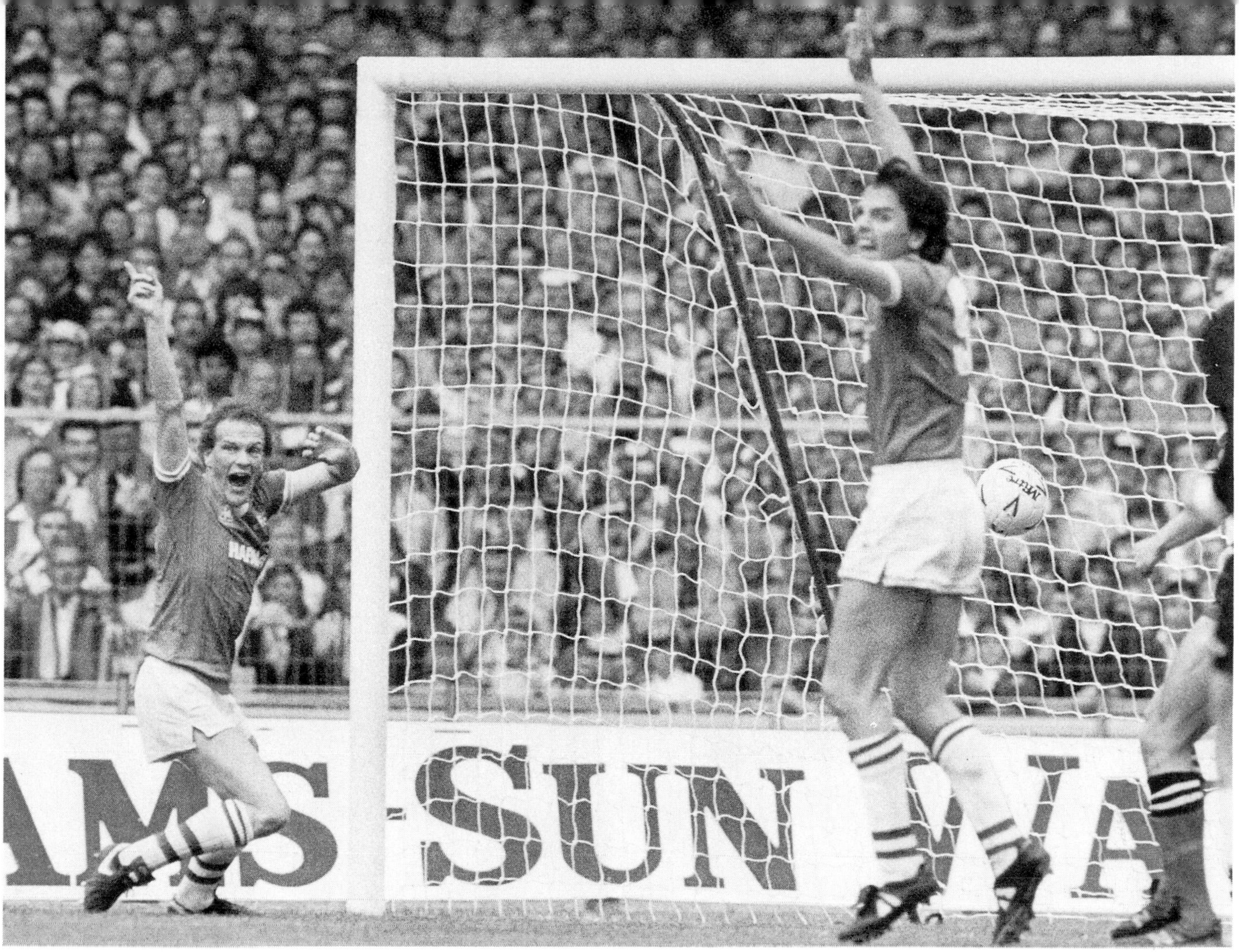
AMS-SUN

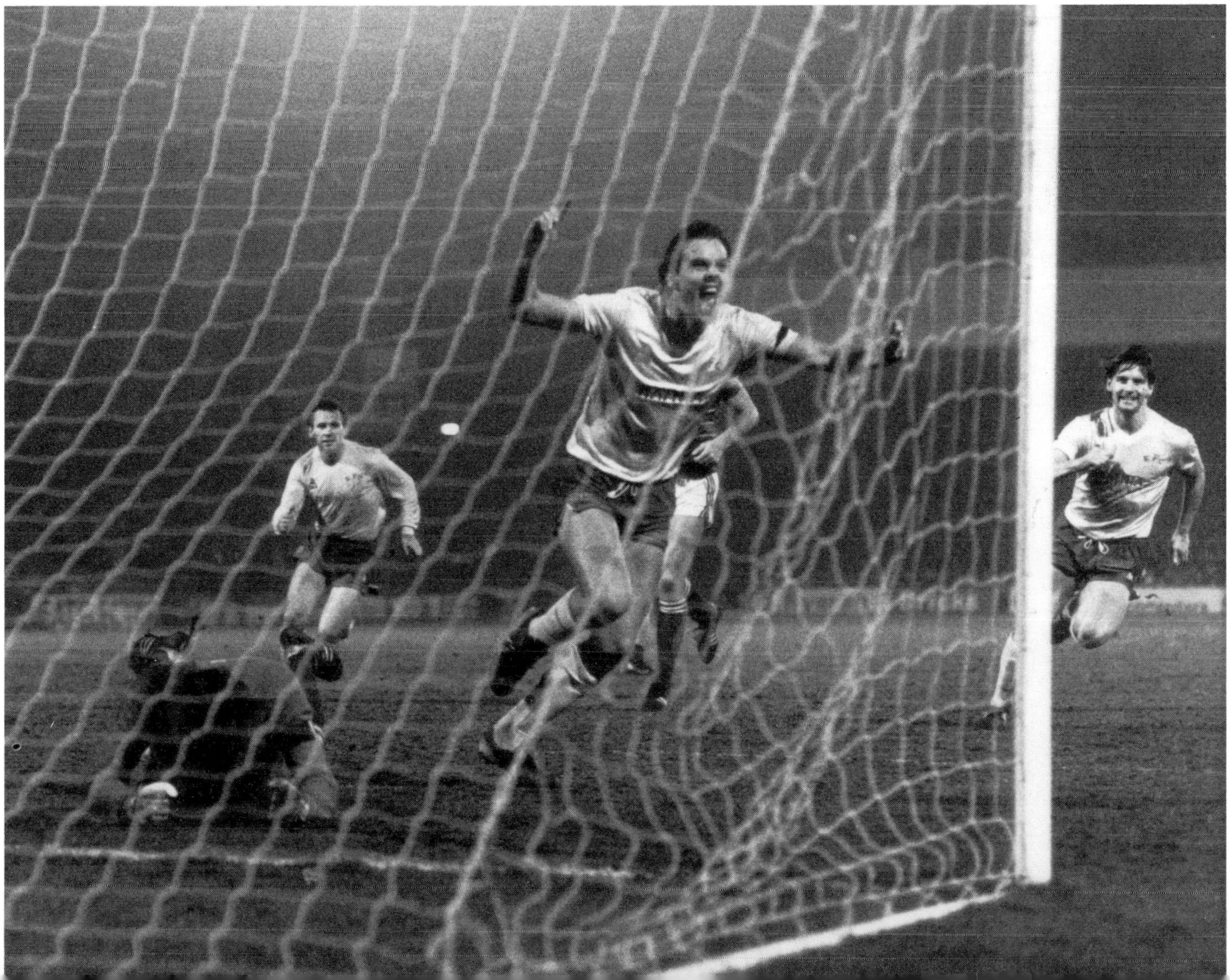

had some skilful and respected performers. It promised to be an entertaining final and above all a friendly one, with two sets of fans dedicated to enjoying their soccer.

19 May was a day for shirtsleeves and open-necked shirts as the sun shone cheerfully across the immaculately clipped turf of Wembley, a far different proposition from Everton's last rain-sodden trip. More than 20,000 Everton supporters had made the return journey, their blue and white banners, scarves and flags dancing in unison on the packed terraces.

Watford began strongly, their hit-and-run style contrasting with Everton's more thoughtful approach. It was a tactic Watford had perfected in their rise up the divisions and one which, although not always attractive to watch, had been highly effective, catching many a speedy defence flatfooted. But Everton were not to be fooled by their style. They held men at the back ready to cut out the adventuresome ball and slowly built up their own attacks. Three times Watford went close, but Southall and his defence were equal to the challenge. It was in the midfield that Everton dominated, with Heath and Reid combining tirelessly to open up the Watford defence. Everton's first goal arrived shortly before the interval, when a mix-up in the Watford goal-mouth saw Graeme Sharp's hard, low drive rebound off the post and into the net. It was an opportunist shot and the kind of goal any side can concede. But that hardly mattered, for Everton were one up.

Six minutes into the second half they added another, when Andy Gray recklessly flew into the six-yard box to challenge the Watford keeper, Steve Sherwood, for a 50–50 ball. Sherwood landed unceremoniously on his back while the ball landed luckily in the back of the goal. The Watford players protested that Sherwood had been fouled, but the referee would have none of it, and Everton, two goals up, were in an unassailable lead. Watford fought back courageously, but the Everton back four were far too experienced to concede two goals.

When the final whistle blew, Wembley erupted. The Cup was coming home to Goodison after an absence of 16 years and for only the fourth time in the club's 106-year history. The captain, Kevin Ratcliffe, lifted the famous trophy aloft just as Brian Labone, Dixie Dean and Jack Taylor had done years before, to celebrate a remarkable five months in the history of the club. And as Howard Kendall's name was chanted around the stadium, that grim Saturday back in the cold of the winter when his name was abused around Goodison was a distant memory, best forgotten.

Everton Southall, Stevens, Bailey, Ratcliffe, Mountfield, Reid, Steven, Heath, Sharp, Gray, Richardson.
Watford Sherwood, Bardsley, Price (Atkinson), Terry, Perry, Sinnott, Callaghan, Johnston, Reilly, Jackett, Barnes.

The 1984/85 season could hardly have kicked off to a more inauspicious start. Spurs, visitors to Goodison for the opening fixture, thrashed the Cup-holders by four goals to one, while two days later West Brom took another three points, beating them 2–1. Everton's championship prospects suddenly looked grim.

Paul Bracewell, a young midfield acquisition from Sunderland for £250,000, had joined the club during Cup Final week, making his debut at Wembley a few months later in the Charity Shield against Liverpool. Everton wreaked sweet revenge that stifling August afternoon in the second Wembley meeting with their neighbours in six months by beating the champions one goal to nil.

That victory had alerted the pundits to Everton's League chances and their name was soon being touted as likely champions. But by the end of August even their most ardent admirers were having second thoughts. The arrival of Bracewell had seen the exit of Andy King, who after seven seasons in Everton's midfield waved goodbye to the club for the second time and ventured abroad to Dutch football. His earlier spell with the Blues under Billy Bingham had been by far the more successful, and he ended his Goodison days with a total of 234 appearances and 68 goals.

With the visit of Chelsea, however, for a live televised match, Everton pulled themselves together, with Kevin Richardson snatching the only goal of the game. That victory began a sequence of six League fixtures without defeat that pulled them back up the table. Five goals were knocked in against Watford at

Vicarage Road in an exciting tussle that brought a four-goal reply. Arsenal then got the better of them at Highbury, but that was followed by six straight wins, including a 5–0 thrashing of Manchester United, reckoned by Joe Mercer to be the finest Everton performance he had ever witnessed, and a 4–0 defeat of Stoke that put them top of the table. They then uncharacteristically conceded four goals at Norwich to go down 4–2, but soon found their winning ways again with another 5–0 win at Nottingham Forest. In their next game they conceded four more goals as Chelsea surprisingly won 4–3 at Goodison, and Everton slipped from their perch at the top of the division. But that was to be their last League defeat for some considerable time.

Progress in the Milk Cup meanwhile had been halted in the fourth round, somewhat unpredictably, by Grimsby Town, who came to Goodison and won by the only goal of the game, scored in the final minute after Everton had totally dominated the other 89 minutes.

But there was better news in the European Cup-Winners' Cup, where Everton were renewing an acquaintance after an 18 year wait. Europe had been a disaster for Everton as it had for so many English clubs (barring their neighbours, of course), and they had never progressed beyond three games in any of the various competitions they had entered. Nor did it look as if it would be very different this time as they came away from Ireland with only a goalless draw against the gallant part-timers University College, Dublin. This was followed by the narrowest of victories at Goodison, thanks to a Graeme Sharp goal, with the Dubliners refusing to die gracefully. At the end of their campaign Everton could honestly say that the plucky Irish team had given them more trouble than any other in Europe.

New signing Pat Van den Hauwe, a £100,000 buy from Birmingham, made his debut that evening, taking over from John Bailey, and barring injury has retained the left-back spot ever since. In the second round Everton faced the useful Czech outfit Inter Bratislava, and although no trip to East Europe is ever easy they returned with an important one-goal lead. They added to that in the second leg to finish comfortable 4–0 winners on aggregate, and with no further European games until the spring they settled once more to the domestic championship.

After their 4–3 defeat at the hands of Chelsea, Everton strung together an astonishing 18 League games without defeat, the best run in their history. Everyone anticipated that they would hit a bad patch,

Fullback Pat Van den Hauwe proved to be another bargain buy at £100,000 from Birmingham City.

but as the weeks came and went Everton simply continued winning. Of those 18 games, no fewer than 16 ended in victory, with 10 consecutive wins notched up between mid-March and mid-May that saw Everton clinch the championship. It was not until the title had been firmly wrapped up with a 2–0 win over QPR at Goodison that they suffered their first defeat. But with the championship trophy now adorning the Everton boardroom again, three defeats in their next four matches hardly mattered. During their 28-game run only nine goals had been conceded, and at the end of the season their record was 88 goals for and 43 against. The Goodison crowds had been treated to 58 home goals, with Graeme Sharp hitting a season's total of 21. By any standards it had been a magnificent performance, with Liverpool relegated to second place and beaten twice by the new champions.

Everton's FA Cup run began on the frozen wastes of Elland Road with a 2–0 win, followed by another

2–0 win against another Yorkshire side, this time Fourth Division Doncaster Rovers. When non-Leaguers Telford United gathered around their transistors to hear the draw for the fifth round of the Cup they must hardly have believed their luck. They had drawn the plum game, a tie with the Cup-holders, the mighty Everton, and like every giant-killing side they must have fancied their chances of another famous scalp, even though it was on Merseyside. But, bravely though they performed for an hour before a frightening Goodison, it was not to be their day, as Everton lashed in three goals in the final 30 minutes.

Ipswich Town in the quarter-finals were a very different proposition. Packed with experienced internationals, they held the Blues to a 2–2 draw at Portman Road before going out to the only goal of the replay. That win put Everton into the semi-finals, with Luton Town as the opposition at Villa Park. Luton had not long returned to the First Division, and their lowly League position made them long-shots for the final, but they still made Everton fight for their place. In the first half they looked the better side, going into a surprise lead shortly before half-time, and Everton must have wondered if they had foolishly underestimated their opponents. But in the second half the Blues came out and gradually grew in confidence while Luton defended stubbornly. With only minutes remaining it looked as if Luton were about to produce the surprise of the day, but then Everton were awarded a free-kick on the edge of the area and Kevin Sheedy, stepping up to take it, slammed the ball past Les Sealey in the Luton goal for the equaliser. The goal stunned Luton, whose supporters were already dreaming of Wembley's twin towers, and left them with everything to do again. Everton now had the upper hand, and as the game drifted into extra time they began to dominate and discover ways through a weary-looking Luton defence. Six minutes from time Derek Mountfield made one of his measured runs into the penalty area to meet a timely cross from Kevin Sheedy and book Everton's place for their fourth Wembley appearance in two years. With the League championship looking certain, there was now the distinct possibility of a League and Cup double. All they had to do was beat Manchester United in the final.

Everton's reputation was spreading not just through the Football League but across Europe as well. In the quarter-finals of the European Cup-Winners' Cup they entertained Fortuna Sittard of Holland at Goodison, and after a goalless first half Andy Gray struck a hat-trick to give them a comfort-able lead for the journey across the North Sea. In the return leg you might have expected Everton to relax a little, but far from it. Instead they attacked the Dutch side just as keenly as they had at Goodison and finished up 2–0 winners.

Bayern Munich, Everton's opponents in the semi-final, were one of the strongest teams in Europe. Three times winners of the European Cup, countless times winners of the Bundesliga, as well as winners of the European Cup-Winners' Cup, they boasted a team littered with German internationals such as Matthaus, Hoeness and Eder and were among that season's challengers for the West German championship. Everton travelled to Germany aware that they would have to defend stubbornly if they were to retain any hope of reaching their first European final. And in front of a 70,000 crowd packed into the Munich Olympic Stadium they did precisely that. It was a magnificent performance that would have suggested it was Everton who boasted years of experience in European football rather than Bayern.

The return leg on Merseyside was a night for Goodison to remember. All those famous European soccer spectaculars in the city had been monopolised by Liverpool, but now it was Everton's turn as 50,000 squeezed into Goodison to roar the Blues on to another final and a possible treble. It was a rugged and passionate affair, but with 38 minutes gone it looked as if Everton's European dream was about to turn into a nightmare when Hoeness put the Germans one goal up. Crucially, it was an away goal, which meant that Everton would have to score twice. Three minutes into the second half, however, Bayern's Belgian goalkeeper, Jean-Marie Pfaff, fumbled a long throw-in from Stevens and Graeme Sharp was on the spot to snatch Everton's equaliser. Twenty-five minutes later Andy Gray, playing what many rated his finest performance at Goodison, hit a fierce drive to put Everton into the lead. But with that vital away goal against them Everton could not relax, and it was Trevor Steven who finally settled the issue just four minutes from time.

Everton were into two finals and about to be crowned League champions. The focus had at last turned from Anfield to Goodison. It had taken a long time but above all it had taken the thoughtful influence of one man – Howard Kendall. The one sadness of the season was that the last manager to lead Everton to glory, Harry Catterick, had collapsed and died one evening at Goodison. A few more weeks and he would have lived to see Everton reclaim that glory.

The European Cup-Winners' Cup Final 1985 Everton v Rapid Vienna

Rapid Vienna had reached the final of the European Cup-Winners' Cup even though they had been knocked out of the competition by Glasgow Celtic. This strange quirk of fortune had arisen when the UEFA authorities decided that, as a Celtic fan had struck a Rapid player with a missile, the game should be replayed. Celtic had won the first match 3–0, but in the replayed game, at neutral Old Trafford, Vienna won by a single goal and went on to play Moscow Dynamo in the semi-final and clinch a place in the final.

Like Everton, Rapid had never won a European trophy, but had been champions of Austria on 27 occasions and were well drilled in European football, having played over a hundred matches in a variety of European competitions. They were not to be taken lightly, and with a player of the calibre of Hans Krankl in their ranks were always liable to forge victory out of defeat.

Some 50,000 spectators gathered in Rotterdam for the final, played at the ultra-modern Feyenoord stadium, with many of them having made the long journey across the North Sea from Merseyside. It was a tribute to Everton that so many should undertake the expensive trip when only three days later they would be appearing in another final, at Wembley.

Everton were always the better side but could not turn their superiority into goals during the opening 45 minutes. Andy Gray did put the ball in the back of the net, but the linesman flagged for an offside, while Sharp and Steven always looked dangerous. Everton's first goal arrived not long into the second half, when a disastrous back pass left Graeme Sharp clear. He rounded the goalkeeper, took the ball to the byline and sent a simple cross over for Gray to slam home.

In desperation, Rapid pulled off two defenders and pushed on a couple of attackers, but that only left their defence even more vulnerable to Everton's quick accurate attack. And before long the Blues had exploited their substitution when Kevin Sheedy's corner was driven homewards by an unmarked

Everton on their way to winning their first European trophy in the European Cup-Winners' Cup final against Rapid Vienna.

Trevor Steven. With ten minutes remaining Rapid pulled a goal back through Krankl, but within a minute Sheedy broke free of the Rapid defence and shot from the edge of the box to make it 3–1.

Everton had won their first European trophy and 100 million viewers throughout the Continent had been able to watch them win in style. All Europe now knew about the 'School of Science'. They had played 62 games, but there was still one more important match remaining before they could emulate their neighbours by winning the treble.

Everton Southall, Stevens, Van den Hauwe, Ratcliffe, Mountfield, Reid, Steven, Sharp, Gray, Bracewell, Sheedy.
Rapid Vienna Konsel, Lainer, Brauneder, Weber, Garger, Kranjcar, Kienast, Hrstick, Pacult (Groess), Krankl, Weinhofer (Panenka).

FA Cup Final 1985 Everton v Manchester United

Everton had twice beaten Manchester United that season. In a League fixture at Goodison they had thrashed Ron Atkinson's team 5–0 in what many rated the finest single Everton performance since the war, while in the Milk Cup they had won 2–1 at Old Trafford. The odds were in Everton's favour and, with the European Cup-Winners' Cup gleaming from their sideboard as well as the League championship trophy, few would have bet on United. But as so often happens in the Cup, the favourites can take a fall.

Everton were in fine spirits after their European triumph on the Wednesday evening, and returned to Britain itching to play the final. But in the end their sixty-third game of the season proved to be just one too many.

Everton began well enough and might have gone a goal up in the first 15 minutes when Peter Reid hit a post, but the match soon settled into a midfield battle with neither side really creating any advantage. At half-time the two teams trooped off the field looking exhausted, but they returned to continue where they had left off. Norman Whiteside had one effort saved by Southall but again both defences refused to concede any space. Then with just thirteen minutes remaining the game sprang into life, though not from any worthy cause, when Kevin Moran was sent off after a clumsy foul on Reid. It was his second offence, and the referee had little option but to give the United man his marching orders, the first-ever sending off in a Cup final.

BELOW Peter Reid shrugs off a challenge from Manchester United's Danish international, Jesper Olsen, during the 1985 Cup final. Reid, who arrived from Bolton Wanderers for £60,000, quickly became the inspiration behind Everton's revival.

OVERLEAF LEFT In his one season with Everton Gary Lineker scored 30 goals in 41 League appearances to make him one of the most feared strikers in Europe.

OVERLEAF RIGHT Graeme Sharp and Liverpool's Barry Venison battle for possession during the 1986 FA Cup final.

With United down to ten men, Everton must have fancied their chances even more, but typically it only incensed United and made them all the more determined. Full-time came with the two teams level, and they kicked off for an extra 30 minutes. Then, with just five minutes gone, Irish international Norman Whiteside attacked down the right and with the Everton defence scurrying back, half expecting a cross, he let fly with an opportunist shot. Unfortunately for Everton it was low and on target, just beyond the stretching arms of Southall. It was a lucky shot that could so easily have gone skidding past the post, but it was enough to win the Cup for United.

The Everton supporters had been magnificent all season, passionately roaring them on at Goodison and loyally following them away from home and across Europe. And as Everton trooped sadly away from the celebration that had engulfed United, they turned and saluted those supporters who now packed the Wembley terraces in their thousands and who were refusing to budge even in the face of defeat. Yet it could hardly be described as defeat. They may have missed the League and Cup double as well as a treble, but they were still the League champions and winners of a European trophy.

Everton Southall, Stevens, Van den Hauwe, Ratcliffe, Mountfield, Reid, Steven, Sharp, Gray, Bracewell, Sheedy.

Manchester United Bailey, Gidman, Albiston (Duxbury), Whiteside, McGrath, Moran, Robson, Strachan, Hughes, Stapleton, Olsen.

Long before the new season kicked off English football was plunged into despair when rioting Liverpool supporters at the European Cup Final in Brussels caused a panic that led to the deaths of 39 spectators, mainly supporters of the Italian club Juventus. It was a night of shame for Britain, and in particular for the city of Liverpool, as millions of television viewers throughout the world watched with horror as the events unfolded before their eyes.

In Rotterdam the Everton fans had been applauded for their fine behaviour, but Liverpool's shame could not help but smear their neighbours. Indeed all English clubs suffered as UEFA imposed a ban on their playing in European competitions. For Everton it was a particular disappointment, as their League championship win would have entitled them to a crack at the most coveted of all European trophies, the European Cup.

Like all British football clubs, Everton had experienced their share of crowd trouble. And while the city's football fans were regarded as among the best behaved and best humoured in the League, there had nevertheless been incidents and senseless violence in the past that could only be forthrightly condemned. Over the years Everton had taken steps to control such violence, yet a minority still persisted in causing trouble.

During the close season Everton created a sensation by selling their Scottish international striker Andy Gray back to his old club, Aston Villa, for £150,000. Gray had been the backbone of Everton's rise to glory yet had been with the club only two seasons. During that time he had scored 22 goals in 61 appearances and had probably enjoyed his best years in football. His transfer shocked the Everton faithful, reminding an older generation of the dramatic transfers of Dean, Lawton and Mercer when the club had previously been at its height. Gray, who would venture anywhere in the six-yard box in search of a goal, irrespective of danger, had inspired all those around him, and his transfer confused his admirers, who had assumed he would be wearing the number nine shirt for years to come.

In his place Everton splashed out on the Leicester City and England striker Gary Lineker. In just over 200 games with Leicester he had scored 100 goals, and a number of clubs throughout the season had been linked with his name. All seemed reluctant, however, to make a firm move for the young striker, but shortly before the new season began Howard Kendall, possibly to appease those who had been so critical of the transfer of Gray, stepped in and paid a club record fee of £800,000 for him.

Lineker's introduction to the side was hardly an overnight success as they journeyed to his old club and promptly lost by three goals to one. He had to wait until the fourth game before putting his name on the scoresheet, with the only goal against Spurs. Five days later, against Birmingham City, he hit a hat-trick and then scored a couple more in an impressive 5–1 win at Sheffield Wednesday. Lineker had arrived, but the champions were still floundering in the top half of the table, and it was not until the New Year that they crept into the top three.

At the beginning of February they shot to the number-one spot and looked all set to remain there until the season was over. Manchester United, who earlier in the campaign had appeared to be running away with the title, were still their principal opponents, with Liverpool handily placed behind them. Everton seemed the likely champions as they enjoyed a run which saw them lose only one game in 18. At one stage they notched up nine wins and one draw in 10 fixtures, but somehow they could not shake off Liverpool, who seemed to have by far the more difficult end-of-season fixtures. Everton's challenge, however, finally came unstuck with a goalless draw at Manchester United and defeat at Oxford, where a late goal cost them their championship. A few days later Everton beat Southampton 6–1, while Liverpool, away to Chelsea, simply had to win to take the title. A 1–0 victory was enough and Everton had to be content with second place. Nevertheless, it had been an impressive end to the season, with only six goals conceded in their final 16 League games. Lineker, who had formed a devastating partnership with Graeme Sharp, finished the season with 30 League goals and could justifiably claim his chapter in the history of outstanding Everton centre-forwards.

FA Cup Final 1986 Everton v Liverpool

The Milk Cup Final clash between the two Merseyside giants in 1984 had been a memorable occasion, although the Wembley match itself had failed to live up to expectations by producing a goalless draw. Now, after so many years of escaping each other in various finals, they suddenly found themselves lining up for the third time within two years on the hallowed turf of Wembley. Sandwiched in between the Milk Cup Final and the FA Cup Final

had been another Wembley appearance, in the Charity Shield, with a Liverpool own-goal enough to give Everton a deserved victory.

When 90 minutes were up in the semi-final against Sheffield Wednesday at Villa Park, most of the Everton supporters had half an ear cocked to their radios, listening for the other semi-final score from White Hart Lane, where Liverpool faced Southampton. The score there was 0–0, and as the two semi-finals kicked off into extra time the dream of a Merseyside final was still possible.

Everton's road to Wembley had begun at Goodison against Fourth Division Exeter City, with fullback Gary Stevens scoring the only goal of a tight match. Howard Kendall's old club, Blackburn Rovers, provided the opposition for the fourth round but were no match for a dangerous-looking Everton, and in particular for the devastating Gary Lineker, whose two goals ended any dreams the east Lancashire side might have been harbouring. In the fifth round Everton were forced to travel to White Hart Lane to face a Tottenham side going through a bad patch. And with Spurs' League dreams in ruins, their only hope of glory lay in the Cup, making them an even tougher proposition. Everton, however, showed all their usual resilience as they battled stubbornly, with Neville Southall outstanding in goal. In the end Everton just about deserved their 2–1 victory, but they could hardly have been delighted when they drew another First Division side, Luton Town, out of the bag for a quarter-final at Kenilworth Road. They faced a mammoth task, and many fancied Luton to go all the way to Wembley. When Luton went two goals up, Everton's chances of a third successive Cup Final looked to have disappeared. But Everton fought back bravely, with substitute Adrian Heath hitting the equaliser after Graeme Sharp had pulled one back. In the replay at Goodison it was Gary Lineker's day again, as he scored his fourth Cup goal and gave Everton a 1–0 victory and a place in their twenty-first semi-final.

With the injured Gary Lineker missing, Everton kicked off into extra time in their semi-final at Villa Park against Sheffield Wednesday with the scores level at 1–1. Everton had struggled through much of the first half, with Trevor Steven limping off with a groin strain to be replaced by the former Liverpool man Alan Harper. In the second half Everton had begun to pull their game together, but, when Alan Harper fired them into the lead in the forty-ninth minute, Wednesday equalised three minutes later.

Extra time, however, proved to be the undoing of the gallant Yorkshire side as Everton, scenting the prospect of their sixth Wembley appearance since 1984, threw everything into attack. In the end it was Graeme Sharp, who had so successfully linked up with Lineker that season, who shot the Blues into their tenth FA Cup Final. And as the final whistle blew, the electric atmosphere inside Villa Park exploded. Everton's 20,000 travelling supporters anxiously tuned in to their radios to hear the result from White Hart Lane. Liverpool had beaten Southampton 2–0 and for the first time in history Everton and Liverpool would face each other in the FA Cup final.

The two teams had come close to such a showdown on many occasions: they had met four times in the semi-final, and when they had been drawn apart one or other had fallen at the penultimate hurdle. The whole of Merseyside was abuzz with the prospect. Tickets were impossible to obtain and black-market prices soared into three figures for standing places alone. In the city itself the streets and shop windows had become a sea of blue and red, with scarves, rosettes, flags and decorations festooned everywhere. And as the mass exodus out of Liverpool began on the morning of Saturday 10 May 1986 it seemed that an army of blue and red was heading away down the M6 and M1 towards the capital. Scarves waved freely out of car windows, and often the same vehicle would be displaying both blue and red colours. The two sets of supporters mingled together happily and it was clearly going to be the friendliest final Wembley had seen in years. There had rarely been any open hostility between the rival teams' supporters, with families divided down the middle rather than family against family. At the top of Wembley Way fathers decked in blue waved goodbye to their sons in red as they wandered off to opposite ends of the stadium. It was that kind of occasion.

A week before the final, Liverpool had pipped Everton to the League championship by beating Chelsea 1–0 and now stood on the brink of a famous double. Only Everton stood between them and a new chapter in the history books. Everton reported a clean bill of health for their regulars, although Southall, injured since mid-March, was always a non-starter. His place had been ably filled by the former Halifax and Rotherham keeper Bobby Mimms, signed a year earlier for £150,000. Indeed, since stepping into the Welsh international's boots he had conceded only four goals in 10 games, but to be on the safe side Howard Kendall had also signed the veteran Irish international Pat Jennings as cover for Mimms.

Watford chairman and pop singer, Elton John, presents Peter Reid with the 1985 PFA award for Footballer of the Year.

The roar that greeted the two sides as they proudly marched out together into the Wembley sun was deafening. The chant of '*Mer-sey-side, Mer-sey-side*' echoed around the stadium, while the blue and red colours mixed freely and amiably on the terraces.

Everton, starting anxiously, soon settled into their usual rhythm, with Peter Reid powerfully initiating attacks while blocking the threatening skills of Dalglish and Craig Johnston. A few early sorties by Everton gave due warning that they had come to Wembley intent on winning, and after 30 minutes it looked as if that would be the case when Gary Lineker raced away from Liverpool's captain, Alan Hansen, and sent a low drive beyond Bruce Grobbelaar's reach to put the Toffees a goal in front. It was his thirty-eighth goal of the season and, although no one knew it at the time, it was to be his last for the club. Everton

155

now began to dominate and went into the dressing-room at half-time confident that, provided they could maintain the pressure on Liverpool's defence, they would be lifting the trophy.

The second half began precisely where the first had left off, with Everton dominating. Gary Stevens, Pat Van den Hauwe and Derek Mountfield had effect-ively contained the Liverpool strike force of Rush and Dalglish, and when Grobbelaar and Beglin exchanged angry words in the Liverpool penalty area the Reds stood in unusual disarray. A moment later the Liverpool keeper saved magnificently from Graeme Sharp to thwart what would have almost certainly been the killer goal. But, as so often happens, a single event or even a stroke of luck can swing a match in the opposite direction. And on that warm afternoon it was a loose ball out of the Everton defence which was seized upon by Ronnie Whelan that led to Liverpool's equaliser and Everton's down-fall. Whelan, collecting the poor clearance, played the ball to the Dane Jan Molby, who slipped a neat pass through to Ian Rush, and the Welsh striker made no mistake. That goal pumped new confidence into Liverpool, who added a further two goals in the next twenty minutes and destroyed Everton. Although the Blues came back at Liverpool in the final quarter of an hour, there was little they could do to put right the injustice.

Everton had dominated for all but 20 minutes of the final yet came away 3–1 losers. What's more, Liverpool had become only the third side to achieve the double since 1900, and they had done it at the expense of Everton, who finished not only runners-up in the League but runners-up in the Cup as well. Under any other circumstances it would have been a highly successful season, but it was little use trying to convince any of the Everton players or supporters of that.

Everton Mimms, Stevens (Heath), Van den Hauwe, Ratcliffe, Mountfield, Reid, Steven, Lineker, Sharp, Bracewell, Sheedy.
Liverpool Grobbelaar, Lawrenson, Beglin, Nicol, Whelan, Hansen, Dalglish, Johnston, Rush, Molby, MacDonald.

Who would have guessed that Manchester City's Paul Power would prove to be such an effective signing? Yet at 32, fullback Power, seen here with Liverpool's Ronnie Whelan, was an inspired purchase.

The goalscoring feats of Gary Lineker had not gone unnoticed on the Continent, and a host of Italian and Spanish clubs were soon trailing the young Everton striker. Money seemed to be no problem and Everton, not one to stand in the way of a player's ambition, came to an agreement with Barcelona shortly after the Cup Final that made Lineker the most expensive British player in history, at a cost of £2.3 million. His departure left yet another question mark, similar to that of the previous close season, when Everton had sold striker Andy Gray to Aston Villa. Where would they find a replacement?

Kendall, however, had other positional worries on his mind at that moment. Paul Power, the 32-year-old Manchester City fullback, was signed for £65,000 in what at the time seemed an unlikely purchase, but by the end of the season Power had more than repaid his transfer fee and proved to be the best transaction made by any club all season. But there were other additions, notably Dave Watson, the powerful Norwich City centre-half, who arrived in a blaze of publicity for £1 million. Six-figure fees were also

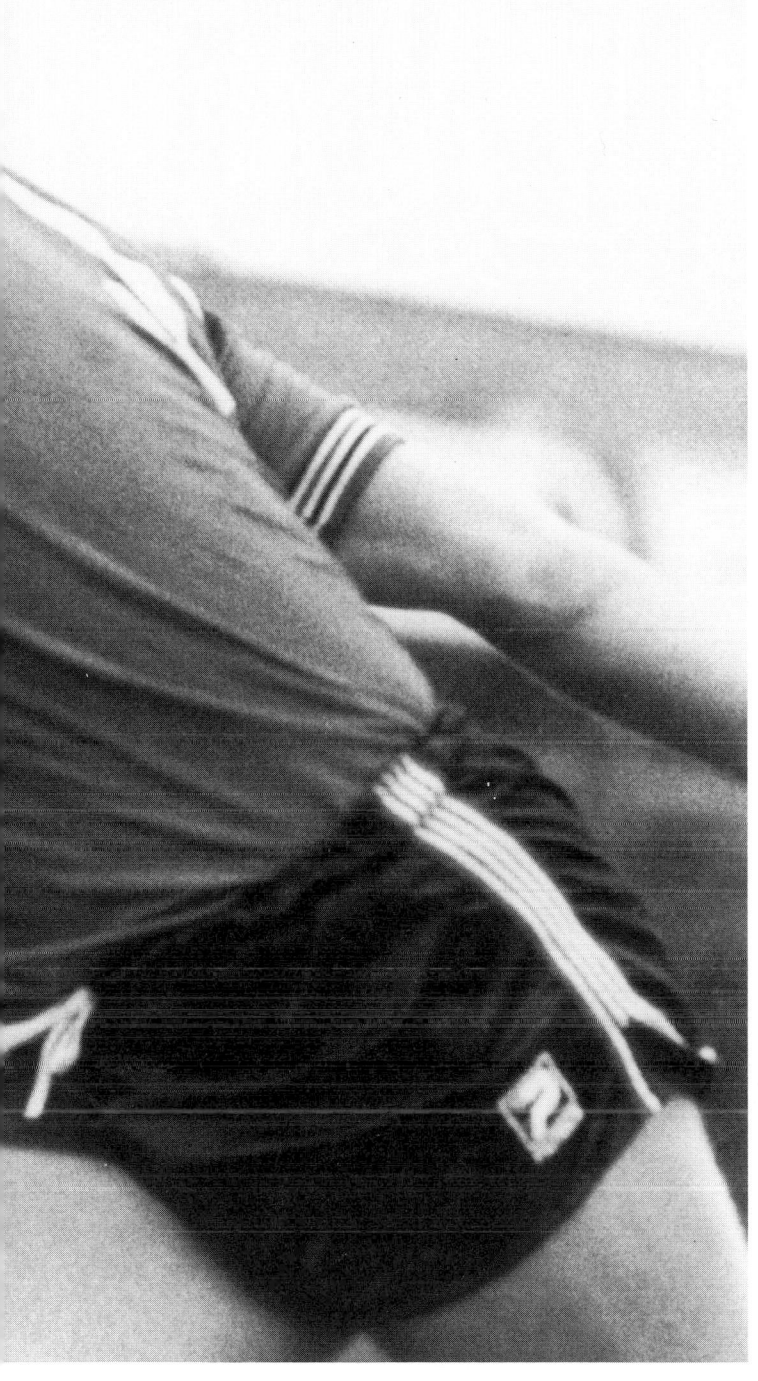

paid for Neil Adams of Stoke and for Wigan's Kevin Langley, while later in the season midfielder Ian Snodin came from Leeds United for £840,000, and just beating the deadline were Wayne Clarke and Stuart Storer, the young Birmingham pair. At the same time, with competition for first-team places now becoming intense, Kevin Richardson, Warren Aspinall and Paul Wilkinson all left for fresh pastures.

Everton began the 1986/87 season with a casualty list as long as Neville Southall's reach. Peter Reid,

ABOVE LEFT £1 million signing Dave Watson beats Southampton's Colin Clarke to the ball. Watson, Everton's most expensive buy, settled quickly and looks set to hold the centre-half slot for years to come.

ABOVE Ian Snodin joined Everton from Leeds in 1987. A midfielder, he has already made his presence felt, playing an important role in Everton's championship triumph.

159

Paul Bracewell, Pat Van den Hauwe, Gary Stevens, Derek Mountfield and Southall himself were all spectators when Brian Clough's Nottingham Forest kicked off the season at Goodison. But even a makeshift Everton side managed to run up a 2–0 win, thanks to Kevin Sheedy. Indeed, it was not until late September, when Everton visited Spurs, that they suffered their first defeat. There may have been a clutch of draws among some of their earlier fixtures, but at least they kept themselves in contention, although when a sprightly looking young Arsenal side won 1–0 at Goodison it seemed as if injuries would be the undoing of the Blues that season as they slipped down the table into eighth place. As Christmas approached they were back in contention, holding Liverpool to a goalless draw and then defeating Manchester City 3–1, Newcastle 5–2, where Graeme Sharp hit a hat-trick, and Norwich 4–0. Lineker may have departed, but Graeme Sharp, ably supported by Adrian Heath, was finding the extra responsibility to his liking.

On Boxing Day they thrashed Newcastle again, this time 4–0 at St James's Park, and climbed into second spot, their highest yet all season. Arsenal still led the table, with Liverpool threatening in third place, and what was more, Everton's walking wounded were slowly climbing off the treatment bench. Neville Southall had replaced his fine young deputy, Bobby Mimms, and Gary Stevens was now back in the number two shirt, with Alan Harper relegated to the reserves once more. Everton, like Liverpool, had now become a squad club, where players were expected to fulfil a role and where nobody had a guaranteed place in the first team.

The Littlewoods Cup, alias the League Cup or the Milk Cup, was proving to be a goalscoring delight for Everton. They opened their offensive back in the autumn with a 4–0 home win over Newport County followed by a 5–1 win in the second leg, with Paul Wilkinson helping himself to five goals over the two games. In the third round they faced far tougher opposition, in First Division Sheffield Wednesday, yet won comfortably by four goals to nil as Paul Wilkinson again bagged a couple. In the next round they faced Norwich City at Carrow Road and against

Wayne Clarke, the former Birmingham City player, has added further bite to the Everton attack since his purchase in 1987.

all expectations hammered the East Anglian side 4–1. That victory gave them a home tie against none other than Liverpool, who were already haunting the Blues again. In the Super Cup played earlier that season Liverpool had beaten them 3–1 and 4–1 over two legs to win the newly created trophy. And back in August at Wembley, in the Charity Shield, Liverpool had held them to a 1–1 draw. Now at Goodison on a cold January evening Liverpool again won, this time by a single goal, in a match that was marred by a tragic accident to the Liverpool fullback Jim Beglin which clearly disturbed the Everton team.

The FA Cup began with a 2–1 home victory over Southampton followed by a battling 1–0 win at Second Division Bradford City in the fourth round. The fifth round brought an away tie in front of the TV cameras at Wimbledon. The south London side, which would have presented few problems a season or two earlier, were newly promoted to the First Division and had already demonstrated their intent to remain there. Everton shot into the lead, and it looked as if they might be going all the way to a record-breaking fourth final in succession. But it was not to be, as Wimbledon's forceful tackling and long, searching balls produced the three goals that won the tie.

With the Littlewoods Cup and the FA Cup out of their reach, Everton could at least concentrate on the League trophy, where prospects looked more hopeful. At the beginning of February, as the harsh winter took its toll of football fixtures and particularly those of Arsenal, the Gunners lost their top spot to Everton. Liverpool, however, still hung on worryingly behind them and the Anfield side remained most people's favourites for the title. The rest of that month brought little luck as Everton drew at Oxford and Manchester United before losing at Watford. As Everton slipped from first to second, Liverpool climbed above them and began to stretch their lead to nine points.

It looked as if it was all over, but Everton were not to be fobbed off quite so easily. With the gritty Peter Reid now returned to full fitness and Ian Snodin beginning to display his midfield talents, while the ebullient Wayne Clarke was adding bite to the forward line, Everton simply carried on, notching up seven victories in succession. Liverpool meanwhile stumbled and lost their winning ways. Within a few weeks the positions were reversed, and although Everton lost 3–1 at Anfield there was never any doubt now that they would win the title. The trophy was duly handed over at Norwich City, where a 1–0 win

brought thousands of journeying Evertonians onto the pitch to celebrate the club's ninth championship.

Everton's triumph was due primarily to their consistency and the depth of their squad. Even when injuries had racked their automatic line-up, others stepped in ably to support their colleagues – in all, 20 players appeared in League fixtures during the season. Even the goals were shared, with Kevin Sheedy hitting 13 League goals, Trevor Steven 14 and Adrian Heath 11, proving that there was still life after Gary Lineker. Everton were champions with 86 points, nine ahead of Liverpool.

It was their second title win under Howard Kendall and, after so many years of living in the shadow of Liverpool, Everton were now being spoken of naturally as the premier side in the Football League.

It was all the more surprising then that on 19 June 1987 Kendall should dramatically reveal that he was to leave Everton. Gary Lineker's transfer to Barcelona in the summer of 1986 had been accompanied by stories in the press that Howard Kendall was about to take over as manager of the affluent Spanish club. In the event, the Barcelona manager, Terry Venables decided to remain at the Nou Camp stadium and any notion of Kendall leaving had long been forgotten by the time Everton clinched their ninth League title. When the news of his appointment as manager of Athletico Bilbao was disclosed, the whole of Merseyside was stunned, but even though they were losing one of the finest managers in their long history, all Evertonians wished him well in his new venture.

At a press conference to confirm his departure, the Everton chairman, Philip Carter also announced that Kendall would be succeeded by his number two and former midfield colleague, Colin Harvey. Liverpool-born Harvey had been a decisive influence on the rise of Everton since 1983 after being promoted to first-team coach as Everton hit rock bottom. His appointment coincided with a dramatic turnaround in their fortunes and Kendall was always the first to acknowledge the guiding authority of Harvey.

Harvey had been a long-time favourite at Goodison, making his debut in Milan when Everton opened their European Cup exploits on foreign soil. After 380 games, 24 goals and just one England cap, he moved to Sheffield Wednesday in 1974 but was forced into premature retirement through injury. He returned to Goodison two years later as youth-team coach, moving up to first-team coach in 1983 where he brought his thoughtful support to bear.

Within weeks of his appointment as manager, Harvey had assembled his backroom staff of Peter Reid, Graham Smith, Terry Darracott and Mick Lyons. It was a team that seemed capable of taking on the challenge of Everton's long tradition.

Under Kendall Everton had won two League titles, the FA Cup and a European trophy as well as appearing in two other FA Cup finals and a League Cup final. It was an outstanding record, but Colin Harvey could at least feel that his predecessor had left the club well endowed with talented young players and that he could look optimistically to the future, knowing that any team winning the First Division would have to beat Everton. A new 'School of Science' had been established at Goodison that was there to stay. And the motto of this proud club, Everton, will remain *Nil Satis Nisi Optimum* – 'Nothing but the best is good enough'.

Colin Harvey, the fifth Everton player to become manager of the club, now faces the daunting task of emulating Howard Kendall's outstanding success.

13

EVERTON PROGRAMMES

The oldest known Everton programme in existence dates back to the days when the club played at Anfield. It is an olive green, single folded sheet measuring about six inches by four and dated 4 October 1890. Everton entertained Derby County in a Division One fixture that day with Fred Geary at centre-forward, the flamboyant Edgar Chadwick alongside him and Johnny Holt at centre-half. By the end of that season it was a line-up that had clinched its first League championship. The game kicked off at 4 p.m. and despite the windy autumn weather Everton ran out 7–0 winners. There were some unusual teams on the fixture list printed in the programme with matches scheduled against Third Lanark, Corinthians, the Vale of Leven, Renton and Bootle; another interesting point was that the linesmen were known

as umpires. Otherwise the programme was much as would be expected with advertisements for coal merchants, jewellers, tobacconists, tailors, football cards and the Monstre Empire Billiard Saloon in Islington where two could play an hour's billiards for just one shilling.

Two years later when Everton moved to Goodison the programme was much the same except that the single folded sheet was now pink in colour. Burton Swifts, Heart of Midlothian and Middlesbrough Ironopolis were listed among the visitors in that first season. The programme for the reserve game against Gorton Villa on 29 October 1892 carried an advertisement for Noblett's Everton Toffees and it was clear that even by then, after only seven weeks at Goodison, they had became known as 'The Toffees'.

No. 8.　　Volume 9.

EVERTON FOOTBALL CLUB

FOOTBALL LEAGUE — DIVISION 1.

EVERTON versus **LIVERPOOL**

AT GOODISON PARK, SATURDAY, 16th SEPTEMBER, 1950, KICK-OFF 3-15 p.m.

SEASON 1950-1951

OFFICIAL PROGRAMME 2D

The ONLY Programme issued by authority of the Everton FOOTBALL CLUB CO. Ltd.

OFFICIAL PROGRAMME

SATURDAY, MARCH 6th, 1937

Everton F.C.

Vol. 1, No. 37, (Regd.) Price: Twopence

The Only Programme Published by Authority of the Everton Football Club Co., Ltd.

Everton v. Middlesborough

EVERTON F.C.

Official Programme.

The only Official Programme issued by the authority of THE EVERTON FOOTBALL CLUB CO., LTD.

FOOTBALL LEAGUE—NORTH SECTION.

EVERTON versus **BURY**

NEW YEAR'S DAY, JANUARY 1st, 1946.

KICK-OFF 2-30 p.m.

Programme - - One Penny

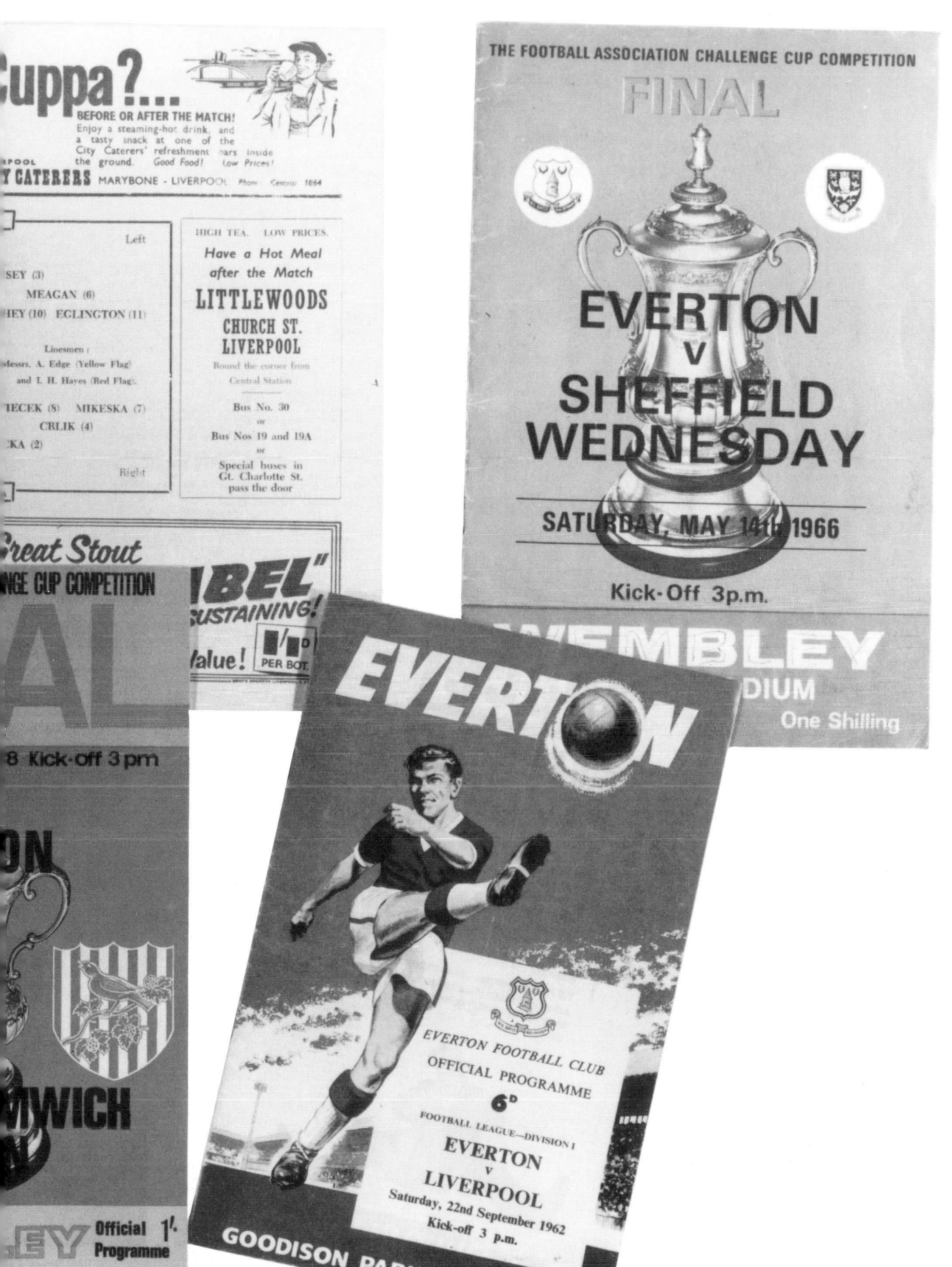

EUROPA CUP 2

FINALE

EVERTON
—
RAPID WIEN

Woensdag 15 mei '85 FEYENOORD-STADION ROTTERDAM

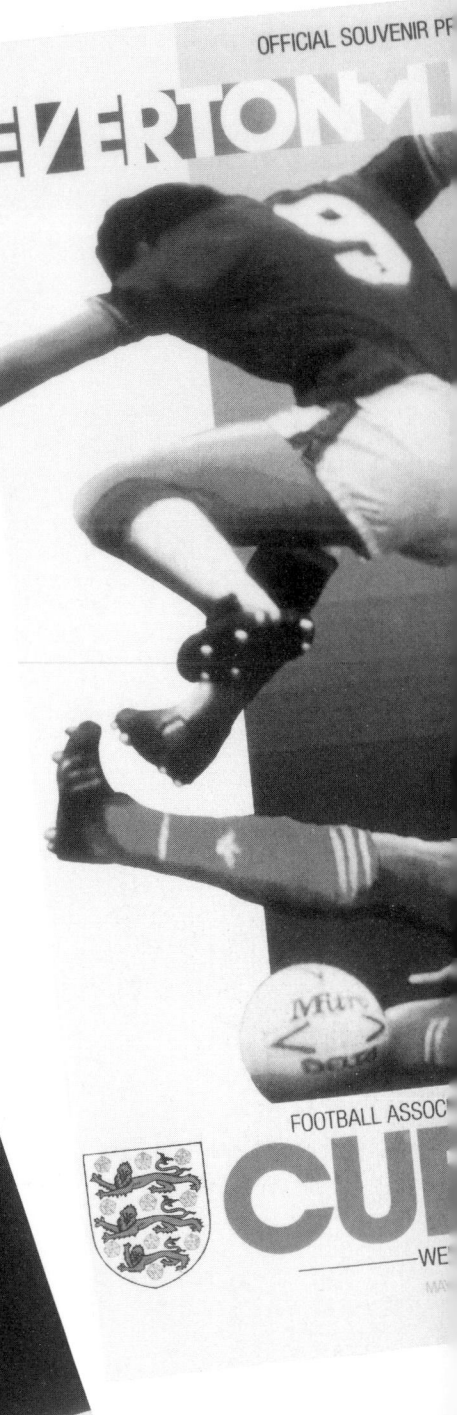

OFFICIAL SOUVENIR PR

EVERTON

FOOTBALL ASSOC

CUP

WE

MA

CUP FIN

Aston Villa
v
Everton

Kick-off
3 pm

Saturday
12th March
1977

WEMBLEY
STADIUM

Official Souvenir Programme 25p

By the turn of the century Everton and Liverpool had joined forces to produce a single weekly programme covering one club's first team game and the other's reserve match. By now the programme had expanded to take up a dozen pages and measured nine inches by six but still cost only one penny. There were the usual advertisements with one offering season tickets at Goodison for 21 shillings while another promoted Jack Sharp's sports shop. There was also plenty of reading material with notes about the team's performances and pen pictures of the various players and the opposition as well as the ever-popular statistics. And unusually there were also theatre reviews. To the modern football programme connoisseur the most surprising aspect would probably be the frankness of the programme editor's notes. As 1905 wound to an end the editor slammed Everton for their mediocre performance. 'They were as depressing as could possibly be imagined,' he wrote, accusing the team selectors of 'trying to fit round pegs in square holes'. Three and a half months later they had won the FA Cup for the first time in their history.

A couple of years after that the programme was looking even grander with a smart front cover showing an Everton and a Liverpool player shaking hands. It was still a joint programme so that when it came to derby matches the editor was forced to tread a delicate path. For the 1908 derby he rubbished both teams equally but diplomatically predicted that the match would end in a draw. As far as Everton were concerned, he suggested that 'a complete change of representation is necessary in the forward line . . . and the fullback division will also need strengthening'. They were brave words and any programme editor being so forthright today would not last too long in his job.

The programe changed little between then and the First World War and was still printed at the offices of the *Bootle Times*. By 1915 there were advertisements imploring men to enlist with Lord Kitchener's army although you had to be a minimum of 5 ft 3 in in height and with a $34\frac{1}{2}$ in chest. As the war became grimmer, so the programme became leaner, reverting to its single folded page format. But once peace returned it was back to normal and even began to boast the occasional team photograph. The programme then remained much the same until the early 1930s when the clubs decided to go their own ways and produce separate programmes.

The Everton programme took on a highly polished look and became one of the most stylish in the Football League. Not surprisingly there was a blue cover with a neat drawing of Goodison and although the size remained at nine inches by six, it now ran to 34 pages and could be bought at any number of newsagents in the Everton area for just 2*d*. By now the club had also opened a shop selling team photographs at 3*d*. each as well as club ties for 2*s* 6*d*. Advertisements for cars also began to appear, and even the occasional crossword puzzle.

With the advent of the Second World War and the postponement of League football the programme reverted to a single folded sheet once more. Priced at one penny, it remained blue in colour, measuring seven inches by four and carried only the barest of information. It improved very little after the war, reflecting the austerity of the times. The number of pages increased to a dozen or more but information was kept to a minimum. It was not until the 1951/52 season that a more lavish style was produced that was to last throughout that decade. It sported an attractive blue cover with a photograph of Goodison and plenty of notes, cartoons and statistics, as well as an increase in price to 3*d*. In the late 1950s it again changed, this time for the worse, as it was reduced to eight pages with the front cover illustrated simply by the club badge. It was drab and unimaginative and hardly worthy of a club with such a fine tradition. But fortunately the 1960s brought an improvement, with a drawing on the cover of an anonymous Everton player kicking for goal, although the inside remained unchanged. A few years later Goodison returned to the cover and the contents improved, though only marginally.

The 1970s brought a far more professional approach, and layout and photographs improved beyond recognition. There was a different picture on the front cover of each edition, while statistics and notes increased to satisfy the eager programme collectors. By the 1980s the programme was a handsome design, running to 36 pages and packed with team information and statistics as well as lavish colour photographs, making it one of the finest in the League and one to rival those splendid, eagerly sought-after editions of the 1930s.

14

A HISTORY OF GOODISON PARK

If you stroll up the hill towards the Anfield end of Stanley Park and then turn and glance back, the magnificent sight of Goodison Park is sprawled out before you. Its triple-decker stand towers above the back-to-back houses in the narrow terraced streets below, making it a landmark for miles around. On match days, when Goodison is throbbing with a packed house, there are few finer experiences than to look down on this famous ground and listen to the roar that rises out of it. It wasn't always so, of course.

When Everton moved to Goodison in 1892 it was their fourth home. They had begun life at Stanley Park in 1878 and then shifted to Priory Road in 1882 for a couple of seasons before the owner turfed them

BELOW Goodison Park today, one of the most modern and comfortable stadiums in the football league.

OVERLEAF In 1948 more than 78,000 crammed into Goodison to watch the league derby with Liverpool. But today Everton's ultra-smart stadium has a limited capacity for 56,000 spectators, all of whom can watch in safety and comfort.

out because of the disturbing noise. So, on the recommendation of one of their members, John Houlding, they moved in 1884 to a pitch at Anfield Road owned by Houlding's friend John Orrell. They stayed until 1892, even winning their first championship there, until a row that year led to their purchasing a ground of their own for £8,090 12s 6d from Colonel Naylor-Leyland. The dispute had blown up over rent, and with John Houlding set to reap a considerable profit from the proposed purchase of Anfield the club members decided to quit the ground and find their own home.

The 30,000-square-yard site which they had bought was known as Mere Green Field and was described by the *Sporting Chronicle* as 'originally farmland, but with the development of Walton it degenerated into a mere brickfield, and was nothing but a waste dotted with dirty cesspools when Everton took it in hand'. The name was soon changed to Goodison Park, and the Walton building firm of Kelly Brothers moved in to start constructing two uncovered stands, each of which could hold 4,000 spectators, and a covered stand to accommodate an additional 3,000. There were even a small press stand, spacious dressing-rooms, large double-baths and a changing-room for the referee. The cost of all this work amounted to £4,000.

When the ground was formally opened by Lord Kinnaird, president of the Football Association, on 24 August 1892, it was the finest football stadium in the land. More than 12,000 spectators turned up to see the opening procession and athletic events which culminated in a spectacular firework display. A few days later, on Thursday, 1 September 1892, Everton played their first game at Goodison, a friendly against Bolton Wanderers that they duly won 4–2. The first League match played at Goodison was two days later, when the visitors, Nottingham Forest, held Everton to a 2–2 draw. Lord Kinnaird and the officials of the Football Association were so impressed with Goodison that it was chosen as the venue of the 1894 Cup Final between Notts County and Bolton and a crowd of 37,000 watched County win the Cup.

A year later the Bullens Road stand was constructed and more money was spent on covering the previously open Goodison Road stand. The next major changes began in 1907 when a double-decker stand was built at the Park end, and two years later the main stand on Goodison Road was opened, at a cost of £28,000.

Goodison soon became the venue for internationals. The first was played there in April 1895,

when England beat Scotland 3–0, and in 1910 it was again honoured, when the Cup Final replay between Newcastle and Barnsley drew an audience of 69,000. Semi-finals also became a regular feature at the ground. In 1913 Goodison became the first League ground to be visited by a reigning monarch, when King George V and Queen Mary dropped in during a visit to Liverpool. There were no further changes to the ground until 1926, when David Leitch designed another double-decker stand on the Bullens Road end, at a cost of £30,000. A few years later, after visiting Aberdeen for a friendly, Everton copied an idea they had seen at Pittodrie by adopting the trainer's dug-out on the touchline. Within a few years dug-outs began to appear throughout the Football League.

There was a second royal visit in 1938 paid by King George VI and Queen Elizabeth to the final double-decker stand, just completed on the Gladwys Street side, which made Everton the only club in the country to have double-decker stands on all four sides. During the war the ground suffered some damage through aerial bombing, though it was nowhere near as badly hit as some grounds and fixtures continued as normal while repairs were carried out. There were no further developments to the ground until 1957, when floodlights were erected, and a year later undersoil heating was installed.

Throughout this period Goodison continued to stage internationals and FA Cup semi-finals and was the unfortunate venue for England's first defeat on English soil by a non-British side, when Eire won 2–0 in September 1949, thanks to a goal by Everton's own Peter Farrell. In 1966 Goodison was chosen as one of the grounds for the World Cup Finals, with Bulgaria, Brazil, Hungary and Portugal playing their group matches there. In the quarter-finals Portugal defeated North Korea at Everton in one of the competition's most memorable games, while in one of the least noteworthy West Germany defeated the Soviet Union for a place in the final.

In 1971 David Leitch's fine old stand on the Goodison Road was pulled down and a new triple-decker stand with executive boxes was erected in its place.

The tunnel that leads out on to the Goodison pitch. Over the years Goodison has changed dramatically but this sign is a reminder to all that Everton remains one of Britain's greatest clubs.

At a cost of £1 million, it was the largest in the country and provided seating for just over 15,000 spectators. During the 1987 close season a new shelter was constructed to cover the Gladwys Street end for the first time in its history. Following the Safety of Sports Grounds Act the stadium's capacity was dramatically cut to 53,000, a considerable reduction on the highest gate recorded, in September 1948, when 78,299 turned up to see Everton and Liverpool in a League match. The record score at Goodison remains the 11–2 victory over Derby County in the FA Cup in January 1890, while the record defeat on the ground was the 7–3 beating that Newcastle United handed out on Boxing Day 1933.

In recent years Goodison has staged few internationals, with all England's home fixtures now being played at Wembley, but it has remained a regular choice for FA Cup semi-final matches. Goodison has also been used for other sporting activities – for athletics during its early years, for army drill practice during the First World War, and for an exhibition baseball game between the New York Whitesocks and the Chicago Giants in the early twenties.

Today, half Goodison's capacity crowd of 53,000 are seated, in one of the most luxurious grounds in the country. And yet the stadium still retains some of its old character and tradition. The church of St Luke the Evangelist is still squeezed into one corner, while the old clock in the opposite corner is as prominent as ever. Both have stood witness to some of the finest matches and some of the finest teams to have graced football, and doubtless will continue to do so as long as Goodison remains the home of Everton Football Club.

15

EVERTON RECORDS

EVERTON IN THE FOOTBALL LEAGUE
1888–89 to 1986–87

Season	P	W	D	L	F	A	Pts.	Pos.
FOOTBALL LEAGUE								
1888–89	22	9	2	11	35	46	20	8
1889–90	22	14	3	5	65	40	31	2
1890–91	22	14	1	7	63	29	29	1
1891–92	26	12	4	10	49	49	28	5
DIVISION ONE								
1892–93	30	16	4	10	74	51	36	3
1893–94	30	15	3	12	90	57	33	6
1894–95	30	18	6	6	82	50	42	2
1895–96	30	16	7	7	66	43	39	3
1896–97	30	14	3	13	62	57	31	7
1897–98	30	13	9	8	48	39	35	4
1898–99	34	15	8	11	48	41	38	4
1899–1900	34	13	7	14	47	49	33	11
1900–01	34	16	5	13	55	42	37	7
1901–02	34	17	7	10	53	35	41	2
1902–03	34	13	6	15	45	47	32	12
1903–04	34	19	5	10	59	32	43	3
1904–05	34	21	5	8	63	36	47	2
1905–06	38	15	7	16	70	66	37	11
1906–07	38	20	5	13	70	46	45	3
1907–08	38	15	6	17	58	64	36	11
1908–09	38	18	10	10	82	57	46	2
1909–10	38	16	8	14	51	56	40	10
1910–11	38	19	7	12	50	36	45	4
1911–12	38	20	6	12	46	42	46	2
1912–13	38	15	7	16	48	54	37	11
1913–14	38	12	11	15	46	55	35	15
1914–15	38	19	8	11	76	47	46	1
1919–20	42	12	14	16	69	68	38	16
1920–21	42	17	13	12	66	55	47	7
1921–22	42	12	12	18	57	55	36	20
1922–23	42	20	7	15	63	59	47	5
1923–24	42	18	13	11	62	53	49	7
1924–25	42	12	11	19	40	60	35	17
1925–26	42	12	18	12	72	70	42	11
1926–27	42	12	10	20	64	90	34	20
1927–28	42	20	13	9	102	66	53	1
1928–29	42	17	4	21	63	75	38	18
1929–30	42	12	11	19	80	92	35	22
DIVISION TWO								
1930–31	42	28	5	9	121	66	61	1
DIVISION ONE								
1931–32	42	26	4	12	116	64	56	1
1932–33	42	16	9	17	81	74	41	11
1933–34	42	12	16	14	62	63	41	14
1934–35	42	16	12	14	89	88	44	8
1935–36	42	13	13	16	89	89	39	16
1936–37	42	14	9	19	81	78	37	17
1937–38	42	16	7	19	79	75	39	14
1938–39	42	27	5	10	88	52	59	1
1946–47	42	17	9	16	62	67	43	10
1947–48	42	17	6	19	52	66	40	14
1948–49	42	13	11	18	41	63	37	18
1949–50	42	10	14	18	42	66	34	18
1950–51	42	12	8	22	48	86	32	22
DIVISION TWO								
1951–52	42	17	10	15	64	58	44	7
1952–53	42	12	14	16	71	75	38	16
1953–54	42	20	16	6	92	58	56	2
DIVISION ONE								
1954–55	42	16	10	16	62	68	42	11
1955–56	42	15	10	17	55	69	40	15
1956–57	42	14	10	18	61	79	38	15
1957–58	42	13	11	18	63	75	37	16
1958–59	42	17	4	21	71	87	38	16
1959–60	42	13	11	18	73	78	37	15
1960–61	42	22	6	14	87	69	50	5
1961–62	42	20	11	11	88	54	51	4
1962–63	42	25	11	6	84	42	61	1
1963–64	42	21	10	11	84	64	52	3
1964–65	42	17	15	10	69	60	49	4
1965–66	42	15	11	16	56	62	41	11
1966–67	42	19	10	13	65	46	48	6
1967–68	42	23	6	13	67	40	52	5
1968–69	42	21	15	6	77	36	57	3
1969–70	42	29	8	5	72	34	66	1
1970–71	42	12	13	17	54	60	37	14
1971–72	42	9	18	15	37	48	36	15
1972–73	42	13	11	18	41	49	37	17
1973–74	42	16	12	14	50	48	44	7
1974–75	42	16	18	8	56	42	50	4
1975–76	42	15	12	15	60	66	42	11
1976–77	42	14	14	14	62	64	42	9
1977–78	42	22	11	9	76	45	55	3
1978–79	42	17	17	8	52	40	51	4
1979–80	42	9	17	16	43	51	35	19
1980–81	42	13	10	19	55	58	36	15
1981–82	42	17	13	12	56	50	64	8
1982–83	42	18	10	14	66	48	64	7
1983–84	42	16	14	12	44	42	62	7
1984–85	42	28	6	8	88	43	90	1
1985–86	42	26	8	8	87	41	85	2
1986–87	42	26	8	8	76	31	86	1

EVERTON IN THE FA CUP

1886–87
Round 1
v Glasgow Rangers (h) 0–1
Everton scratched prior to the match, knowing they would field ineligible players.

1887–88
Round 1 1st leg
v Bolton Wanderers (a) 0–1*
Round 1 2nd leg
v Bolton Wanderers (h) 2–2
Round 1 replay, 1st leg
v Bolton Wanderers (a) 0–0
Round 1 replay, 2nd leg
v Bolton Wanderers (h) 2–1**
Round 2
v Preston North End (a) 0–6
*Everton protest over eligibility of Bolton player upheld
**Bolton protest over eligibility of seven Everton players upheld. Bolton duly played Preston

1888–89
Did not compete

1889–90
Round 1
v Derby County (h) 11–2
Round 2
v Stoke City (a) 2–4

1890–91
Round 1
v Sunderland (a) 1–2

1891–92
Round 1
v Burnley (h) 2–4

1892–93
Round 1
v West Bromwich Albion (h) 4–1
Round 2
v Nottingham Forest (h) 4–2
Round 3
v Sheffield Wednesday (h) 3–0
Semi-final
v Preston North End (Bramall Lane) 2–2
Replay
v Preston North End (Ewood Park) 0–0
Second Replay
v Preston North End (Trent Bridge) 2–1

Final
v Wolverhampton Wanderers (Fallowfield) 0–1

1893–94
Round 1
v Stoke City (a) 0–1

1894–95
Round 1
v Southport (a) 3–0
Round 2
v Blackburn Rovers (h) 1–1
Replay
v Blackburn Rovers (a) 3–2
Round 3
v Sheffield Wednesday (a) 0–2

1895–96
Round 1
v Nottingham Forest (a) 2–0
Round 2
v Sheffield United (h) 3–0
Round 3
v Sheffield Wednesday (a) 0–4

1896–97
Round 1
v Burton Wanderers (h) 5–2
Round 2
v Bury (h) 3–0
Round 3
v Blackburn Rovers (h) 2–0
Semi-final
v Aston Villa (Crystal Palace) 2–3

1897–98
Round 1
v Blackburn Rovers (h) 1–0
Round 2
v Stoke City (a) 0–0
Replay
v Stoke City (h) 5–1
Round 3
v Burnley (a) 3–1
Semi-final
v Derby County (Molineux) 1–3

1898–99
Round 1
v Jarrow (h) 3–1
Round 2
v Nottingham Forest (h) 0–1

1899–1900
Round 1
v Southampton (a) 0–3

1900–01
Round 1
v Southampton (h) 3–1

Round 2
v Sheffield United (a) 0–2

1901–02
Round 1
v Liverpool (a) 2–2
Replay
v Liverpool (h) 0–2

1902–03
Round 1
v Portsmouth (h) 5–0
Round 2
v Manchester United (h) 3–1
Round 3
v Millwall (a) 0–1

1903–04
Round 1
v Tottenham Hotspur (a) 1–2

1904–05
Round 1
v Liverpool (a) 1–1
Replay
v Liverpool (h) 2–1
Round 2
v Stoke City (a) 4–0
Round 3
v Southampton (h) 4–0
Semi-final
v Aston Villa (Victoria Ground) 1–1
Replay
v Aston Villa (Trent Bridge) 1–2

1905–06
Round 1
v West Bromwich Albion (h) 3–1
Round 2
v Chesterfield (h) 3–0
Round 3
v Bradford City (h) 1–0
Round 4
v Sheffield Wednesday (h) 4–3
Semi-final
v Liverpool (Villa Park) 2–0
Final
v Newcastle United (Crystal Palace) 1–0

1906–07
Round 1
v Sheffield United (h) 1–0
Round 2
v West Ham United (a) 2–1
Round 3
v Bolton Wanderers (h) 0–0
Replay
v Bolton Wanderers (a) 3–0
Round 4
v Crystal Palace (a) 1–1

Replay
v Crystal Palace (h) 4–0
Semi-final
v West Bromwich Albion (Burnden Park) 2–1
Final
v Sheffield Wednesday (Crystal Palace) 1–2

1907–08
Round 1
v Tottenham Hotspur (h) 1–0
Round 2
v Oldham Athletic (a) 0–0
Replay
v Oldham Athletic (h) 6–1
Round 3
v Bolton Wanderers (a) 3–3
Replay
v Bolton Wanderers (h) 3–1
Round 4
v Southampton (h) 0–0
Replay
v Southampton (a) 2–3

1908–09
Round 1
v Barnsley (h) 3–1
Round 2
v Manchester United (a) 0–1

1909–10
Round 1
v Middlesbrough (a) 1–1
Replay
v Middlesbrough (h) 5–3
Replay 2
v Woolwich Arsenal (h) 5–0
Round 3
v Sunderland (h) 2–0
Round 4
v Coventry City (a) 2–0
Semi-final
v Barnsley (Elland Road) 0–0
Replay
v Barnsley (Old Trafford) 0–3

1910–11
Round 1
v Crystal Palace (a) 4–0
Round 2
v Liverpool (h) 2–1
Round 3
v Derby County (a) 0–5

1911–12
Round 1
v Clapton Orient (a) 2–1
Round 2
v Bury (h) 1–1

Replay
v Bury (h) 6–0
Round 3
v Oldham Athletic (a) 2–0
Round 4
v Swindon Town (a) 1–2

1912–13
Round 1
v Stockport County (h) 5–1
Round 2
v Brighton & Hove Albion (a) 0–0
Replay
v Brighton & Hove Albion (h) 1–0
Round 3
v Bristol Rovers (a) 4–0
Round 4
v Oldham Athletic (h) 0–1

1913–14
Round 1
v Glossop (a) 1–2

1914–15
Round 1
v Barnsley (h) 3–0
Round 2
v Bristol City (h) 4–0
Round 3
v Queens Park Rangers (a) 2–1
Round 4
v Bradford City (a) 2–0
Semi-final
v Chelsea (Villa Park) 0–2

1919–20
Round 1
v Birmingham (a) 0–2

1920–21
Round 1
v Stockport County (h) 1–0
Round 2
v Sheffield Wednesday (h) 1–1
Replay
v Sheffield Wednesday (a) 1–0
Round 3
v Newcastle United (h) 3–0
Round 4
v Wolverhampton Wanderers (h) 0–1

1921–22
Round 1
v Crystal Palace (h) 0–6

1922–23
Round 1
v Bradford (h) 1–1
Replay
v Bradford (a) 0–1

1923–24
Round 1
v Preston North End (h) 3–1
Round 2
v Brighton & Hove Albion (a) 2–5

1924–25
Round 1
v Burnley (h) 2–1
Round 2
v Sunderland (a) 0–0
Replay
v Sunderland (h) 2–1
Round 3
v Sheffield United (a) 0–1

1925–26
Round 1
v Fulham (h) 1–1
Replay
v Fulham (a) 0–1

1926–27
Round 3
v Poole Town (h) 3–1
Round 4
v Hull City (a) 1–1
Replay
v Hull City (h) 2–2
Second Replay
v Hull City (Villa Park) 2–3

1927–28
Round 3
v Preston North End (a) 3–0
Round 4
v Arsenal (a) 3–4

1928–29
Round 3
v Chelsea (a) 0–2

1929–30
Round 3
v Carlisle United (a) 4–2
Round 4
v Blackburn Rovers (a) 1–4

1930–31
Round 3
v Plymouth Argyle (a) 2–0
Round 4
v Crystal Palace (a) 6–0
Round 5
v Grimsby Town (h) 5–3
Round 6
v Southport (h) 9–1
Semi-final
v West Bromwich Albion (Old Trafford) 0–1

1931–32
Round 3
v Liverpool (h) 1–2

1932–33
Round 3
v Leicester City (a) 3–2
Round 4
v Bury (h) 3–1
Round 5
v Leeds United (h) 2–0
Round 6
v Luton Town (h) 6–0
Semi-final
v West Ham United (Molineux) 2–1
Final
v Manchester City (Wembley) 3–0

1933–34
Round 3
v Tottenham Hotspur (a) 0–3

1934–35
Round 3
v Grimsby Town (h) 6–3
Round 4
v Sunderland (a) 1–1
Replay
v Sunderland (h) 6–4
Round 5
v Derby County (h) 3–1
Round 6
v Bolton Wanderers (h) 1–2

1935–36
Round 3
v Preston North End (h) 1–3

1936–37
Round 3
v Bournemouth (h) 5–0
Round 4
v Sheffield Wednesday (h) 3–0
Round 5
v Tottenham Hotspur (h) 1–1
Replay
v Tottenham Hotspur (a) 3–4

1937–38
Round 3
v Chelsea (a) 1–0
Round 4
v Sunderland (h) 0–1

1938–39
Round 3
v Derby County (a) 1–0
Round 4
v Doncaster Rovers (h) 8–0
Round 5
v Birmingham (a) 2–2

Replay
v Birmingham (h) 2–1
Round 6
v Wolverhampton Wanderers (a) 0–2

1945–46
Round 3 1st leg
v Preston North End (a) 1–2
Round 3 2nd leg
v Preston North End (h) 2–2 agg 3–4

1946–47
Round 3
v Southend United (h) 4–2
Round 4
v Sheffield Wednesday (a) 1–2

1947–48
Round 3
v Grimsby Town (a) 4–1
Round 4
v Wolverhampton Wanderers (a) 1–1
Replay
v Wolverhampton Wanderers (h) 3–2
Round 5
v Fulham (a) 1–1
Replay
v Fulham (h) 0–1

1948–49
Round 3
v Manchester City (h) 1–0
Round 4
v Chelsea (a) 0–2

1949–50
Round 3
v Queens Park Rangers (a) 2–0
Round 4
v West Ham United (a) 2–1
Round 5
v Tottenham Hotspur (h) 1–0
Round 6
v Derby County (a) 2–1
Semi-final
v Liverpool (Maine Road) 0–2

1950–51
Round 3
v Hull City (a) 0–2

1951–52
Round 3
v Leyton Orient (a) 0–0
Replay
v Leyton Orient (h) 1–3

1952–53
Round 3
v Ipswich Town (h) 3–2
Round 4
v Nottingham Forest (h) 4–1
Round 5
v Manchester United (h) 2–1
Round 6
v Aston Villa (a) 1–0
Semi-final
v Bolton Wanderers (Maine Road) 3–4

1953–54
Round 3
v Notts County (h) 2–1
Round 4
v Swansea Town (h) 3–0
Round 5
v Sheffield Wednesday (a) 1–3

1954–55
Round 3
v Southend United (h) 3–1
Round 4
v Liverpool (h) 0–4

1955–56
Round 3
v Bristol City (h) 3–1
Round 4
v Port Vale (a) 3–2
Round 5
v Chelsea (h) 1–0
Round 6
v Manchester City (a) 1–2

1956–57
Round 3
v Blackburn Rovers (h) 1–0
Round 4
v West Ham United (h) 2–1
Round 5
v Manchester United (a) 0–1

1957–58
Round 3
v Sunderland (a) 2–2
Replay
v Sunderland (h) 3–1
Round 4
v Blackburn Rovers (h) 1–2

1958–59
Round 3
v Sunderland (h) 4–0
Round 4
v Charlton Athletic (a) 2–2
Replay
v Charlton Athletic (h) 4–1

Round 5
v Aston Villa (h) 1–4

1959–60
Round 3
v Bradford City (a) 0–3

1960–61
Round 3
v Sheffield United (h) 0–1

1961–62
Round 3
v King's Lynn (h) 4–0
Round 4
v Manchester City (h) 2–0
Round 5
v Burnley (a) 1–3

1962–63
Round 3
v Barnsley (a) 3–0
Round 4
v Swindon Town (a) 5–1
Round 5
v West Ham United (a) 0–1

1963–64
Round 3
v Hull City (a) 1–1
Replay
v Hull City (h) 2–1
Round 4
v Leeds United (a) 1–1
Replay
v Leeds United (h) 2–0
Round 5
v Sunderland (a) 1–3

1964–65
Round 3
v Sheffield Wednesday (h) 2–2
Replay
v Sheffield Wednesday (a) 3–0
Round 4
v Leeds United (a) 1–1
Replay
v Leeds United (h) 1–2

1965–66
Round 3
v Sunderland (h) 3–0
Round 4
v Bedford Town (a) 3–0
Round 5
v Coventry City (h) 3–0
Round 6
v Manchester City (a) 0–0
Replay
v Manchester City (h) 0–0

Second Replay
v Manchester City (Molineux) 2–0
Semi-final
v Manchester United (Burnden Park) 1–0
Final
v Sheffield Wednesday (Wembley) 3–2

1966–67
Round 3
v Burnley (a) 0–0
Replay
v Burnley (h) 2–1
Round 4
v Wolverhampton Wanderers (a) 1–1
Replay
v Wolverhampton Wanderers (h) 3–1
Round 5
v Liverpool (h) 1–0
Round 6
v Nottingham Forest (a) 2–3

1967–68
Round 3
v Southport (a) 1–0
Round 4
v Carlisle United (a) 2–0
Round 5
v Tranmere Rovers (h) 2–0
Round 6
v Leicester City (a) 3–1
Semi-final
v Leeds United (Old Trafford) 1–0
Final
v West Bromwich Albion (Wembley) 0–1

1968–69
Round 3
v Ipswich Town (h) 2–1
Round 4
v Coventry City (h) 2–0
Round 5
v Bristol City (h) 1–0
Round 6
v Manchester United (a) 1–0
Semi-final
v Manchester City (Villa Park) 0–1

1969–70
Round 3
v Sheffield United (a) 1–2

1970–71
Round 3
v Blackburn Rovers (h) 2–0
Round 4
v Middlesbrough (h) 3–0

Round 5
v Derby County (h) 1–0
Round 6
v Colchester United (h) 5–0
Semi-final
v Liverpool (Old Trafford) 1–2

1971–72
Round 3
v Crystal Palace (a) 2–2
Replay
v Crystal Palace (h) 3–2
Round 4
v Walsall (h) 2–1
Round 5
v Tottenham Hotspur (a) 0–2

1972–73
Round 3
v Aston Villa (h) 3–2
Round 4
v Millwall (h) 0–2

1973–74
Round 3
v Blackburn Rovers (h) 3–0
Round 4
v West Bromwich Albion (h) 0–0
Replay
v West Bromwich Albion (a) 0–1

1974–75
Round 3
v Altrincham (h) 1–1
Replay
v Altrincham (Old Trafford) 2–0
Round 4
v Plymouth Argyle (a) 3–1
Round 5
v Fulham (h) 1–2

1975–76
Round 3
v Derby County (a) 1–2

1976–77
Round 3
v Stoke City (h) 2–0
Round 4
v Swindon Town (a) 2–2
Replay
v Swindon Town (h) 2–1
Round 5
v Cardiff City (a) 2–1
Round 6
v Derby County (h) 2–0
Semi-final
v Liverpool (Maine Road) 2–2
Replay
v Liverpool (Maine Road) 0–3

1977–78
Round 3
v Aston Villa (h) 4–1
Round 4
v Middlesbrough (a) 2–3

1978–79
Round 3
v Sunderland (a) 1–2

1979–80
Round 3
v Aldershot (h) 4–1
Round 4
v Wigan Athletic (h) 3–0
Round 5
v Wrexham (h) 5–2
Round 6
v Ipswich Town (h) 2–1
Semi-final
v West Ham United (Villa Park) 1–1
Replay
v West Ham United (Elland Road)
    1–2

1980–81
Round 3
v Arsenal (h) 2–0
Round 4
v Liverpool (h) 2–1
Round 5
v Southampton (a) 0–0
Replay
v Southampton (h) 1–0
Round 6
v Manchester City (h) 2–2
Replay
v Manchester City (a) 1–3

1981–82
Round 3
v West Ham United (a) 1–2

1982–83
Round 3
v Newport County (a) 1–1
Replay
v Newport County (h) 2–1
Round 4
v Shrewsbury Town (h) 2–1
Round 5
v Tottenham Hotspur (h) 2–0
Round 6
v Manchester United (a) 0–1

1983–84
Round 3
v Stoke City (a) 2–0
Round 4
v Gillingham (h) 0–0

Replay
v Gillingham (a) 0–0
Second Replay
v Gillingham (a) 3–0
Round 5
v Shrewsbury Town (h) 3–0
Round 6
v Notts County (a) 2–1
Semi-final
v Southampton (Highbury) 1–0
Final
v Watford (Wembley) 2–0

1984–85
Round 3
v Leeds United (a) 2–0
Round 4
v Doncaster Rovers (h) 2–0
Round 5
v Telford United (h) 3–0
Round 6
v Ipswich Town (h) 2–2
Replay
v Ipswich Town (a) 1–0
Semi-final
v Luton Town (Villa Park) 2–1

Final
v Manchester United (Wembley)
    0–1

1985–86
Round 3
v Exeter City (h) 1–0
Round 4
v Blackburn Rovers (h) 3–1
Round 5
v Tottenham Hotspur (a) 2–1
Round 6
v Luton Town (a) 2–2
Replay
v Luton Town (h) 1–0
Semi-final
v Sheffield Wednesday (Villa Park)
    1–2
Final
v Liverpool (Wembley) 1–3

1986–87
Round 3
v Southampton (h) 2–1
Round 4
v Bradford City (a) 1–0
Round 5
v Wimbledon (a) 1–3

EVERTON IN THE FOOTBALL LEAGUE CUP
(1982–86 the Milk Cup, now the Littlewoods Cup)

1960–61
Round 1
v Accrington Stanley (h) 3–1
Round 2
v Walsall (h) 3–1
Round 3
v Bury (h) 3–1
Round 4
v Tranmere Rovers (a) 4–0
Round 5
v Shrewsbury Town (a) 1–2

1967–68
Round 2
v Bristol City (a) 5–0
Round 3
v Sunderland (h) 2–3

1968–69
Round 2
v Tranmere Rovers (h) 4–0
Round 3
v Luton Town (h) 5–1
Round 4
v Derby County (h) 0–0
Replay
v Derby County (a) 0–1

1969–70
Round 2
v Darlington (a) 1–0
Round 3
v Arsenal (a) 0–0
Replay
v Arsenal (h) 1–0
Round 4
v Manchester City (a) 0–2

1971–72
Round 2
v Southampton (a) 1–2

1972–73
Round 2
v Arsenal (a) 0–1

1973–74
Round 2
v Reading (h) 1–0
Round 3
v Norwich (h) 0–1

1974–75
Round 2
v Aston Villa (a) 1–1

Replay
v Aston Villa (h) 0–3

1975–76
Round 2
v Arsenal (h) 2–2
Replay
v Arsenal (h) 1–0
Round 3
v Carlisle United (h) 2–0
Round 4
v Notts County (h) 2–2
Replay
v Notts County (a) 0–2

1976–77
Round 2
v Cambridge United (h) 3–0
Round 3
v Stockport County (a) 1–0
Round 4
v Coventry City (h) 3–0
Round 5
v Manchester United (a) 3–0
Semi-final 1st leg
v Bolton Wanderers (h) 1–1
Semi-final 2nd leg
v Bolton Wanderers (a) 1–0
Final
v Aston Villa (Wembley) 0–0
Replay
v Aston Villa (Hillsborough) 1–1
Second Replay
v Aston Villa (Old Trafford) 2–3

1977–78
Round 2
v Sheffield United (a) 3–0
Round 3
v Middlesbrough (h) 2–2
Replay
v Middlesbrough (a) 2–1
Round 4
v Sheffield Wednesday (a) 3–1
Round 5
v Leeds United (a) 1–4

1978–79
Round 2
v Wimbledon (h) 8–0
Round 3
v Darlington (h) 1–0
Round 4
v Nottingham Forest (h) 2–3

1979–80
Round 2 1st leg
v Cardiff City (h) 2–0
Round 2 2nd leg
v Cardiff City (a) 0–1 agg 2–1

Round 3
v Aston Villa (a) 0–0
Replay
v Aston Villa (h) 4–1
Round 4
v Grimsby Town (a) 1–2

1980–81
Round 2 1st leg
v Blackpool (h) 3–0
Round 2 2nd leg
v Blackpool (a) 2–2 agg 5–2
Round 3
v West Bromwich Albion (h) 1–2

1981–82
Round 2 1st leg
v Coventry City (h) 1–1
Round 2 2nd leg
v Coventry City (a) 1–0 agg 2–1
Round 3
v Oxford United (h) 1–0
Round 4
v Ipswich Town (h) 2–3

1982–83
Round 2 1st leg
v Newport County (a) 2–0
Round 2 2nd leg
v Newport County (h) 2–2 agg 4–2
Round 3
v Arsenal (h) 1–1
Replay
v Arsenal (a) 0–3

1983–84
Round 2 1st leg
v Chesterfield (a) 1–0
Round 2 2nd leg
v Chesterfield (h) 2–2 agg 3–2
Round 3
v Coventry City (h) 2–1
Round 4
v West Ham United (a) 2–2
Replay
v West Ham United (h) 2–0
Round 5
v Oxford United (a) 1–1
Replay
v Oxford United (h) 4–1
Semi-final 1st leg
v Aston Villa (h) 2–0
Semi-final 2nd leg
v Aston Villa (a) 0–1 agg 2–1
Final
v Liverpool (Wembley) 0–0
Replay
v Liverpool (Maine Road) 0–1

1984–85
Round 2 1st leg
v Sheffield United (a) 2–2
Round 2 2nd leg
v Sheffield United (h) 4–0 agg 6–2
Round 3
v Manchester United (a) 2–1
Round 4
v Grimsby Town (h) 0–1

1985–86
Round 2 1st leg
v Bournemouth (h) 3–2
Round 2 2nd leg
v Bournemouth (a) 2–0 agg 5–2
Round 3
v Shrewsbury Town (a) 4–1
Round 4
v Chelsea (a) 2–2
Replay
v Chelsea (h) 1–2

1986–87
Round 2 1st leg
v Newport County (h) 4–0
Round 2 2nd leg
v Newport County (a) 5–1 agg 9–1
Round 3
v Millwall (a) 4–1
Round 4
v Norwich City (a) 4–1
Round 5
v Liverpool (h) 0–1

EVERTON IN EUROPE

European Cup

1963–64
Round 1 1st leg
v Inter Milan (h) 0–0
Round 1 2nd leg
v Inter Milan (a) 0–1 agg 0–1

1970–71
Round 1 1st leg
v Keflavik (h) 6–2
Round 1 2nd leg
v Keflavik (a) 3–0 agg 9–2
Round 2 1st leg
v Borussia Moenchengladbach (a) 1–1
Round 2 2nd leg
v Borussia Moenchengladbach (h) 1–1 agg 1–1
Everton won 4–3 on penalties
Round 3 1st leg
v Panathinaikos (h) 1–1
Round 3 2nd leg
v Panathinaikos (a) 0–0 agg 1–1
Panathinaikos won on away goals

European Cup-Winners' Cup

1966–67
Round 1 1st leg
v Aalborg (a) 0–0
Round 1 2nd leg
v Aalborg (h) 2–1 agg 2–1
Round 2 1st leg
v Real Zaragoza (a) 0–2
Round 2 2nd leg
v Real Zaragoza (h) 1–0 agg 1–2

1984–85
Round 1 1st leg
v UC Dublin (a) 0–0
Round 1 2nd leg
v UC Dublin (h) 1–0 agg 1–0
Round 2 1st leg
v Bratislava (a) 1–0
R und 2 2nd leg
v Bratislava (h) 3–0 agg 4–0
Round 3 1st leg
v F Sittard (h) 3–0
Round 3 2nd leg
v F Sittard (a) 2–0 agg 5–0
Semi-final 1st leg
v Bayern Munich (a) 0–0
Semi-final 2nd leg
v Bayern Munich (h) 3–1 agg 3–1
Final
v Rapid Vienna (Rotterdam) 3–1

Inter-Cities Fairs' Cup

1962–63
Round 1 1st leg
v Dunfermline A (h) 1–0
Round 1 2nd leg
v Dunfermline A (a) 0–2 agg 1–2

1964–65
Round 1 1st leg
v Valerengen (a) 5–2
Round 1 2nd leg
v Valerengen (h) 4–2 agg 9–4

Round 2 1st leg
v Kilmarnock (a) 2–0
Round 2 2nd leg
v Kilmarnock (h) 4–1 agg 6–1
Round 3 1st leg
v Manchester U (a) 1–1
Round 3 2nd leg
v Manchester U (h) 1–2 agg 2–3

1965–66
Round 1 1st leg
v IFC Nuremberg (a) 1–1
Round 1 2nd leg
v IFC Nuremberg (h) 1–0 agg 2–1
Round 2 1st leg
v Ujpest Dozsa (a) 0–3
Round 2 2nd leg
v Ujpest Dozsa (h) 2–1 agg 2–4

UEFA Cup

1975–76
Round 1 1st leg
v AC Milan (h) 0–0
Round 1 2nd leg
v AC Milan (a) 0–1 agg 0–1

1978–79
Round 1 1st leg
v Finn Harps (a) 5–0
Round 1 2nd leg
v Finn Harps (h) 5–0 agg 10–0
Round 2 1st leg
v Dukla Prague (h) 2–1
Round 2 2nd leg
v Dukla Prague (a) 0–1 agg 2–2
Dukla Prague won on away goals

1979–80
Round 1 1st leg
v Feyenoord (a) 0–1
Round 1 2nd leg
v Feyenoord (h) 0–1 agg 0–2

TEXACO CUP

1973–74
Round 1 1st leg
v Heart of Midlothian (h) 0–1
Round 1 2nd leg
v Heart of Midlothian (a) 0–0 agg 0–1

FA CHARITY SHIELD

1928
v Blackburn Rovers (Old Trafford) 2–1

1932
v Newcastle United (a) 5–3

1933
v Arsenal (h) 0–3

1963
v Manchester United (h) 4–0

1966
v Liverpool (h) 0–1

1970
v Chelsea a) 2–1

1984
v Liverpool (Wembley) 1–0

1985
v Manchester United (Wembley) 2–0

1986
v Liverpool (Wembley) 1–1

1987
v Coventry City (Wembley) 1–0

BRITISH CHAMPIONSHIP

1963
v Glasgow Rangers (a) 3–1
v Glasgow Rangers (h) 1–1 agg 4–2

EVERTON'S INTERNATIONALS

ENGLAND

Abbott W. 1902 v Wales (1).
Baker B. H. 1921 v Belgium; 1925 v N. Ireland (2).
Ball A. J. 1966 v N. Ireland, Czechoslovakia, Wales; 1967 v Scotland, Spain, Austria, Wales, USSR; 1968 v Scotland, Spain (twice), W. Germany, Yugoslavia, Romania; 1969 v Romania, N. Ireland, Wales, Scotland, Mexico, Uruguay, Brazil, Portugal; 1970 v Belgium, Wales, Scotland, Colombia, Ecuador, Romania, Brazil, Czechoslovakia (sub), W. Germany, E. Germany; 1971 v Malta, Greece, Malta (sub), N. Ireland, Scotland, Switzerland, Greece (39).
Balmer W. 1905 v Ireland (1).
Booth T. 1903 v Scotland (1).
Boyes W. 1938 v Wales, Rest of Europe (2).
Bracewell P. 1985 v W. Germany (sub), USA; 1986 v N. Ireland (3).
Britton C. S. 1934 v Wales, Italy; 1935 v N. Ireland, Scotland; 1936 v N. Ireland, Hungary, Scotland, Norway, Sweden (9).
Chadwick E. 1891 v Wales, Scotland; 1892 v Scotland; 1893 v Scotland; 1894 v Scotland; 1896 v Ireland; 1897 v Scotland (7).
Chedgzoy S. 1920 v Wales, Ireland; 1921 v Wales, Scotland, Ireland; 1923 v Scotland; 1924 v Wales, N. Ireland (8).
Cresswell W. 1929 v N. Ireland (1).
Cunliffe J. N. 1936 v Belgium (1).
Dean W. R. 1927 v Wales, Scotland, Belgium, France, Luxembourg, N. Ireland, Wales; 1928 v Scotland, France, Belgium, N. Ireland, Wales; 1929 v Scotland; 1931 v Scotland, Spain; 1932 v N. Ireland (16).
Dobson M. 1974 v Czechoslovakia (1).
Downs R. W. 1920 v Ireland (1).
Freeman B. C. 1909 v Wales, Scotland (2).
Geary F. 1890 v Ireland; 1891 v Scotland (2).
Gee C. W. 1931 v Wales, Spain; 1936 v N. Ireland (3).
Geldard A. 1933 v Italy, Switzerland; 1935 v Scotland; 1937 v N. Ireland (4).
Hardman H. P. 1905 v Wales; 1907 v Ireland, Scotland; 1908 v Wales (4).
Harrison G. 1921 v Belgium, Ireland (2).
Harvey J. C. 1971 v Malta (1).
Holt J. 1890 v Wales; 1891 v Wales, Scotland; 1892 v Ireland, Scotland; 1893 v Scotland; 1894 v Ireland, Scotland; 1895 v Scotland (9).
Howarth R. H. 1894 v Ireland (1).
Jefferis F. 1912 v Wales, Scotland (2).
Johnson T. C. F. 1931 v Spain; 1932 v Scotland, N. Ireland (3).
Kay A. H. 1963 v Switzerland (1).
Labone B. L. 1963 v France, N. Ireland, Wales; 1967 v Spain, Austria; 1968 v Scotland, Spain, Sweden, W. Germany, Yugoslavia, USSR, Romania, Bulgaria; 1969 v N. Ireland, Scotland, Mexico, Uruguay, Brazil; 1970 v Belgium, Wales, Scotland, Colombia, Ecuador, Romania, Brazil, W. Germany (26).
Latchford R. D. 1977 v Italy; 1978 v Brazil, Wales, Denmark, Republic of Ireland, Czechoslovakia (sub); 1979 v Republic of Ireland, N. Ireland, Wales, Scotland, Bulgaria, Austria (12).
Lawton T. 1938 v Wales, Rest of Europe, Norway, N. Ireland; 1939 v Scotland, Italy, Yugoslavia, Romania (8).
Lineker G. 1986 v Romania, Turkey, N. Ireland, E. Germany, USSR, Canada, Portugal, Morocco, Poland, Paraguay, Argentina (11).
Makepeace H. 1906 v Scotland; 1910 v Scotland; 1912 v Wales, Scotland (4).
Mercer J. 1938 v N. Ireland; 1939 v Scotland, Italy, Yugoslavia, Romania (5).
Milward A. 1891 v Wales, Scotland, 1897 v Wales, Scotland (4).
Newton K. R. 1970 v Holland, N. Ireland, Scotland, Colombia, Ecuador, Romania, Czechoslovakia, W. Germany (8).
Pickering F. 1964 v USA, N. Ireland, Belgium (3).
Reid P. 1985 v Mexico (sub), W. Germany, USA (sub); 1986 v Romania, Scotland (sub), Poland, Paraguay, Argentina; 1987 v Brazil (10).
Royle J. 1971 v Malta; 1972 v Yugoslavia (2).
Sagar E. 1935 v N. Ireland; 1936 v Scotland, Austria, Belgium (4).
Settle J. 1902 v Ireland, Scotland; 1903 v Ireland (3).
Sharp J. 1903 v Ireland; 1905 v Scotland (2).
Steven T. 1984 v N. Ireland; 1985 v Republic of Ireland, Romania, Finland, Italy, USA (sub); 1986 v Turkey (sub), E.Germany, USSR (sub), Mexico (sub), Poland, Paraguay, Argentina; 1987 v Sweden, Yugoslavia (sub), Spain (sub) (16).
Stevens G. 1985 v Italy, W. Germany; 1986 v Romania, Turkey, N. Ireland, E. Germany, Israel, Scotland, Canada, Portugal, Morocco, Poland, Paraguay, Argentina; 1987 v Brazil, Scotland (16).
Temple D. W. 1965 v W. Germany (1).
Watson D. 1987 v N. Ireland (1).
West G. 1968 v Bulgaria; 1969 v Wales, Mexico (3).
White T. A. 1933 v Italy (1).
Wilson R. 1965 v Scotland, Hungary, Yugoslavia, W. Germany, Sweden, Wales, Austria, N. Ireland, Spain; 1966 v Poland, W. Germany (sub), Yugoslavia, Finland, Denmark, Poland, Uruguay, Mexico, France, Argentina, Portugal, W. Germany, N. Ireland, Czechoslovakia, Wales; 1967 v Scotland, Austria, N. Ireland, USSR; 1968 v Scotland, Spain (twice), Yugoslavia, USSR (33).
Wolstenholme S. 1904 v Scotland (1).
Wright T. J. 1968 v USSR, Romania; 1969 v Romania, Mexico (sub), Uruguay, Brazil, Holland; 1970 v Belgium, Wales, Romania (sub), Brazil (11).

ENGLAND 'B'

Lyons M. 1979 v Czechoslovakia (1).
Wright W. 1979 v Austria; 1981 v Australia (2).

SCOTLAND

Bell J. 1896 v England; 1897 v England; 1898 v England; 1899 v Wales, Ireland, England; 1900 v Wales, England (8).
Brewster G. 1921 v England (1).

Collins R. Y. 1958 v Wales, N. Ireland; 1959 v England, W. Germany, Holland, Portugal (6).
Connolly J. 1973 v Switzerland (1).
Dunn J. 1928 v Wales (1).
Gabriel J. 1960 v Wales; 1963 v Norway (sub) (2).
Gillick T. 1937 v Austria, Czechoslovakia; 1938 v N. Ireland, Wales, Hungary (5).
Gray A. 1985 v Iceland (1).
Hartford A. 1979 v Peru, Belgium; 1981 v N. Ireland (sub), Israel, Wales, N. Ireland, England (7).
McBain N. 1923 v Ireland; 1924 v Wales (2).
Parker A. 1958 Paraguay (1).
Rioch B. D. 1977 v Wales, N. Ireland, England, Chile, Brazil, Czechoslovakia (6).
Robertson J. T. 1898 v England (1).
Scott A. S. 1963 v Wales, Norway; 1964 v Finland; 1966 v Portugal, Brazil (5).
Sharp G. 1985 v Iceland; 1986 v Wales, Australia (sub and sub), Israel, Romania, Uraguay; 1987 v Republic of Ireland (8).
Thomson J. R. 1932 v Wales (1).
Troup A. 1926 v England (1).
Wilson G. W. 1907 v England (1).
Wood G. 1979 v N. Ireland, England, Argentina (sub) (3).
Young A. 1961 v Republic of Ireland; 1966 v Portugal (2).
Young A. 1905 v England; 1907 v Wales (2).

WALES

Arridge S. 1894 v Ireland; 1895 v Ireland; 1896 v England (3).
Davies J. 1899 v Scotland, Ireland (2).
Davies S. 1921 v Scotland, England, Ireland (3).
Davies W. D. 1975 v Hungary, Luxembourg, Scotland, England, N. Ireland; 1976 v Yugoslavia, England, N. Ireland, Yugoslavia, W. Germany, Scotland; 1977 v Czechoslovakia, Scotland, England, N. Ireland, Kuwait (16).
Griffiths T. P. 1927 v England, N. Ireland; 1928 v England; 1929 v England; 1931 v N. Ireland, Scotland, England, N. Ireland (8).
Hughes E. 1899 v Ireland, Scotland (2).
Humphreys J. V. 1947 v N. Ireland (1).
Jones R. S. 1894 v Ireland (1).
Jones T. G. 1938 v N. Ireland, England, Scotland; 1939 v N. Ireland; 1946 v Scotland, England; 1947 v England, Scotland; 1948 v N. Ireland, England; 1949 v N. Ireland, Portugal, Belgium, Switzerland, England, Scotland, Belgium (17).
Parry C. F. 1891 v England, Scotland; 1893 v England; 1894 v England; 1895 v England, Scotland (6).
Powell A. 1948 v England; 1949 v Belgium (2).
Ratcliffe K. 1981 v Czechoslovakia, Republic of Ireland, Turkey, Scotland, England, USSR; 1982 v Czechoslovakia, Iceland, USSR, Spain, England, Yugoslavia; 1983 v England, Bulgaria, Scotland, N. Ireland, Brazil, Norway, Romania, Bulgaria, Yugoslavia; 1984 v Scotland, England, N. Ireland, Norway, Israel, Iceland, Spain, Iceland; 1985 v Norway, Scotland, Spain; 1986 v Scotland, Hungary, Saudi Arabia, Uruguay; 1987 v Finland, USSR, Finland, Czechoslovakia (40).
Roose L. R. 1905 v Scotland, England (2).
Smallman D. P. 1975 v Hungary (sub), England, N. Ireland (sub), Austria (4).

Southall N. 1982 v N. Ireland, Norway; 1983 v England, Bulgaria, Scotland, N. Ireland, Brazil, Norway, Romania, Bulgaria, Yugoslavia; 1984 v Scotland, England, N. Ireland, Norway, Israel, Iceland, Spain, Iceland; 1985 v Norway, Scotland, Spain, Norway; 1986 v Scotland, Hungary, Saudi Arabia, Republic of Ireland; 1987 v USSR, Finland, Czechoslovakia (30).
Thomas M. 1981 v Czechoslovakia (1).
Van den Hauwe P. 1984 v Spain; 1986 v Scotland, Hungary; 1987 v USSR, Finland, Czechoslovakia (6).
Vernon T. R. 1960 v N. Ireland, Republic of Ireland, Scotland, England; 1962 v N. Ireland, Brazil (twice), Mexico, Scotland, Hungary, England; 1963 v England, Scotland (13).
Williams B. D. 1931 v N. Ireland, England; 1932 v Scotland, England, N. Ireland; 1935 v N. Ireland (6).

NORTHERN IRELAND (and Ireland before 1924)

Bingham W. P. 1960 v W. Germany, Scotland; 1961 v Italy, Greece, W. Germany, Greece, England; 1962 v Poland, England, Scotland, Poland; 1963 v Spain (12).
Clements D. 1973 v Bulgaria, Portugal; 1974 v Scotland, England, Wales, Norway, 1975 v Yugoslavia, England, Scotland, Wales, Sweden, Yugoslavia (12).
Cook W. 1935 v England, Scotland; 1936 v Wales, Scotland, England; 1937 v Wales, England, Scotland, 1938 v Wales, Scotland, England; 1939 v Wales (12).
Coulter J. 1934 v Scotland; 1935 v England, Wales; 1936 v Scotland; 1937 v Wales (5).
Eglington T. J. 1946 v Scotland; 1947 v Wales, Scotland, England; 1948 v Wales, Scotland (6).
Farrell P. D. 1946 v Scotland; 1947 v Wales, Scotland, England; 1948 v Wales, England; 1949 v Wales (7).
Hamilton B. 1976 v Israel, Scotland, England, Wales, Holland, Belgium; 1977 v W. Germany, England, Scotland, Wales, Iceland (11).
Harris V. 1909 v England, Scotland, Wales; 1910 v England, Scotland, Wales; 1911 v Wales, England, Scotland; 1912 v England; 1913 v England, Scotland; 1914 v Wales, Scotland (14).
Hill M. J. 1963 v Scotland, Spain, England (3).
Houston J. 1913 v England, Scotland; 1914 v Scotland (3).
Irvine R. W. 1922 v Scotland, England; 1923 v Wales, England; 1924 v Scotland, England; 1925 v England; 1926 v England; 1927 v Wales, England; 1928 v Scotland (11).
Jackson T. 1968 v Israel; 1969 v England, Scotland, Wales, USSR (twice, once as sub) (6).
Lacey W. 1909 v England, Scotland, Wales; 1910 v England, Scotland, Wales; 1911 v Wales, England, Scotland; 1912 v England (10).
Scott P. W. 1975 v Wales, Yugoslavia (2).
Scott W. 1905 v England, Scotland; 1907 v England, Scotland; 1908 v England, Scotland, Wales; 1909 v England, Scotland, Wales; 1910 v England, Scotland; 1911 v Wales, England, Scotland; 1912 v England (16).
Sheridan J. 1903 v England, Scotland, Wales; 1904 v England, Scotland (5).
Stevenson A. E. 1934 v Scotland; 1935 v England, Scotland; 1936 v Wales, England; 1937 v Wales, England; 1938 v Wales, Scotland, England; 1939 v Wales; 1946 v Scotland; 1947 v Wales, Scotland (14).

REPUBLIC OF IRELAND

Clinton T.J. 1951 v Norway; 1953 v France, Luxembourg (3).
Corr P.J. 1949 v Portugal, Spain, England, Sweden (4).
Donovan D. 1954 v Norway; 1955 v Holland, Norway, W. Germany; 1957 v England (5).
Eglington T.J. 1946 v England; 1947 v Spain, Portugal; 1948 v Portugal, Switzerland; 1949 v Portugal, Sweden; 1950 v Norway; 1951 v Argentina, W. Germany; 1952 v W. Germany, Austria, Spain, France; 1953 v Austria, France, Luxembourg, France; 1954 v Norway; 1955 v Holland, W. Germany, Spain (22).
Farrell P.D. 1947 v Spain, Portugal; 1948 v Portugal, Spain, Switzerland; 1949 v Portugal (sub), Spain, England, Finland, Sweden; 1951 v Argentina, Norway, West Germany; 1952 v W. Germany, Austria, Spain, France; 1953 v Austria, France (twice); 1954 v Norway; 1955 v Holland, W. Germany, Yugoslavia, Spain; 1957 v England (26).
McDonagh J. 1981 v Wales, Belgium, Czechoslovakia (3).
Meagan M.K. 1961 v Scotland; 1962 v Austria, Iceland; 1964 v Spain (4).
O'Keefe E. 1981 v Wales (1).
O'Neill J.A. 1952 v Spain, France; 1953 v Austria, France, Luxembourg, France; 1954 v Norway; 1955 v Holland, Norway, W. Germany, Yugoslavia, Spain; 1956 v Denmark; 1958 v Mexico, Poland; 1959 v Czechoslovakia (twice) (17).
Sheedy K. 1983 v Holland (sub), Malta; 1984 v Denmark; 1985 v Italy, Israel, Switzerland; 1986 v Switzerland, Denmark; 1987 v Scotland, Poland (10).
Walsh M.A. 1978 v N. Ireland (sub) (1).
Walsh M. 1982 v Chile, Brazil, Trinidad & Tobago, Spain (4).

VICTORY AND WARTIME INTERNATIONALS

1919 and 1946 Victory Internationals. 1939–45 Wartime Internationals. No caps were awarded for these matches.

ENGLAND

Britton C.S. 1941 v Wales (twice); 1942 v Scotland, Wales (twice); 1943 v Scotland (twice), Wales (three times); 1944 v Scotland, Wales (12).
Fleetwood T. 1919 v Scotland (twice) (2).
Greenhalgh N.H. 1939 v Scotland (1).
Grenyer A. 1919 v Wales (1).
Lawton T. 1939 v Scotland; 1941 v Scotland; 1942 v Scotland (three times), Wales (twice); 1943 v Scotland; 1944 v Scotland (three times), Wales (twice); 1945 v France, Scotland (twice), Wales, N. Ireland (18).
Mercer J. 1939 v Scotland; 1940 v Scotland; 1941 v Scotland (three times), Wales; 1942 v Scotland (twice), Wales; 1943 v Scotland (twice), Wales (twice); 1944 v Scotland (three times), Wales (twice); 1945 v Scotland (twice), Wales (twice), France, N. Ireland; 1946 v Belgium, Scotland (26).

SCOTLAND

Caskie J. 1939 v England; 1941 v England (three times); 1942 v England; 1944 v England (three times) (8).
Gillick T. 1941 v England; 1942 v England; 1943 v England (3).
Note: Although Jimmy Caskie is listed as an Everton player for wartime internationals, it should be noted that he made only four wartime appearances for the club.

WALES

Jones T.G. 1939 v England; 1940 v England (twice); 1941 v England (twice); 1942 v England (twice); 1943 v England (three times); 1946 v N. Ireland (11).

NORTHERN IRELAND

Stevenson A.E. 1946 v Scotland (1).

INDEX

BIBLIOGRAPHY

Graham, Matthew *Everton* (Hamlyn, 1986)

Hodgson, Derek *The Everton Story* (Arthur Barker, 1979)

Inglis, Simon *The Football Grounds of England and Wales* (Willow, 1983)

Inglis, Simon *Soccer In The Dock* (Willow Books, 1985)

Keates, Thomas *History of the Everton Football Club, 1878–1928* (Thomas Brakell, 1928)

Roberts, John *Everton, The Official Centenary History* (Granada, 1978)

Rollins, Jack *Soccer At War* (Willow Books, 1985)

Ross, Ian, and Smailes, Gordon *Everton, A Complete Record 1878–1985* (Breedon Books, 1985)

Walsh, Nick *Dixie Dean* (Macdonald and Jane's, 1977)

Young, Percy *Football On Merseyside* (Stanley Paul, 1963)

PICTURE CREDITS

Action Plus: 159R, 160

All-Sport: frontis., 99T (Simon Bruty), 64B, 138/9 (David Cannon), 61B, 153

Associated Sports Photography/George Herringshaw: Endpapers, 119, 121, 126, 130, 131, 141T, 145

BBC Hulton Picture Library: 45, 51T, 53, 57, 60B, 67, 74, 76, 80, 87, 93R, 110

Colorsport: 29T, 31, 32, 34T, 46, 47, 49, 55, 58, 59, 77B, 79, 94T, 98, 100T, 101R, 106, 107, 108/9, 111, 115, 116, 117, 118, 120, 122/3, 125, 128/9, 132/3, 150, 152, 156/7, 158/9, 172/3, 175

Taken from *Dixie Dean* by Nick Walsh. Macdonald & Jane's, 1977: 51B

Taken from *Everton: A Complete Record 1878–1985* by Ian Ross and Gordon Smailes. Breedon Books Sport, 1985: 15, 16, 20, 27L & R, 33, 37, 43, 72

Taken from *Football On Merseyside* by Percy M. Young. Soccer Book Club, 1963: 12, 19, 52

Taken from *Football On Merseyside* by Percy M. Young. Soccer Book Club, 1963: 12, 19, 52

George Higham: 164/9

Illustrated London News Picture Library: 21, 22/3, 24, 29B, 38, 60T, 65

Stephen Kelly: 27C, 69

Liverpool City Libraries: 17

Liverpool Post and Daily Echo: 75, 162, 163

Mail Newspapers plc: 93L, 101L

Harry Ormesher: 124

Photosource: 84, 88

S. & G. Press Agency Ltd: 48, 77T, 82, 83, 85, 86, 100B, 137

Sporting Pictures (UK) Ltd: 61T, 62, 63T & B, 64T, 97T & B, 99B, 112, 127, 134, 140, 146, 148, 155

Topham Picture Library: 34B, 70, 71, 89, 90, 94B, 103, 104/5, 141B, 142/3